Too Much
Free Speech?

Too Much Free Speech?

Randall P. Bezanson

University of Illinois Press
Urbana, Chicago, and Springfield

Manufactured in the United States of America
C 5 4 3 2 1
∞ This book is printed on acid-free paper.

Library of Congress Cataloging-in-Publication Data
Bezanson, Randall P.
Too much free speech? / Randall P. Bezanson.
p. cm.
ISBN 978-0-252-03711-5 (hardback)
1. Freedom of speech—United States.
2. Freedom of speech—United States—Cases.
I. United States. Supreme Court. II. Title.
KF4772.B49 2012
342.7308'53—dc23 2012022919

Contents

Too Much Free Speech?

1 Introduction

In 1994 Stanley Fish, a peripatetic and controversial scholar at Duke, published a book titled *There's No Such Thing as Free Speech, and It's a Good Thing, Too.* It was the *free* part of free speech that he challenged. His claim was that, unbeknownst to defenders of speech freedom, speech occupies and is bounded by a realm of values and politics in which the speakable and unspeakable are defined and beyond which speech is unspeakable—and usually illegal. As speakers we are trapped by our politics and predispositions; what we say inside the safe realm cannot be called free. Speech that might rightly count as free—speech outside of the dominant domain at a point in time, like hate speech or obscene art or blasphemy—doesn't count as speech. It is instead outside the domain of acceptable discourse, indeed often illegal. Thus, there is no such thing as free speech.

In 2003 Justice Antonin Scalia penned a spirited separate opinion in the case challenging the McCain-Feingold campaign finance act. There he famously wrote that in the American democracy "*there is no such thing as too much speech.*"[1] For Justice Scalia, it seems, speech is a political and individual good of itself, a largely benign force not, as Fish would have it, because it doesn't rattle the cage, but instead because it does. Justice Scalia is neither an absolutist nor a pure libertarian. There are limits: trees and polar bears, he has said, have no free speech rights; speech that is imminently coupled with illegal conduct can be prohibited. But beyond that he sees a free world of opinion and ideas, even hateful ones falling outside of Fish's speakable domains.

In the real world of human behavior and constitutional law, of course, the speech picture is more complex. And lately the Supreme Court has been hard at work on the complexities, and more specifically on the meaning of "speech" covered by the First Amendment, not the amount of protection afforded to speech—that is, the Amendment's *coverage*, not its standard of freedom. In the process the Court has expanded the meaning of "speech" dramatically and fundamentally. The cases that do so represent the purest measure by which to address this book's central question: Is there such a thing as too much free speech? And they allow us to answer that question in terms that transcend partisan politics and personal preferences.

The cases we will focus on include the much-discussed *Citizens United* decision, which granted the full measure of constitutional protection to speech by corporations; the *Summum* decision, holding that the decision to select a monument for a public park and to reject another based on the government's disagreement with the monument's message is an act of government speech immunized from challenge under the First Amendment; the *Hurley* and *Dale* cases that recognize free speech claims for messages and meanings that arise "out of thin air": speech without an author (a parade); an author without a message (the Boy Scouts); and the *Doe v. Reed* case from Washington State that recognized the acts of signing petitions and voting in elections as acts of free speech.

Between Stanley Fish's claim that there really is no free speech and Justice Scalia's view that we can't get enough of it lie such difficult and largely definitional puzzles that make the relevant questions in real life not Fish's nor Scalia's, but mine: What limits should apply to the Supreme Court in its singular capacity of creator, interpreter, and enforcer of the free speech guarantee? Are there costs involved in expanding the meaning of "speech" and the scope of its freedom: costs of assuming that free speech is a quantitative good, not, as Stanley Fish would have it, a qualitative one; costs in subverting principle; costs to the structural characteristics of government and the Constitution; costs to the separation of powers; costs to the independence and scope of judicial power; costs to governments' practical capacity to achieve important ends and formulate important policy?

In exploring each of the selected Supreme Court cases, we will ask whether the Court's decision to expand the meaning of First Amendment free speech has important consequences that transcend the specific outcome of the case and our personal preferences or feelings. The recent uproar following the Court's extension of First Amendment protection to corporate political speech has rested almost entirely on personal political, economic, and ideological grounds. This is, of course, fair enough in a democracy. But the fact is that we don't expect the Supreme Court justices to make decisions based on our, or their, personal preferences. We would—or at least we should—be shocked if the Court were to announce that it would reconsider the case because of the overwhelming public sentiment against it. The Supreme Court is politically independent, and it is the *Constitution* that the justices are interpreting, one that binds all of government and all of the rest of us. So when we explore the Court's First Amendment decisions, we must ask not whether the decisions rest on an interpretation of the Constitution with which we disagree, but instead whether the way the Court conducted itself in its search for meaning was fitting for the independent judicial branch and consistent with the larger constitutional expectations that should surround the power claimed by the nonelected, secure, intellectually elite, and independent judicial branch in a representative democracy.

The Supreme Court is a unique institution in our democracy: independent, small, intellectually elite, charged with the power and duty to enforce law and the Constitution, and committed to openness, reason, prudence, and consistency in the exercise of its power. With the First Amendment, especially, it is obliged as the almost single-handed creator, interpreter, and enforcer of freedom of speech to engage in full and independent reasoning from the constitutional text applied faithfully over time and based on principles that transcend any particular case. Its opinions, to be sure, are not always pretty. With nine fully independent minds, getting five votes to form a majority in difficult cases can be a challenge, as multiple concurrences and dissents often signify. But the practice of multiple opinions from justices is of a piece with the Court's commitment to open public reason by each justice. This is an expectation that cannot be breached by a branch whose stock in trade, constitutionally speaking, is principled and full reason.

My own conclusion about the Court's fidelity to its constitutional responsibilities is mixed but often also grim, as the reader will see. My aim, however, is not simply to supply my own conclusions, but also to arm the reader with the capacity to reach her or his own decisions. The issue, after all, is not strictly speaking a "legal" one. It is one with which every citizen should be concerned, for it goes to the form of government we have in America and the way in which it should operate. This is a matter on which all of us can and should have informed opinions.

1 New Speakers

The First Amendment coverage question involves a number of linked questions: Who is a speaker, if there need be one? What counts as "speech"? What acts, including group relationships with others, are also swept into "speech"? What constitutional purposes must qualifying free speech serve? And there are others. In the pages that follow we will separate these pieces out in order to isolate specific definitions and issues, though we will always see the shadows of the other dimensions of free speech and we will regularly stitch the relevant pieces back together as we assess the Court's work.

We start with the speaker, and specifically with the Court's expansion of speakers whose expression qualifies for First Amendment protection. The new speakers we will explore are, at first glance, quite unlikely ones. The first new speakers are corporations, and specifically business corporations, who claim freedom to speak for themselves as entities independent of the shareholders and members and other people who comprise the legally constructed organization that we refer to as a corporation. The second and perhaps more surprising new speaker is government, which claims protection under the

First Amendment in the form of immunity from competing speech claims by individuals and other private speakers. The First Amendment protects individuals from government restrictions on speech. Should it also protect government from people under the First Amendment?

Our two decisions, the *Citizens United* and the *Summum* cases, are highly controversial and perhaps even radical. Our job will be to understand them and the Supreme Court that decided them.

CHAPTER ONE

Corporations as Speakers

Citizens United v. Federal Election Commission, 130 S. Ct. 876 (2010)

The Supreme Court's *Citizens United* decision was announced on January 21, 2010. Just weeks later it moved President Barack Obama in his State of the Union Address to make a special point of criticizing the Court, which had declared the prohibition on corporate and union electioneering within thirty days of a federal election unconstitutional, and in the process conferred broad First Amendment rights on corporate and union political speech. The decision, he said, "is nothing less than a vote to allow corporate and special interest takeovers of our elections. It is damaging to our democracy. It is precisely what led a Republican president named Theodore Roosevelt to tackle this issue a century ago."[1] Justice Samuel Alito broke the code of sobriety and expressed shock at the president's statement. Great controversy followed, with most, but not all, voices supporting the president's view.

This was not much ado about nothing.

Campaign finance reform has a long history in the United States. Calls for reform began in the late 1800s and first took hold in the early 1900s with a prohibition on corporate campaign contributions. At mid-century contribution limits were also placed on unions, and federal government employees were prohibited from active participation in federal campaigns. The issue again gained legislative momentum in the 1970s. The Federal Election Campaign Act (FECA) of 1972 implemented rules requiring political donors to disclose the amount given to campaigns as well as the recipients of the gifts. Subsequent reports of financial abuses in the 1972 presidential election, however, prompted further congressional action. In 1974, FECA was amended to include limits on contributions from individuals, political parties, and political action committees (PACs). The 1974 amendments also provided for the creation of an independent federal agency, the Federal Election Commission (FEC), to oversee enforcement of campaign finance laws.

Following the 1974 amendments, FECA remained untouched until 2002, when renewed public concern over campaign spending—especially unregulated contributions made to national political parties (so-called "soft money" donations)—prompted the passage of the Bipartisan Campaign Reform Act of 2002, better known as the McCain-Feingold bill. Though the bill modestly raised limits for contributions to a particular candidate, it is chiefly remembered for eliminating soft-money donations. It also prohibited the use of corporate or union funds in paying for an "electioneering communication" within thirty days of a primary election or caucus and within sixty days of a general election.

Then the law of unintended consequences set in. While Congress sought to closely regulate contributions to candidates and parties in McCain-Feingold, Congress also shifted the balance of power in campaign spending from established political parties to independent organizations rallying around a particular ideology or political cause. The bill placed comparatively few restrictions on independent expenditures made in support of a political belief, candidate, or cause. Groups organized under alternative structures thus had even broader latitude to become actively involved in elections.

Congress's aim, however, was to limit the two groups it deemed most likely to spend large sums of money on electioneering communications—corporations and unions—from exercising too much influence in the last weeks of the election cycle. That limit is the issue in the *Citizens United* case. Citizens United is a nonprofit corporation dedicated to championing conservative political causes. During the 2008 presidential election cycle, Citizens United produced a feature-length documentary titled "Hillary: The Movie" that portrayed Hillary Clinton in a negative light and sought to discredit her as a viable presidential candidate. To ensure that the program would reach the broadest possible audience, Citizens United wanted to air commercials advertising the documentary's availability through the free on-demand service offered by some cable providers. Citizens United was prevented from airing those commercials, however, because of the McCain-Feingold provision restricting corporations from engaging in electioneering communications within thirty days of a primary election. Following a lower court ruling that upheld McCain-Feingold's restrictions on corporate-funded political advertising, Citizens United appealed to the

Supreme Court, alleging that those restrictions violated the corporation's constitutionally protected right to freedom of speech.

The Supreme Court placed the case on the docket on August 18, 2008, and heard oral arguments on March 24, 2009. Citing the need for further development, the Court then took the exceedingly rare step of ordering the parties to reargue their case on September 9, 2009. On January 1, 2010, the Court handed down the landmark *Citizens United* decision. Our interest in the *Citizens United* case will be limited to its core holding, without which none of the fuss would have occurred. The holding was that corporations, just like individuals, have full First Amendment rights to speak, at least on political matters. This, in turn, meant that government restrictions on corporate speech would be subject to the highest level of constitutional scrutiny, a standard that could rarely be satisfied and that, if applied to the electioneering provision, would without a doubt lead to its invalidation on First Amendment grounds.

The electioneering prohibition was far from perfect. It exempted media companies. And it didn't limit individuals, who remained free to spend their vast fortunes at a rate dwarfing corporations. Yet it included within its grasp small and individual- or family-owned corporations, nonprofit corporations, and political and ideological organizations that used the corporate form or received funding from corporations. These included most "ma and pa" businesses, churches, nonprofit and charitable organizations, major advocacy groups such as right-to-life organizations, the NRA, the ACLU, the NAACP, and so on. Congress's action in enacting the electioneering provision was based, at best, on limited evidence of undue influence or corruption by corporations. Congress's judgment was intuitive and experience based, and the line it drew between corporations and unions, on the one hand, and rich people and organizations not using the corporate form, was a political compromise—that is, it was imperfect, ugly, and grossly overbroad and underinclusive. Such a law could not claim that the government's interest was compelling—a high risk of actual corruption or crippling loss of faith in the democratic process—or that the electioneering provision was narrowly tailored toward preventing those harms in the least speech-restrictive manner. Given the Court's conclusion that corporations are First Amendment speakers and their speech is fully protected at the highest level, the result was foreordained.

In the pages that follow we will examine the justices' views and the reasoning behind Court's the 5–4 decision. We will do so through a review of the second oral argument before the Court and an analysis of the Court's opinion. After the Court had first heard oral argument in 2009, it scheduled a second argument and instructed the parties to brief and argue the general question of the constitutional status of corporate speech. The Court had ruled in prior cases that much corporate speech was protected by the First Amendment, but as a general rule the protection afforded such speech was weak and limited. We will see the justices arguing about exactly what the Court had decided in the prior cases. And we will see the sources and assumptions underlying their very different views in the second oral argument and, most critically, in their opinions.

After taking full stock of the Court's decision, and in light of the virtual absence of serious *constitutional* analysis of the core question of the First Amendment's meaning, we will then step back and consider from a fresh and broader perspective whether corporations should be fully protected speakers under the First Amendment, drawing on the Constitution's text, its history, and the structural, philosophical, and practical considerations that bear on this central question.

▪ ▪ ▪

We begin with the second oral argument, held in the Supreme Court at 10:00 A.M. on Wednesday, September 9, 2009, before the official beginning of the 2009 term on the first Monday of October. Justice John Roberts was the chief justice. Justice John Paul Stevens was the most senior justice, who would retire at the end of the coming term, to be replaced by Justice Elena Kagan. The other justices, in order of seniority, were Justices Antonin Scalia, Anthony M. Kennedy, Clarence Thomas, Ruth Bader Ginsburg, Stephen Breyer, and Samuel Alito. The Court was deeply divided on a jurisprudential level, with differing views of the role and power of the Court, the methodology of constitutional interpretation, and, based on a ten-year record of decisions, the scope of the First Amendment freedom of speech.

The lawyers arguing the case were U. S. Solicitor General (now Justice) Kagan, who defended the electioneering provision of the campaign law on behalf of the United States. She was joined by Seth Waxman, who had been the solicitor general from 1997 to 2001. He represented Senator McCain (co-sponsor with Senator Feingold) and other senators who sponsored and supported the campaign reform act in Congress. The lawyers arguing against the constitutionality of the electioneering provision were, first, Theodore Olson, who also served as solicitor general from 2001 to

2004. He represented Citizens United, the corporation that had produced and distributed the allegedly prohibited electioneering film that was highly critical of Senator Hillary Clinton, then a presidential candidate and now secretary of state. Olson was joined by Floyd Abrams of New York City, perhaps the most prominent First Amendment lawyer in the United States. Abrams represented Senator Mitch McConnell, Republican minority leader and opponent of the McCain-Feingold campaign reform bill, which was enacted in 2002. Senator McConnell was not a party to the Citizens United case but instead appeared as amicus curiae (friend of the court, literally), with the consent of Olson. He had been the named party in a previous and important case that challenged the entire McCain-Feingold bill, enacted as BCRA, which of course included the electioneering provision at issue in *Citizens United*, and which was upheld by the Supreme Court. Dubbed the *McConnell* case in Supreme Court parlance, it was one of the prior decisions the Court brought into question in the Court's announcement of the new briefing and second oral argument in *Citizens United.*

The oral argument attracted much national attention, and the case involved a quite remarkable and prominent cast of litigants and lawyers. Justice Roberts announced the case and called on Olson for his oral argument shortly after 10:00.

CHIEF JUSTICE ROBERTS: We'll hear reargument this morning in Case 08-205, *Citizens United v. The Federal Election Commission*. Mr. Olson.

MR. OLSON: Mr. Chief Justice and may it please the Court: Robust debate about candidates for elective office is the most fundamental value protected by the First Amendment's guarantee of free speech. Yet that is precisely the dialogue that the government has prohibited if practiced by unions or corporations, any union or any corporation.

The government claims it may do so based upon the *Austin* decision that corporate speech is by its nature corrosive and distorting because it might not reflect actual public support for the views expressed by the corporation. The government admits that that radical concept of requiring public support for the speech before you can speak would even authorize it to criminalize books and signs.

This Court needs no reminding that the government, when it is acting to prohibit, particularly when it is acting to criminalize, speech that is at the very core of the First Amendment, [it] has a heavy burden to prove that there is a compelling governmental

> interest that justifies that prohibition and that the regulation adopted, in this case a criminal statute, is the most narrowly tailored necessary to accomplish that compelling governmental interest.

A number of points should be made here. First, following the first oral argument, the Court specifically requested supplemental briefs and a second oral argument on whether *Austin* and part of the *McConnell* case, which upheld restrictions on electioneering (candidate-focused) communications by corporations or unions within thirty days of a federal election, should be overruled.

Second, Olson's characterization of the *Austin* case is extreme. *Austin* involved a candidate endorsement by the Michigan Chamber of Commerce, a corporation. Michigan's prohibition on corporate endorsement ads was upheld. Olson says that, under the *Austin* case, corporate speech must "reflect actual public support" for its content before it will be protected by the First Amendment. It is clear, however, that while language to that effect is contained in the *Austin* opinion—it was actually "popular support," a more ambiguous word than "public"—that's not what the Court meant. Instead, it seems to have meant that a *corporation*'s speech must reflect the actual views (popular support) of the members or owners (stockholders) for whom the corporation is speaking, and the Michigan Chamber did not have membership support for the endorsement. The *Austin* opinion was very loose in its language, a fact that will bedevil the Court and the lawyers throughout the oral argument.

Third, Mr. Olson argues that speech by corporations (and unions) should be treated as fully protected by the First Amendment, just like speech by individuals. If this is so, restrictions on corporate speech would be subject to "strict scrutiny," which means that the government's reason for restricting (or prohibiting) the speech must be a compelling one that is unrelated to the content of the speech itself, and that the restrictions imposed must be narrowly tailored toward accomplishing the government's speech-unrelated purpose and the least restrictive of available means of accomplishing the government's purpose. This is such a demanding standard that it is only rarely satisfied.

> JUSTICE GINSBURG: Mr. Olson, are you taking the position that there is no difference in the First Amendment rights of an individual? A corporation, after all, is not endowed by its creator with inalienable rights.
>
> MR. OLSON: What the Court has said in the First Amendment context

is that corporations are persons entitled to protection under the First Amendment.

That's a bit of an overstatement. The Court has not said that corporations are speakers, just like individuals, under the First Amendment. It has said that corporations are "persons" for constitutional purposes, but only for such purposes as due process protection and the like. It is, however, the case that corporate speech in the form of advertising is protected by the First Amendment under the "commercial speech" doctrine, but the protection afforded that speech is considerably more modest than the strict scrutiny protection given to fully protected speech by individuals, and the "speech right" is the public's right to receive accurate and useful commercial information, not, strictly speaking, the corporate advertiser's liberty.

JUSTICE GINSBURG: In the view that you are putting forth—that there is no distinction between an individual and a corporation for First Amendment purposes—could any mega-corporation, even if most of the investors are from abroad, take the position that Congress could not limit their spending?

MR. OLSON: I'm not saying that, Justice Ginsburg. I'm saying that the First Amendment applies. Then the next step is to determine whether Congress and the government [have] established a compelling governmental interest and a narrowly tailored remedy to that interest. There is no record of that in this case of which I am aware. Certainly the government has not advanced it in its briefs.

Claiming on the one hand that "the First Amendment applies," as Olson does, and on the other that therefore strict scrutiny applies to corporate speech, is a legal non sequitur, for the First Amendment provides many gradations of protection. Olson elides the possible distinctions, arguing that strict scrutiny would apply without really having to defend or explain why. The Court seems to let him get away with it.

JUSTICE STEVENS: Mr. Olson, would you answer Justice Ginsburg's question yes or no? Does the First Amendment permit any distinction between corporate speakers and individual speakers?

MR. OLSON: I would not rule that out, Justice Stevens. I mean, there may be. I can't imagine all of the infinite varieties of potential problems that might exist, but we would eventually come back to the [strict scrutiny] narrow-tailoring problem anyway.

What the government has done here is prohibit speech. I don't know how many unions there are in this country, but there are something like 6 million corporations that filed tax returns in 2006. Ninety-seven percent of the 6 million corporations that filed tax returns in 2006 had assets less than $5 million—assets, not net worth. So we are talking about a prohibition that covers every corporation in the United States, including nonprofit corporations, limited liability corporations, Subchapter S corporations and every union in the United States.

JUSTICE ALITO: Well, Mr. Olson, do you think that media corporations that are owned or principally owned by foreign shareholders have fewer First Amendment rights than other media corporations in the United States?

MR. OLSON: I don't think so, Justice Alito. And I come back to the language of the First Amendment: "Congress shall make no law."

JUSTICE GINSBURG: But you have used the word "prohibition," Mr. Olson. One answer to that is that no entity is being prohibited from speaking. Corporations can use PACs and that way we assure that the people who contribute are really supportive of the issue, of the candidate.

MR. OLSON: I respectfully disagree. The corporation may not expend money. It might find people, stockholders or officers, who wanted to contribute to a separate fund, who could then speak. That in the words of one Justice, is ventriloquist-speak. I would say that it is more like surrogate speech. If you can find some other people that will say what you want to say and get them to contribute money through a process that this just—

JUSTICE GINSBURG: Who is the "you": the directors, the CEO, not the shareholders? We don't know what they think.

MR. OLSON: Well, this statute is not limited to cases where the shareholders agree or don't agree with what the corporation says.

This is true in terms of the terms of the law being challenged, but it is not necessarily true in terms of the Constitution, and this case is about the Constitution. As we will see, the Court in the past has carved out exceptions to the law's prohibition for ideological groups that speak for their members, much like political and religious organizations were treated before the rise of the corporation as a form of organization. This is what was done in the *Austin* case, involving a candidate endorsement by the Chamber of Commerce with which the members had not agreed. Mr. Olson's statement is an evasion of the constitutional issue that Justice Ginsburg was raising: whether the Constitution requires that the prohibition on electioneering before an election by corporations and unions would apply only to corporations that can't claim to speak for their investor shareholders. The question will arise again later in the argument.

JUSTICE BREYER: So here the obvious argument is: Look, they said the compelling interest is that people think that representatives are being bought, okay? That's to put it in a caricature, but you understand what I'm driving at, okay? So Congress now says precisely that [the same] interest leads us to want to limit the expenditures that corporations can make on electioneering communication in the last 30 days of a primary, over-the-air television, but not on radio, not on books, not on pamphlets, not on anything else. All right? So in what respect is there not conceptually at least a compelling interest and narrow tailoring?

MR. OLSON: Well, in the first place, I accept what the Court said in *Buckley* [*v. Valeo*, the Court's 1974 decision that set the foundation of First Amendment principles for campaign regulations] that expenditures do not raise that concern [that people are being bought] at all. Congress has not made [a contrary] finding.

JUSTICE KENNEDY: But in furtherance of Justice Breyer's point, you have two cases, one in which an officeholder goes to a corporation and says: Will you please give me money? They say: We can't do that. The other is in which a corporation takes out an ad for the candidate, which relieves that candidate of the responsibility of substantial television coverage. Isn't that about the same? As a practical matter, is that always true?

MR. OLSON: Well, it may not always be true. In the infinite potential applications of something like that, Justice Kennedy, anything might possibly be true. And Justice Breyer said, well, what if Congress thought the people might think that that was somehow suspect? That is not a basis for prohibiting speech by a whole class of individuals—

JUSTICE BREYER: Is the argument in this case about the existence of a compelling interest? Because Congress seemed to think that there was certainly that; it's this concern about the perception that people are, say, buying candidates.

Are we arguing about narrow tailoring? Congress thought it was narrow tailoring. Or are we arguing about whether we should second-guess Congress on whether there is enough of a compelling interest and the tailoring is narrow enough?

MR. OLSON: You must always second-guess Congress when the First Amendment is in play. And that we are arguing—we are not—we are *discussing*–

(Laughter.)

MR. OLSON: —both the compelling governmental interest and the narrow tailoring, and there is not a sufficient record [to support the government's argument on either basis].

JUSTICE GINSBURG: But what about the district court's finding? Wasn't there a finding before the three-judge court that Federal officials know of and feel indebted to corporations or unions who finance ads urging their election or the defeat of their opponent? There was a finding of fact to that effect, was there not?

MR. OLSON: Yes, there is something to that effect in the district court opinion, but it doesn't cover all corporations. It didn't focus in specifically on expenditures.

JUSTICE GINSBURG: So if they just covered large corporations, so you take out the mom-and-pop single shareholder–

MR. OLSON: Well, that is 97 percent of the corporations.

JUSTICE GINSBURG: Not 97 percent of the contributions. I mean, the contributions that count are the ones from the corporations that can amass these huge sums in their treasuries.

MR. OLSON: Under some circumstances an expenditure might coincide or resonate with what the candidate wishes to do, but the Court looked at that very carefully in *Buckley v. Valeo* and said that might not be the case. It might, in fact, be [the case that] these expenditures might be counterproductive [for the candidate] when they are independent, they are not coordinated with the candidate, they are more directly expression by the party spending the money, they are not like a contribution, so they are more of an infringement on the right to speak. And they are less of a threat of corruption because there is no quid pro quo there, and if there is, it would be punishable as a crime.

The basic point is getting drowned out here. It can easily be stipulated that if strict scrutiny applies, the electioneering law and its corporate speech distinction will fall. Olson is a very good lawyer and advocate. He doesn't mind getting into the details, because the questions all assume that strict scrutiny applies and the only real issue is whether it can be satisfied. He wins if the assumption holds. The same is true of the turn the questions now take. Starting with Justice Roberts, the justices engage in a detailed discussion of prior cases which Olson argues have already decided the corporate speech question, a discussion which draws attention away from the more basic question of *should* corporations be treated just like individuals under the First Amendment and, if so, why and when.

CHIEF JUSTICE ROBERTS: Counsel, in your discussion of *Austin*, you rely on its inconsistency with *Bellotti*.[2] *Bellotti*, of course, involved a referendum and *Austin* expenditures in an individual election. Why isn't that a significant distinction?

MR. OLSON: Well, what the *Bellotti* Court said is that the Court was not deciding [whether a corporation's right to speak about a referendum that directly affects its business applies more generally to non-referendum settings, such as elections]. And *Austin* did address, you are correct, expenditures, [not contributions]. What *Bellotti* also said is—and I think this is also in many decisions of this Court—the inherent worth of speech in terms of its capacity for informing the public does not depend upon the identity of the source, whether corporation, association, union, or individual.

CHIEF JUSTICE ROBERTS: Now that we've cleared up that *Bellotti* didn't decide the question, why don't you think that distinction makes sense? In other words, you don't have a potential for corruption if a corporation is simply speaking on a referendum that may directly affect its interest. If you are dealing with a candidate, what the Court has said in the past is that you do have that problem of corruption. In other words, why isn't that distinction a way to reconcile *Bellotti* and *Austin*?

MR. OLSON: There is a distinction, but the line dissolves on practical application. The distinction is very hard to draw between the interest that the speaker is addressing and whether it's a candidate or an issue, because issues are wrapped up in candidates. It's all First Amendment freedom.

CHIEF JUSTICE ROBERTS: Thank you, Mr. Olson.

Not much can be said about Olson's argument. He avoided the central question of whether corporations should have *full First Amendment protection* just like individual speakers by simply claiming that the question was whether regulating corporate political speech presented a First Amendment question—which it surely does, if for no other reason than that a corporation's advertising receives First Amendment protection, though very modest protection indeed—and then simply invoking strict scrutiny as the test. The central question, however, was whether corporate speech should be protected *in the same way* and *with the same scrutiny* as individual speech, and what the basis for such a conclusion would be in light of the history and purposes of the First Amendment.

In a sense, though, Olson can hardly be criticized for avoiding the central question, as the justices never pressed him on it. The Court's silence is very surprising, for surely the justices know very well that different types of speech and different speakers receive different levels of protection. The broadcast medium receives lower levels of protection, as does indecent speech, speech in schools, and libelous speech, for example. Why should corporate speech automatically receive the very highest level of protection? Does liberty play a different role with corporate speech than with individual speech? As former Chief Justice William Rehnquist said on more than one occasion, corporations have no mind or free will of their own.[3]

Having raised the central question in its call for additional briefing and reargument, the Justices simply dropped the ball. Maybe they knew the answer and called for reargument simply in order to justify deciding it. If so, a very heavy burden fell on Solicitor General (now Justice) Kagan, who would have to try to change their minds. The Chief Justice calls General Kagan to the podium for her oral argument on behalf of the United States.

GENERAL KAGAN: Mr. Chief Justice and may it please the Court: I have three very quick points to make about the government position. The first is that this issue has a long history. For over 100 years Congress has made a judgment that corporations must be subject to special rules when they participate in elections and this Court has never questioned that judgment.

Number two—

JUSTICE SCALIA: Wait, wait, wait, wait. We never questioned it, but we never approved it, either. And we gave some really weird interpretations to the Taft-Hartley Act in order to avoid confronting the question.

GENERAL KAGAN: I will repeat what I said, Justice Scalia: For 100 years this Court, faced with many opportunities to do so, left standing the legislation that is at issue in this case—first the contribution limits, then the expenditure limits that came in by way of Taft-Hartley—and then of course *Austin* specifically approved those limits.

JUSTICE SCALIA: I don't understand what you are saying. I mean, we are not a self-starting institution here. We only disapprove of something when somebody asks us to. And if there was no occasion for us to approve or disapprove, it proves nothing whatever that we didn't disapprove it.

GENERAL KAGAN: Well, you are not a self-starting institution. But many litigants brought many cases to you in 1907 and onwards and in each case this Court declined the opportunity to invalidate or otherwise interfere with this legislation.

JUSTICE KENNEDY: But that judgment was validated by *Buckley*'s contribution-expenditure line. And you're correct if you look at contributions, but this is an expenditure case. And I think that it doesn't clarify the situation to say that for 100 years—to suggest that for 100 years we would have allowed expenditure limitations, which in order to work at all have to have a speaker-based distinction, exemption from media, content-based distinction, time-based distinction. We've never allowed that.

GENERAL KAGAN: Well, I think Justice Stevens was right in saying that the expenditure limits that are in play in this case came into effect in 1947, so it has been 60 years rather than 100 years. But in fact, even before that the contribution limits were thought to include independent expenditures, and as soon as Congress saw independent expenditures going on, Congress closed what it perceived to be illegal. So in fact for 100 years corporations have made neither contributions nor expenditures, save for a brief period of time in the middle 1940s, which Congress very swiftly reacted to by passing the Taft-Hartley Act.

That's impressive. General Kagan stood firm and faced off with Justice Scalia and set Scalia on his heels. That's rarely done by lawyers in the Supreme Court, and rarely done so directly yet gently. With Justice Kennedy's more peevish question she kept her cool but nearly flattened him as well.

JUSTICE STEVENS: Before you go to your second point, may I ask you to clarify one part of the first, namely, your answer to the question I proposed to Mr. Olson, namely, why isn't the Snowe-Jeffords Amendment,[4] which was picked on by Congress itself, and which is argued by the NRA, an appropriate answer to this case?

GENERAL KAGAN: That was my third point, Justice Stevens.

JUSTICE STEVENS: Oh, I'm sorry.

(Laughter.)

GENERAL KAGAN: So we will just skip over the second.

My third point is that this is an anomalous case in part because this is an atypical plaintiff. And the reason this is an atypical plaintiff is because this plaintiff is an ideological nonprofit and—

CHIEF JUSTICE ROBERTS: So you are giving up—you are giving up the distinction from MCFL that you defended in your opening brief? There you said this doesn't qualify as a different kind of corporation because it takes corporate funds, and now you are changing that position?

The *Massachusetts Citizens for Life, Inc.* (*MCFL*) case involved political speech by an ideological organization that was a corporation formed to speak on right-to-life issues and which used its general treasury funds to endorse candidates. Because *MCFL* was ideological and received all of its funding from its members and none from corporations, the political speech was deemed to be the speech of its individual members and not the corporation itself; thus it was not subject to the campaign law's prohibitions on corporate electioneering. The Court explained that *MCFL* was "more akin to voluntary political organizations than business firms." The government had taken the position, in its original briefs, that because Citizens United received corporate funding (though very limited), it did not qualify for the exception from the electioneering law for corporations.

The *MCFL* decision is largely reflected in the Snowe-Jeffords Amendment to which Justice Stevens alluded.

GENERAL KAGAN: I don't think *MCFL* as written applies in this case, but I think that the Court could, as lower courts have done, adjust *MCFL* potentially to make it apply in this case, although I think that would require a remand. *MCFL* was written in a very strict kind of way so that the organization had to have a policy of accepting no corporate funds whatsoever. Some of the lower courts, including the D.C. Circuit, which, of course, sees a lot of these cases, have suggested that MCFL is too strict—

CHIEF JUSTICE ROBERTS: Do you—do you think it's too strict?

GENERAL KAGAN: The FEC has no objection to *MCFL* being adjusted in order to give it some flexibility.

If the Court were to approve such flexibility—in other words, allowing very limited corporate funding but clear ideological aims to speak for the views of its members (for example, the ACLU, the NRA, the NAACP)—Citizens United may well qualify for the exception from the corporate electioneering ban and, if so, the case would be concluded without reaching other issues.

CHIEF JUSTICE ROBERTS: Counsel, what do you—what do you understand to be the compelling interest that the Court articulated in *Austin*?

GENERAL KAGAN: In the government briefs we have suggested that *Austin* did not articulate what we believe to be the strongest compelling interest, which is the anticorruption interest. But what the Court articulated in *Austin* was essentially a concern about corporations using the corporate form to appropriate other people's money [in other words, shareholders' money] for expressive purposes.

CHIEF JUSTICE ROBERTS: So am I right then in saying that in the supplemental briefing you do not rely at all on the market distortion rationale on which *Austin* relied; in other words, these corporations have a lot of money.

GENERAL KAGAN: We do not rely at all on *Austin* to the extent that anybody takes *Austin* to be suggesting anything about the equalization of a speech market. So I know that that's the way that many people understand the distortion rationale of *Austin*, and if that's the way the Court understands it, we do not rely at all on that.

CHIEF JUSTICE ROBERTS: So if we are going to preserve *Austin* we have to accept your invitation that the quid pro quo interest or the shareholder protection interest supports the holding there.

The Chief Justice is showing his colors a bit too obviously. He seems set on overruling *Austin* and seems to be making the best possible record to support that decision. There's nothing wrong with this; it's just a little transparent.

GENERAL KAGAN: I would say either the quid pro quo corruption interest or the shareholder interest, or what I would say is something related to the shareholder interest that is in truth my view of *Austin*, which is a view that when corporations use other people's money to electioneer, that is a harm not just to the shareholders themselves but a sort of a broader harm to the public that comes from distortion of the electioneering that is done by corporations.

JUSTICE SCALIA: Let's talk about overbreadth. Let's assume that that is a valid interest. What percentage of the total number of corporations in the country are not single shareholder corporations? The local hairdresser, the local auto repair shop, the local new car dealer—I don't know any small business in this country that isn't incorporated, and the vast majority of them are sole-shareholder owned.

Now this statute makes it unlawful for all of them to do the things that you are worried about, you know, distorting the interests of other shareholders. That is vast overbreadth.

GENERAL KAGAN: You know, I think that the single shareholders can present these corruption problems. Many, many closed corporations, single shareholder corporations—

JUSTICE SCALIA: I'm not talking about the corruption interest. You have your quid pro quo argument, that's another one. We get to that when we get there. But as far as the interest you are now addressing, which is those shareholders who don't agree with this political position are being somehow cheated, that doesn't apply probably to the vast majority of corporations in this country.

GENERAL KAGAN: You are quite right, Justice Scalia; we say when it comes to single shareholders, the kind of "other people's money" interests, the shareholder protection interests do not apply. There the strongest justification is the anticorruption interest.

JUSTICE SCALIA: Congress has a self-interest. I mean, we are suspicious of congressional action in the First Amendment area precisely because we—at least I—doubt that one can expect a body of incumbents to draw election restrictions that do not favor incumbents. Now is that excessively cynical of me?

GENERAL KAGAN: I think, Justice Scalia, it's wrong. In fact, corporate and union money go overwhelmingly to incumbents. This may be the single most self-denying thing that Congress has ever done. If you look at the last election cycle and look at corporate PAC money and ask where it goes, it goes ten times more to incumbents than to challengers, and in the prior election cycle even more than that.

And for an obvious reason, because when corporations play in the political process, they want winners, they want people who will produce outcomes for them, and they know that the way to get those outcomes, the way to get those winners is to invest in incumbents, and so that's what they do. So I think that that rationale, which is undoubtedly true in many contexts, simply is not the case with respect to this case.

JUSTICE KENNEDY: But under your position, if corporations A, B, and C, are called to Washington every Monday morning by a high-ranking administrative official or a high-ranking member of the Congress with a committee chairmanship and told to tow the line and to tell their directors and shareholders what the policy ought to be, some other corporation can't object to that during the election cycle. The government silences a corporate objector, and those corporations may have the most knowledge of this on the subject.

Corporations have lots of knowledge about environment, transportation issues, and you are silencing them during the election.

GENERAL KAGAN: Well, to the extent, Justice Kennedy, that you are talking about what goes on in the halls of Congress, of course corporations can lobby members of Congress in the same way that they could before this legislation. What this legislation is designed to do, because of its anticorruption interest, is to make sure that that lobbying is just persuasion and it's not coercion. But in addition to that, of course corporations have many opportunities to speak outside the halls of Congress. Corporations have actually a fiduciary obligation to their shareholders to increase value. That's their single purpose, their goal.

CHIEF JUSTICE ROBERTS: So if a candidate–take a tobacco company—and a candidate is running on the platform that they ought to make tobacco illegal, presumably that company would maximize its shareholders' interests by opposing the election of that individual.

GENERAL KAGAN: But everything is geared through the corporation's self-interest in order to maximize profits, in order to maximize revenue, in order to maximize value. Individuals are more complicated than that. So that when corporations engage the political process, they do it with that set of you know, blinders—I don't mean it to be pejorative, because that's what we want corporations to do, is to—

CHIEF JUSTICE ROBERTS: Well, I suppose some do, but let's say if you have ten individuals and they each contribute $1,000 to a corporation, and they say, "We want this corporation to convey a particular message," why can't they do that, when if they did that as partnership, it would be all right?

GENERAL KAGAN: Well, it sounds to me as though the corporation that you were describing is a corporation of the kind we have in this case, where one can assume that the members all sign on to the corporation's ideological mission, where the corporation in fact has an ideological mission.

Such a corporation would not be restricted in its electioneering speech before the election because of *Austin* and the *MCFL* exception, and because it is "akin to voluntary political associations" that speak for their individual members.

> JUSTICE SCALIA: General Kagan, most corporations are indistinguishable from the individual who owns them, the local hairdresser, the new auto dealer who has just lost his dealership and who wants to oppose whatever Congressman he thinks was responsible for this happening or whatever Congressman won't try to patch it up by getting the auto company to undo it. There is no distinction between the individual interest and the corporate interest. And that is true for the vast majority of corporations. Yet this law freezes all of them out.

This is a weakness in the government's argument. With a single shareholder corporation the entity is always speaking for an individual even though, like the ACLU or NRA, the single owner is speaking by way of the corporation. Single-owner corporations probably shouldn't be covered by the law, at least in the absence of some risk of corruption. But General Kagan resists. She has little choice, since she is duty bound to defend the laws of the United States, and an argument that would gut the vast majority of the campaign act's prohibition on electioneering would not qualify as a "defense" of the law, in all likelihood.

> GENERAL KAGAN: To the extent that we are only talking about single shareholder corporations, I guess I would ask why it's any burden on that single shareholder to make the expenditures to participate in the political process in the way that person wants to outside the corporate forum? So single shareholders aren't suffering any burden here; they can do everything that they could within the corporate form, outside the corporate form. They probably don't get the tax breaks that they would get inside the corporate form, but I'm not sure anything else is very different.
>
> CHIEF JUSTICE ROBERTS: Counsel, could I ask [about] your shareholder protection rationale; isn't it extraordinarily paternalistic for the government to take the position that shareholders are too stupid to keep track of what their corporations are doing and can't sell their shares or object in the corporate context if they don't like it?
>
> GENERAL KAGAN: I don't think so, Mr. Chief Justice. I mean, I, for one, can't keep track of what my—

CHIEF JUSTICE ROBERTS: You have a busy job. You can't expect everybody to do that.

(Laughter.)

CHIEF JUSTICE ROBERTS, continuing: But it is extraordinary—I mean, the idea and as I understand the rationale, we the government, Big Brother, has to protect shareholders from themselves.

GENERAL KAGAN: In a world in which most people own stock through mutual funds, in a world where people own stock through retirement plans in which they have to invest, they have no choice, I think it's very difficult for individual shareholders to be able to monitor what each company they own is doing—

JUSTICE GINSBURG: In that respect, it's unlike the union, because the worker who does not want to affiliate with a union cannot have funds from his own pocket devoted to political causes. But there is no comparable check for corporations.

GENERAL KAGAN: That's exactly right, Justice Ginsburg. In the union context, of course, it's a constitutional right that the unions give back [the portion of dues] that any union member or employee in the workplace does not want used for electoral purposes.

JUSTICE GINSBURG: Does that mean that unions should be taken out, because there isn't the same—the shareholder protection interest doesn't—there is no parallel for the union?

Oops! It would be politically impossible, though maybe constitutionally correct, to allow electioneering by unions and not by business corporations (although some kind of parallel opt-out system could also be designed for corporate shareholders). General Kagan executes a quick step to the corruption justification.

GENERAL KAGAN: You are right about that. But the government believes that with respect to unions, the anticorruption interest is as strong, and that unions should be kept in. But Congress made a judgment that it was an important value that shareholders have this choice, have the ability both to invest in our country's assets and also to be able to choose our country's leaders.

CHIEF JUSTICE ROBERTS: I take it we have never accepted your shareholder protection interest. This is a new argument.

GENERAL KAGAN: I think that's fair.

CHIEF JUSTICE ROBERTS: So to the extent that you abandoned the original rationale in *Austin*, and articulated different rationales, you have two, the quid pro quo corruption interest and the shareholder protection interest—

GENERAL KAGAN: Which we think is in *Austin*.

CHIEF JUSTICE ROBERTS: *Austin*, I thought, was based on the aggregation of immense wealth by corporations.

GENERAL KAGAN: Again, *Austin* is not the most lucid opinion. But the way we understand *Austin*, what *Austin* was suggesting was that the corporate form gave corporations significant assets, other people's money, that when the corporations spent those assets—

CHIEF JUSTICE ROBERTS: Then I get back to my question, which is, you are asking us to support or continue the *Austin* opinion on the basis of two rationales that we have never accepted, shareholder protection and quid pro quo corruption?

GENERAL KAGAN: I would say on the quid pro quo corruption, of course you have accepted that rationale—

CHIEF JUSTICE ROBERTS: In the context of contributions, not expenditures.

GENERAL KAGAN: That's correct. And I think what has changed since—since that time is the BCRA record Congress compiled, which was very strong on the notion that there was no difference when it came to corporate contributions and expenditures, that there actually was no difference between the two. That they—

CHIEF JUSTICE ROBERTS: Is that a yes? Is that a yes?

Hold on, Chief! You seem to be getting a little excited. You've made your point, so why try to force General Kagan into a corner from which she can't escape without being pretty nasty back, which she wisely won't do.

CHIEF JUSTICE ROBERTS, continuing: In other words, you are asking us to uphold *Austin* on the basis of two arguments, two principles, two compelling interests we have never accepted, in expenditure context.

GENERAL KAGAN: In this—in this particular context, fair enough.

CHIEF JUSTICE ROBERTS: Thank you, General.

These questions and this discussion frankly seem silly. It doesn't really matter whether the same theory was used in *Austin*. There is plenty of room for further clarification of the *Austin* opinion. But even if the arguments, or government interests, are different yet support the result in *Austin* and are constitutionally valid, why should this wrangling about different principles and interests matter? There are plenty of cases in which the Supreme Court has later recast or reexplained an earlier opinion. One example is the one-person-one-vote principle, which originally required rather exact equality in population of districts, but was later modified formally to permit 10 percent variations in population on the practical ground that the census was inexact and population mobility often changed the numbers almost as soon as they were recorded.[5] The Court didn't overrule *Reynolds v. Carr* because the Court later modified the rule and principle used in the original case.

The central corporate issue was discussed more thoroughly in General Kagan's argument than in Olson's, but frankly the Court—or more precisely Chief Justice Roberts and Justices Scalia, Alito, and Kennedy—didn't seem very interested. The issue was picked up again and pressed further by Seth Waxman, a former Solicitor General who was also arguing on behalf of Senator McCain and other senators who supported the corporate speech limitation.

The Chief Justice calls on Mr. Waxman.

> MR. WAXMAN: Mr. Chief Justice, and may it please the Court: The requirement that corporations fund electoral advocacy the same way individuals do, that is with money voluntarily committed by people associated with the corporation, is grounded in interests that are so compelling that 52 years ago, before *Buckley* was decided, before FECA was enacted, before *Buckley*-style quid pro quo corruption was ever addressed, this Court explained that, quote: "What is involved here is the integrity of our electoral process and not less the responsibility of the individual citizen for the successful functioning of that process."
>
> If the Court now wishes to reconsider the existence and extent of the interests that underlie that sentiment expressed for the Court by Justice Frankfurter, it should do so in a case in which those interests are forthrightly challenged with a proper and full record below.
>
> When the sober-minded Elihu Root was moved to stand up in 1894 and urged the people of the United States, and urged the Congress of the United States, to enact legislation that would address, quote, "a constantly growing evil which has done more to shake the confidence of plain people of small means of this country in our political institutions than any practice which has ever obtained since the founding of our government," he was not engaging in a high-level discussion about political philosophy.

JUSTICE KENNEDY: But he was talking about contributions in that context. That's quite clear.

Give me a break! Are we to suppose that President Theodore Roosevelt and Justice Frankfurter and Elihu Root had any such hidden distinction in mind?

MR. WAXMAN: With all due respect, Justice Kennedy, I don't think that there was any distinction whatsoever in that time between contributions expenditures. For this reason, Justice Kennedy, what Root said was [that] the idea is to prevent the great companies, the great aggregations of wealth from using corporate funds directly or indirectly to send members of the legislature to these halls in order to vote for their protection and the advancement of their interests as against those of the public.

JUSTICE SCALIA: Great aggregations of wealth. The brief by the Chamber of Commerce, the amicus brief by the Chamber of Commerce, points out that 96 percent of its members employ less than 100 people. These are not aggregations of great wealth. You are not talking about the railroad barons and the rapacious trusts of the Elihu Root era; you are talking mainly about small business corporations.

MR. WAXMAN: Justice Scalia, I take your point and I think you have made this point forcefully many times before. A unanimous court in *National Right to Work Committee* concluded that Congress was entitled to make the judgment that it would treat [business corporations differently] in order to address this root evil, a problem of such concern that it goes to the very foundation of the democratic republican exercise, that is, the notion of integrity in representative government.

And, Justice Scalia, if a small corporation or even any corporation of any sort wants to bring an as-applied challenge to 441b or a State law analogue and say, you know, I am not the problem that Theodore Roosevelt and Elihu Root addressed; there isn't a compelling interest because I only have three employees and $8,000 in my bank account, that's fine. But what is extraordinary, truly extraordinary, given the sentiments that underlay the Tillman Act and the Taft-Hartley Act, is that we would be having a discussion today about the constitutionality of a law that has been on the books forever when no party, no corporation, has ever raised the challenge. I well recall—

JUSTICE KENNEDY: You say it's been on the books forever. But, number one, the phenomenon of television ads where we get information about scientific discovery and environment and transportation issues from corporations who after all have patents because they know something, that is different. And the history you applied [does] apply to contributions, not to those kinds of expenditures.

MR. WAXMAN: Justice Kennedy, first of all, I think it is actually true that patents are owned by individuals and not corporations. But be that as it may, I am not here saying that this Court should reconsider *Bellotti* on first principles any more than I am saying that it shouldn't consider *Austin* on first principles. Corporations can and do speak about a wide range of public policy issues, and since the controlling opinion was issued in *Wisconsin Right to Life*, the kind of campaign-related speech that corporations can't engage in [during] the pre-election period is limited to the functional equivalent of express advocacy and nothing else.

All I am suggesting—and I hope that if you take nothing else from my advocacy today it will be this—is that we have here a case in which the Court has asked a question that essentially goes to the bona fides, that is, the factual predicates of the interests that have been viewed as compelling in *Austin*, in *MCFL*, in *McConnell* itself, whether you call it the corrosive effect of corporate wealth, whether you call it, quote, "shareholder protection"—

CHIEF JUSTICE ROBERTS: Thank you, Mr. Waxman.

Waxman's argument went directly to the deeper core of the corporation-as-speaker issue. In protecting free speech, the First Amendment clearly focused on the individual citizens who composed the democratic self-governing core of the American democracy. Corporations didn't really exist at the time the First Amendment was ratified (except for charters granted by the Crown and later the states). Ideological groups of individuals speaking in common cause did not and could not use the corporate form, for that kind of corporation didn't exist at the time. It wasn't until the late nineteenth century that the voluntary business corporation came into being under the laws of the various states (accompanied, it should be said, with substantial limitations and regulations that continue to this day). So there is really no basis in history or constitutional text for an automatic presumption that corporations have any First Amendment free-speech rights.

Waxman's argument tried to reset, or recast, the issue in the *Citizens United* case from Olson's argument that there must be a compelling reason to deny corporations free speech rights identical with those of individuals, to the question whether there is any good reason to interpret the First Amendment more broadly than its original meaning in order to include corporations as speakers. He is perfectly justified in this effort, historically and textually as well as culturally. Whether hated or not today, corporations have historically been seen as artificial entities with limited rights whose power and privileges should be closely regulated (as they are to this day) by the democratic political process in order to preserve individual liberty and democratic self-government. It would be strange, Waxman argues, to extend full free-speech rights against this background, and especially so in an increasingly information-based (and thus speech-based) society. Thus, no compelling interest test and no narrow tailoring is needed or even relevant to the core interpretive question of whether the "freedom" of speech is possessed by corporations unless those corporations are the functional equivalent of the ideological groups of individuals that had been covered from the beginning by the First Amendment: the Federalists; the Antifederalists; the Sons of Liberty.

Waxman's argument was concise, fundamentally sound, serious, and reflected the way in which the Court *should* approach a case in which a new and expanded interpretation of a constitutional provision is sought. The record in such a case would consist of historical, cultural, political, and economic facts and attitudes over the course of more than two hundred years. It is ironic that the justices most devoted to sticking to the text and its original meaning were the Justices who seemed to have little interest in Mr. Waxman's argument and who spent most of their time asking the same picky and pointed questions that they had asked over and over throughout the argument.

CHIEF JUSTICE ROBERTS: Mr. Olson, five minutes.

MR. OLSON: Thank you, Mr. Chief Justice. The words that I would leave with this Court are the Solicitor General's. The government's position has changed. The way in which the government has changed its position is its rationale for this prohibition in the first place. Is it corruption? Is it shareholder protection? Is it equalization? There was some dispute. I heard the Solicitor General say that the equalization rationale was something the government disavowed. It wasn't what *Austin* said, the government said. And I—

JUSTICE GINSBURG: Justice Marshall said that he was not trying to equalize all voices in the political process. He has a sentence that says that's not what the rationale of this case is.

MR. OLSON: With all due respect Justice Ginsburg, the words that jump out at me are the words from page 665 that say the desire to counterbalance those advantages unique to the corporate forum is the state's compelling interest in this case. That sounds to me like equalization.

I don't know. I am representing an individual who wants to speak about something that's the most important thing that goes on in our democracy. I'm told it's a felony. I don't know what the rational basis is. It's overbroad. Now I hear about protecting shareholders. There is not a word in the congressional record about protecting shareholders.

JUSTICE BREYER: Actually, I read that sentence that you just read as meaning the corporation is an artificial person in respect to which the State creates many abilities and capacities, and the State is free also to create some disabilities and capacities. Not a statement about balancing rich and poor.

MR. OLSON: Well, it strikes me that it is, because it follows the words that say corporations are given unique advantages to aggregate wealth and that we must take away that advantage by equalizing the process.

CHIEF JUSTICE ROBERTS: Thank you, counsel. The case is submitted.

Well, the cards are now on the table for all to see. General Waxman did a very nice job of explaining the constitutional basis for disqualifying corporations from having the same freedom to speak as individuals. Some of the justices tried to pick at his dates, etc., but in the end his argument stood firm and the justices were left tilting at windmills. But none of that seemed to bother the chief justice and Justices Scalia, Kennedy, and Alito. They wanted none of this constitutional principle and political theory. They had made up their minds and, by God, nothing was going to stand in their way. It should be said in their defense that this isn't an entirely unusual thing to happen in oral argument. The Court often has pretty well settled on its views well in advance of argument, and thus uses oral argument to clarify narrower and more technical questions, as it did in *Citizens United.*

All of this was perfectly obvious when the Court announced its opinion in the case. Justice Kennedy was the author of the Court's opinion, and his opinion was, if nothing else, clear and decisive on the constitutional rule to be announced: corporations have full First Amendment freedom of speech and were entitled to the highest measure of protection against government restriction, just like individual speech. It was a take-no-prisoners opinion.

> Justice KENNEDY delivered the opinion of the Court.
>
> Speech is an essential mechanism of democracy, for it is the means to hold officials accountable to the people. The right of citizens to inquire, to hear, to speak, and to use information to reach consensus is a precondition to enlightened self-government and a necessary means to protect it. The First Amendment "'has its fullest and most urgent application' to speech uttered during a campaign for political office."
>
> For these reasons, political speech must prevail against laws that would suppress it, whether by design or inadvertence. Laws that burden political speech are "subject to strict scrutiny," which requires the Government to prove that the restriction "furthers a compelling interest and is narrowly tailored to achieve that interest."
>
> Premised on mistrust of governmental power, the First Amendment stands against attempts to disfavor certain subjects or viewpoints. Prohibited, too, are restrictions distinguishing among different speakers, allowing speech by some but not others. As instruments to censor, these categories are interrelated: Speech restrictions based on the identity of the speaker are all too often simply a means to control content.
>
> Quite apart from the purpose or effect of regulating content, moreover, the Government may commit a constitutional wrong when by law it identifies certain preferred speakers. By taking the right to speak from some and giving it to others, the Government deprives the disadvantaged person or class of the right to use speech to strive to establish worth, standing, and respect for the speaker's voice. The Government may not by these means deprive the public of the right and privilege to determine for itself what speech and speakers are worthy of consideration. The First Amendment protects speech and speaker, and the ideas that flow from each.
>
> The Court has recognized that First Amendment protection extends to corporations. . . . This protection has been extended by explicit holdings to the context of political speech. Under the rationale of these precedents, political speech does not lose First Amendment protection "simply because its source is a corporation." The Court has thus rejected the argument that political speech of corporations or other associations should be treated differently under the First Amendment simply because such associations are not "natural persons."

This is a key paragraph in the opinion, for as we will see Justice Kennedy rests his argument not on how or why the First Amendment should be interpreted to include corporation (and union) speech as the legal equivalent of individual speech, but instead on the argument that the decision to do so had already been decided in prior cases. *McConnell* and *Austin*, under this view, were outlier decisions that needed to be overruled in order to reinstate the prior law that corporations were fully protected speakers. So Justice Kennedy in this paragraph is summarizing his argument based on prior decisions.

In the second sentence Justice Kennedy says that "political speech does not lose First Amendment protection '*simply because* its source is a corporation.'" That is an accurate description of prior cases, even of the *McConnell* and *Austin* cases, because it is qualified by the "simply because" phrase. The statement means only that corporations can be fully protected, but they are not always so protected. They can be excluded from speech protection, but for reasons in addition to the fact of their corporate status—as in *Austin*—because their speech is not an expression of a group of individuals who band together to express their views collectively. The statement also says nothing about the degree of protection, which may be modest for commercial and advertising speech by a corporation, or it may be fully protected just as individual speech is when the corporation acts as an instrument for the collective views of its members (often charitable or nonprofit corporations) or shareholders, such as the ACLU or the NRA.

The last sentence—the key "thus" proposition—simply does not follow clearly from the one before it. If he is saying that corporations as a class therefore enjoy full first amendment protection just as individuals do, the statement is a non sequitur. It just doesn't follow from its more limited predicate. If he's saying only that corporations are not always denied full protection "*simply because* such associations are not natural persons," he is correct, though the statement doesn't necessarily flow from the prior sentence, because, again, fully protected speech rights are given (under *MCFL* and *McConnell* and *Austin* and many other cases) when the corporation's speech reflects its members' collective views whether or not the corporation is a natural person—or, one presumes, an individual. When the paragraph is subjected to careful scrutiny, in other words, it says nothing inconsistent with *McConnell* or *Austin*.

But Justice Kennedy seems to use the sentence as definitive support from prior cases for the proposition that corporations are protected by the First Amendment just as individuals are, at least as to political speech.

> At least since the latter part of the 19th century, the laws of some States and of the United States imposed a ban on corporate direct contributions to candidates. Yet not until 1947 did Congress first prohibit independent

> expenditures by corporations and labor unions in the Labor Management Relations Act of 1947. In passing this Act Congress overrode the veto of President Truman, who warned that the expenditure ban was a "dangerous intrusion on free speech."
>
> For almost three decades thereafter, the Court did not reach the question whether restrictions on corporate and union expenditures are constitutional.
>
> In *Buckley v. Valeo* the Court addressed various challenges to the Federal Election Campaign Act of 1971. These amendments created an independent expenditure ban that applied to individuals as well as corporations and labor unions.
>
> Before addressing the constitutionality of [the broad] independent expenditure ban, *Buckley* first upheld FECA's limits on direct contributions to candidates. The *Buckley* Court recognized a "sufficiently important" governmental interest in "the prevention of corruption and the appearance of corruption." This followed from the Court's concern that large contributions could be given "to secure a political quid pro quo."
>
> The *Buckley* Court explained that the potential for quid pro quo corruption distinguished direct contributions to candidates from independent expenditures. The Court emphasized that "the independent expenditure ceiling . . . fails to serve any substantial governmental interest in stemming the reality or appearance of corruption in the electoral process" because "[t]he absence of prearrangement and coordination . . . alleviates the danger that expenditures will be given as a quid pro quo for improper commitments from the candidate." *Buckley* invalidated [the law's] restrictions on independent expenditures, with only one Justice dissenting.

Justice Kennedy fails to mention what is perhaps the key justification for regulating contributions. That was, according to Chief Justice Rehnquist who authored the Court's opinion in *Buckey*, that "[w]hile contributions may result in political expression if spent by a candidate or an association to present views to the voters, the transformation of contributions into political debate *involves speech by someone other than the contributor*." Therefore, whether the contribution comes from an individual or a corporation or union, it is not speech, and therefore is not protected by the First Amendment.

The omission of this central premise of *Buckley* allows Justice Kennedy to ignore and thus not confront in the *expenditure* cases, the rationale of *Austin* and *McConnell* and other cases, which is that the mere investment in a corporation *without the intention that the corporation speak and express a view for an individual in common cause with other like minded investors* is not an act of speech, and thus any resulting speech by the corporation is not protected as collective individual speech, but instead as speech by an artificial entity without a known or knowable individual author.

This does not mean, of course, that a corporation's speech *can not* be fully protected by the First Amendment, but it does mean that to give it that protection requires a substantial and independent justification not found in *Buckley* or in other prior cases.

> Buckley did not consider [the law's separate ban in § 610 on corporate and union independent expenditures]. Had § 610 been challenged in the wake of *Buckley*, however, it could not have been squared with the reasoning and analysis of that precedent. The *Buckley* Court did not invoke the First Amendment's overbreadth doctrine to suggest that § 608(e)'s expenditure ban would have been constitutional if it had applied only to corporations and not to individuals.

This isn't quite so clear. In 1986 Chief Justice Rehnquist, the author of *Buckley*, said in connection with a public utility company's first amendment claim to be free from a state requirement that it carry messages of other groups in its billing envelopes, "extension of [first amendment protection to corporations based on] individual freedom of conscience strains the rationale beyond the breaking point. To ascribe to such artificial entities an 'intellect' or 'mind' . . . is to confuse metaphor with reality."

> Notwithstanding this precedent, Congress recodified § 610's corporate and union expenditure ban four months after *Buckley* was decided. Now renumbered, the challenged Section 441b is the independent expenditure restriction challenged here.
>
> Less than two years after *Buckley*, [our decision in *First National Bank of Boston v.] Bellotti* reaffirmed the First Amendment principle that the Government cannot restrict political speech based on the speaker's corporate identity. *Bellotti* could not have been clearer when it struck down a state-law prohibition on corporate independent expenditures related to referenda issues:
>
> > We thus find no support in the First . . . Amendment, or in the decisions of this Court, for the proposition that speech that otherwise would be within the protection of the First Amendment loses that protection simply because its source is a corporation that cannot prove, to the satisfaction of a court, a material effect on its business or property. . . . [That proposition] amounts to an impermissible legislative prohibition of speech based on the identity of the interests that spokesmen may represent in public debate over controversial issues and a requirement that the speaker have a sufficiently great interest in the subject to justify communication. . . . In the realm of protected speech, the legislature is constitutionally disqualified from

> dictating the subjects about which persons may speak and the speakers who may address a public issue.
>
> It is important to note that the reasoning and holding of *Bellotti* did not rest on the existence of a viewpoint-discriminatory statute. It rested on the principle that the Government lacks the power to ban corporations from speaking.

Again we confront the "simply because" qualifier. *Austin* can easily be read as in agreement; indeed, its rationale was that corporations and organizations do have full speech rights when the message is one shared by the members or owners. Thus, a corporation is not disqualified from First Amendment speech protection "simply" because it is a corporation, but because it is a certain type of corporation that doesn't express views shared by the owners/stockholders. *Bellotti* is therefore not the strong authority that the Court's opinion suggests. And it is certainly not support for the bald and much more absolutist statement below: that "the First Amendment does not allow political speech restrictions based on a speaker's corporate identity."

> *Bellotti* did not address the constitutionality of the State's ban on corporate independent expenditures to support candidates. In our view, however, that restriction would have been unconstitutional under *Bellotti*'s central principle: that the First Amendment does not allow political speech restrictions based on a speaker's corporate identity.
>
> Thus the law stood until *Austin*. *Austin* "uph[eld] a direct restriction on the independent expenditure of funds for political speech for the first time in [this Court's] history." There, the Michigan Chamber of Commerce sought to use general treasury funds to run a newspaper ad supporting a specific candidate. Michigan law, however, prohibited corporate independent expenditures that supported or opposed any candidate for state office. A violation of the law was punishable as a felony. The Court sustained the speech prohibition.
>
> To bypass *Buckley* and *Bellotti*, the *Austin* Court identified a new governmental interest in limiting political speech: an antidistortion interest. *Austin* found a compelling governmental interest in preventing "the corrosive and distorting effects of immense aggregations of wealth that are accumulated with the help of the corporate form and that have little or no correlation to the public's support for the corporation's political ideas.

It is true that Austin relied in part on a literally untenable standard of public support for the corporation's message. But Justice Kennedy's opinion ignores the alternative rationale of *Austin*, which was that the Chamber's endorsement was not a reflection of the political views of its *members*, nor did the members authorize the Chamber to speak on this issue on their behalf. As the *Austin* opinion put it, "the resources in the treasury of a business corporation [are] not an indication of *popular* support for the corporation's political ideas. They reflect instead the economically motivated decisions of investors and customers." The emphasis here is mine: "popular support" is very different, especially in its context, than "public support" used by Justice Kennedy. The *Austin* Court sustained the flat Michigan ban by carving an exception for corporations that speak for their individual members, thus eliminating the flat ban. The same argument for a qualification of the ban on corporate expenditures in this case was, of course, made by the solicitor general and rejected by the Court. This is what led to the widespread belief—accurate I think—that the Court decided to treat corporations, unions, and other organizations as full First Amendment speakers whether the corporation spoke for its owners or instead spoke just for "the corporation" on matters with which the owner/shareholders neither agreed nor wished the corporation to speak. It is this broad holding that cannot be defended simply on the basis of prior decisions that had already decided it. Other reasons will have to be offered by the Court.

The pejorative treatment of the antidistortion interest also ignores the argument made by Waxman—that for historical reasons the First Amendment should not be interpreted in the first instance to protect speech by corporations. Justice Kennedy ignores this analysis altogether by claiming that the First Amendment's inclusion of corporate speech, and its level of protection, had already been decided prior to *Austin*. This is an assumption that is in very deep trouble based on the reasoning Justice Kennedy offers for it in the opinion.

It should also be mentioned at this point that the Court's heavy reliance on the *Bellotti* case as full support for the conclusion that the corporate speech issue had already been decided is, at best, dicey; at worst, it's simply wrong. The Court in *Bellotti* disavowed any intention to decide the broad corporate speech issue in a footnote in the opinion, a footnote that the *Belotti* Court took very seriously and was likely required to be included in order to get enough votes on the Court for the more limited result that was reached. Since *Bellotti*, the Court has cited and relied on that footnote in a number of important cases. We'll see in due course what Justice Kennedy does with the footnote.

> The Court is thus confronted with conflicting lines of precedent: a pre-*Austin* line that forbids restrictions on political speech based on the speaker's corporate identity and a post-*Austin* line that permits them. No case before

> *Austin* had held that Congress could prohibit independent expenditures for political speech based on the speaker's corporate identity.
>
> Political speech is "indispensable to decisionmaking in a democracy, and this is no less true because the speech comes from a corporation rather than an individual." This protection for speech is inconsistent with *Austin*'s antidistortion rationale. *Austin* sought to defend the antidistortion rationale as a means to prevent corporations from obtaining "'an unfair advantage in the political marketplace' by using 'resources amassed in the economic marketplace.'" But *Buckley* rejected the premise that the Government has an interest "in equalizing the relative ability of individuals and groups to influence the outcome of elections." The First Amendment's protections do not depend on the speaker's "financial ability to engage in public discussion."
>
> It is irrelevant for purposes of the First Amendment that corporate funds may "have little or no correlation to the public's support for the corporation's political ideas."

This was the unfortunate—even simply erroneous—language that the *Austin* opinion used to qualify a corporation's speech rights. The *Citizens United* opinion rightly eviscerated this reason, as it implies that speech can be limited because the public doesn't agree with it. This is anathema to the First Amendment, which is premised in part on the proposition that better decisions will be made if people are able to hear, and thus accept or reject, unwelcomed ideas, having a deeper understanding of their views as a result of confronting their possible weaknesses or alternatives.

But *Austin* also, or even instead, explicitly spoke of political support in the more limited setting of the members or owners of a corporation—individuals for whom the corporation must, as a matter of law, speak. The *Austin* opinion focused attention prominently on the fact that the members of the chamber did not all, or even primarily, support the candidate endorsement speech that was at issue, nor had they licensed the chamber to speak on that question on their behalf. The chamber's expression of views on the interests of business and economic development would be one thing, but endorsement of candidates was quite different in terms of the members' political support.

The *Citizens United* opinion ignores this alternative explanation, though it turns to it later in the narrower and weaker terms of shareholder interest that General Kagan had argued in support of the law. The fate of the later shareholder interest argument seems to have been sealed by what the Court says in this earlier part of its opinion. Justice Kennedy continues:

> All speakers, including individuals and the media, use money amassed from the economic marketplace to fund their speech. The First Amendment protects the resulting speech, even if it was enabled by economic transactions with persons or entities who disagree with the speaker's ideas.

This paragraph literally seals the fate of any exception to the flat ban for certain kinds of corporations or corporate speech. The paragraph is, frankly, a stunningly broad and absolutist statement that corporations, themselves and despite the intentions of their owners, are full rights holders under the First Amendment whose rights cannot be distinguished from *individual* persons who speak.

> *Austin*'s antidistortion rationale would produce the dangerous, and unacceptable, consequence that Congress could ban political speech of media corporations. Media corporations are now exempt from § 441b's ban on corporate expenditures. Yet media corporations accumulate wealth with the help of the corporate form, the largest media corporations have "immense aggregations of wealth," and the views expressed by media corporations often "have little or no correlation to the public's support" for those views. Thus, under the Government's reasoning, wealthy media corporations could have their voices diminished to put them on par with other media entities. There is no precedent for permitting this under the First Amendment.

Frankly, this is a manufactured argument based on a manufactured premise. Media corporations—at least those that publish or broadcast news and opinion—are exempted by legislation. This would be a problem only if granting an exception for those businesses violates the First Amendment by preferring some speakers over others. Indeed, that seems to be what the Court is saying, remarkably enough. But media corporations in the news and opinion publishing business are nevertheless protected by the distinct First Amendment recognition of the "press"—because, presumably, of its distinct functions in the American democracy.

But the Court uses this reasoning to address the meaning of "Freedom of the Press" which might otherwise justify an exception for the media. Having thus manufactured the requirement that it examine press freedom, the Court proceeds to eviscerate the press clause as a distinct constitutional provision. Watch.

> The media exemption discloses further difficulties with the law now under consideration. There is no precedent supporting laws that attempt to distinguish between corporations which are deemed to be exempt as media corporations

> and those which are not. "We have consistently rejected the proposition that the institutional press has any constitutional privilege beyond that of other speakers." With the advent of the Internet and the decline of print and broadcast media, moreover, the line between the media and others who wish to comment on political and social issues becomes far more blurred.

Wow! Without the benefit of briefing or oral argument, the Court makes the already concise Constitution even more concise. Who needs a free press guarantee anyway? For that matter, who needs the press, now that we have corporations speaking? Justice Kennedy then turns ominous and grave.

> The censorship we now confront is vast in its reach. The Government has "muffle[d] the voices that best represent the most significant segments of the economy." And "the electorate [has been] deprived of information, knowledge and opinion vital to its function." By suppressing the speech of manifold corporations, both for-profit and nonprofit, the Government prevents their voices and viewpoints from reaching the public and advising voters on which persons or entities are hostile to their interests. Factions will necessarily form in our Republic, but the remedy of "destroying the liberty" of some factions is "worse than the disease." Factions should be checked by permitting them all to speak, and by entrusting the people to judge what is true and what is false.
>
> When Government seeks to use its full power, including the criminal law, to command where a person may get his or her information or what distrusted source he or she may not hear, it uses censorship to control thought. This is unlawful. The First Amendment confirms the freedom to think for ourselves.
>
> What we have said also shows the invalidity of other arguments made by the Government. For the most part relinquishing the antidistortion rationale, the Government falls back on the argument that corporate political speech can be banned in order to prevent corruption or its appearance. In *Buckley*, the Court found this interest "sufficiently important" to allow limits on contributions but did not extend that reasoning to expenditure limits. When *Buckley* examined an expenditure ban, it found "that the governmental interest in preventing corruption and the appearance of corruption [was] inadequate to justify [the ban] on independent expenditures."

Well, the *Buckley* Court was dealing with a flat ban. The *Citizens United* Court is dealing with a "ban," a loaded term the Court uses, that contains, by way of *Austin* and *MCFL*, an exception to it for corporate speech that represents the views of the individual members or owners. Ironically, it is the government in *Citizens United* that is arguing against a flat ban by trying to preserve *Austin* and *McConnell*.

> With regard to large direct contributions, *Buckley* reasoned that they could be given "to secure a political quid pro quo," and that "the scope of such pernicious practices can never be reliably ascertained." The practices *Buckley* noted would be covered by bribery laws if a quid pro quo arrangement were proved. The Court, in consequence, has noted that restrictions on direct contributions are preventative, because few if any contributions to candidates will involve quid pro quo arrangements. The *Buckley* Court, nevertheless, sustained limits on direct contributions in order to ensure against the reality or appearance of corruption. That case did not extend this rationale to independent expenditures, and the Court does not do so here.

Of course the reason the *Buckley* Court sustained the contribution limitations in the interest of possible corruption was that it concluded that contributions are not speech of contributor, so they are not protected at all by the First Amendment. Therefore any restriction would be permissible constitutionally if the government had a rational (though not compelling and perfectly fitting) basis for it. The Court should have noted this central rationale of *Buckley*'s treatment of contribution limits, as it made *Buckley* irrelevant to the point it was making.

> "The absence of prearrangement and coordination of an expenditure with the candidate or his agent not only undermines the value of the expenditure to the candidate, but also alleviates the danger that expenditures will be given as a quid pro quo for improper commitments from the candidate." Limits on independent expenditures, such as § 441b, have a chilling effect extending well beyond the Government's interest in preventing quid pro quo corruption. The anticorruption interest is not sufficient to displace the speech here in question.
>
> A single footnote in *Bellotti* purported to leave open the possibility that corporate independent expenditures could be shown to cause corruption. For the reasons explained above, *we now conclude that independent expenditures, including those made by corporations, do not give rise to corruption or the appearance of corruption* [emphasis added]. Dicta in *Bellotti*'s footnote suggested that "a corporation's right to speak on issues of general public interest implies no comparable right in the quite different context of participation in a political campaign for election to public office." Citing the portion of *Buckley* that invalidated the federal independent expenditure ban, and a law review student comment, *Bellotti* surmised that "Congress might well be able to demonstrate the existence of a danger of real or apparent corruption in independent expenditures by corporations to influence candidate elections." *Buckley*, however, struck down a ban on independent expenditures to support candidates that

covered corporations, and explained that "the distinction between discussion of issues and candidates and advocacy of election or defeat of candidates may often dissolve in practical application." *Bellotti*'s dictum is thus supported only by a law review student comment, which misinterpreted *Buckley*. See Comment, *The Regulation of Union Political Activity: Majority and Minority Rights and Remedies, 126 U. Pa. L. Rev. 386, 408 (1977)* (suggesting that "corporations and labor unions should be held to different and more stringent standards than an individual or other associations under a regulatory scheme for campaign financing").

Hold on there! We have already discussed the *Buckley* decision striking down a flat ban on expenditures. It simply does not support the weight the Court is placing on it. But the cheap shot in the analysis is that the Court simply dismisses *Bellotti's* footnote as dicta, though it uses other statements in *Belotti* that weren't intended to apply to the *Citizens United* situation (therefore the footnote), which statements in light of the footnote would be dicta when applied to *Citizens United*. And then it eviscerates the argument about the corruption interest as therefore relying only on a (dread word) law review article written by a law student. I'm certainly glad that I didn't write the article, and I feel great sympathy for the student who wrote it. Justice Kennedy may judge its conclusion to be wrong, but the article remains a quite nicely argued piece of scholarship.

But the clincher is the Court's statement that "we now conclude that independent expenditures, including those made by corporations, do not give rise to corruption or the appearance of corruption." It is not usually the Court's function to make findings of fact, which this is, and then to state them as conclusions of law, thus preventing any future fact-based challenge to them in another case. The Court's role is interpreting the meaning of the Constitution and announcing rules of law. Here the Court seems to be having enough trouble with the law part of that function, so it's probably unwarranted to expand its power by taking on questions of fact and giving them the force of rules of law.

The Government contends further that corporate independent expenditures can be limited because of its interest in protecting dissenting shareholders from being compelled to fund corporate political speech. This asserted interest, like *Austin*'s antidistortion rationale, would allow the Government to ban the political speech even of media corporations. Assume, for example, that a shareholder of a corporation that owns a newspaper disagrees with the political views the newspaper expresses. Under the Government's view, that potential disagreement could give the Government the authority to restrict the media corporation's political speech. The First Amendment does not allow that power. There is, furthermore, little evidence of abuse that cannot be corrected by shareholders "through the procedures of corporate democracy."

Having earlier essentially eliminated the "freedom of the Press" clause as freestanding constitutional provision, saying instead that press freedom is no different from speech freedom—a dubitable proposition, and certainly not one to be almost offhandedly announced—Justice Kennedy proceeds to rely on the press's *distinct* interests to dismiss out of hand the "shareholder interest" argument of the solicitor general. And he also misstates the solicitor general's argument as consisting of little more than member or shareholder objection, rather than an argument that the use of shareholder money to express views that are not representative of shareholder intentions or beliefs foreclose the corporation from justifying its speech in the name of its owners or members, leaving it instead as authorless speech by an abstract legal entity.

Then he proceeds to dismiss shareholder interests as fully protected by shareholder self-help, and not in need of government oversight (as in regulation of the securities markets, insider trading, and the like). This is the paternalism point raised in oral argument though clothed in other garb. But the record of shareholder activism affecting corporate decisions is, to be honest, virtually nonexistent. And there is no nonpaternalism clause in the Constitution. If there were, we wouldn't have securities regulations, or clean air and water, or seatbelts (which my mother objected to on philosophical grounds, though not on legal or constitutional ones). Justice Kennedy is covering a very wide terrain in this opinion, making a lot of new law along the way even, it seems, when it isn't required for the decision in the case. Is that activism?

For the reasons above, it must be concluded that *Austin* was not well reasoned. The Government defends *Austin*, relying almost entirely on "the quid pro quo interest, the corruption interest or the shareholder interest," and not *Austin*'s expressed antidistortion rationale. When neither party defends the reasoning of a precedent, the principle of adhering to that precedent through *stare decisis* is diminished.

Austin should be and now is overruled. We return to the principle established in *Buckley* and *Bellotti* that the Government may not suppress political speech on the basis of the speaker's corporate identity. No sufficient governmental interest justifies limits on the political speech of nonprofit or for-profit corporations.

> Given our conclusion we are further required to overrule the part of *McConnell* that upheld restrictions on corporate independent expenditures. This part of *McConnell* is now overruled.

Wow. Right or wrong in result, this is one of the most cleverly constructed and logically flawed arguments I have seen in the Supreme Court. It is a house of cards. One awaits, however, the fully argued and reasoned analysis of why the First Amendment should be read to extend such protections to corporations . . . a principled constitutional justification on the merits. But we wait in vain. Justice Kennedy offers no justification based on the text, history, values, or original intent of "freedom of speech." None.

He is equally brazen about campaign disclosure requirements.

> *Citizens United* next challenges BCRA's disclaimer and disclosure provisions as applied to Hillary and the three advertisements for the movie. Under BCRA § 311, televised electioneering communications funded by anyone other than a candidate must include a disclaimer that "'______ is responsible for the content of this advertising.'" The required statement must be made in a "clearly spoken manner" and displayed on the screen in a "clearly readable manner" for at least four seconds. It must state that the communication "is not authorized by any candidate or candidate's committee"; it must also display the name and address (or Web site address) of the person or group that funded the advertisement. Any person who spends more than $10,000 on electioneering communications within a calendar year must file a disclosure statement with the FEC. That statement must identify the person making the expenditure, the amount of the expenditure, the election to which the communication was directed, and the names of certain contributors.
>
> Disclaimer and disclosure requirements may burden the ability to speak, but they "impose no ceiling on campaign-related activities," and "do not prevent anyone from speaking." In *Buckley*, the Court explained that disclosure could be justified based on a governmental interest in "provid[ing] the electorate with information" about the sources of election-related spending . . . on the ground that they would help citizens "'make informed choices in the political marketplace.'" For these reasons, we reject Citizens United's contention that the disclosure requirements must be limited to speech that is the functional equivalent of express advocacy.
>
> The judgment of the District Court is reversed with respect to the constitutionality of restrictions on corporate independent expenditures. The judgment is affirmed with respect to the law's disclaimer and disclosure requirements. The case is remanded for further proceedings consistent with this opinion.
>
> It is so ordered.

The disclaimer and disclosure requirements addressed in the final paragraphs of Justice Kennedy's opinion are not directly related to the corporation as speaker issue. A brief portion of that part of the opinion is included, however, because the issue is directly relevant to Chapter 5, Voting as Speech, which follows later. It is also a matter now in litigation following the *Citizens United* case, and it may reach the Supreme Court fairly quickly. The difficulty for the Court will be that individual speech includes a right to anonymous speech that can only be overridden by compelling state interests that are narrowly tailored. If the First Amendment protects a speaker's choice of anonymity, and if the Court really meant what it said in *Citizens United* when it stated that corporate speech is protected just as individual speech is, the Court is going to have some difficulty explaining its decision in *Citizens United*—and its statement that disclosure requirements do not prevent anyone from speaking.

Viewing the opinion as a whole, there is good reason to find it logically wanting, historically and textually arid, given to grand and broad statements of law, and ultimately dissatisfying. The Court's opinion never really gets to the substance of the corporate speech issue, instead escaping the need to grapple with text and history and theory by what proved to be a weak and unconvincing expedient of claiming that the decision had already been made in many Supreme Court decisions, with *Austin* and *McConnell* cast as the recent and radical roadblocks that turned the clock back. With all respect, nothing could be further from the truth.

Before turning in earnest to the core underlying issues of corporate speech and the First Amendment, we will briefly sample the concurring and dissenting opinions. A couple of things should be noted at the outset. There were four concurring or dissenting opinions. Three of the concurring opinions were by, or joined by, four of the five justices who joined Justice Kennedy's opinion and gave it a majority. There was widespread implicit and explicit "joining" of Kennedy's opinion "on the assumption that it means what I say." The five-member majority, in short, seems to have been very delicately cobbled together. The four dissenters, in contrast, spoke with a single voice.

We will sample all of the opinions, but for most of them just a few key sentences or paragraphs will be included. The exceptions are, most importantly, Justice Scalia, who seems downright discontented with many of the Kennedy opinion's absolutist statements, and who may therefore be the least stable member of the majority because he sees the case in a different and broader way; and Justice Stevens, who writes a very long and scathing dissent. We will look at some of the dissent, but we have already seen many of the misgivings about the majority opinion in the commentary I have interlaced with it. We start with Chief Justice Roberts.

> Chief Justice ROBERTS, with whom Justice ALITO joins, concurring:
>
> The Government urges . . . [that] First Amendment rights could be confined to individuals, subverting the vibrant public discourse that is at the foundation of our democracy. The Court properly rejects that theory, and I join its opinion in full.
>
> None of this is to say that the Government is barred from making new arguments to support the outcome in *Austin*. On the contrary, it is free to do so. And of course the Court is free to accept them. But the Government's new arguments must stand or fall on their own; they are not entitled to receive the special deference we accord to precedent.
>
> Because continued adherence to *Austin* threatens to subvert the "principled and intelligible" development of our First Amendment jurisprudence, I support the Court's determination to overrule that decision.

All that needs be said is that this is a peculiar and qualified concurring opinion, joining the majority opinion, it seems, largely because it overrules *Austin*. *Austin*, to be sure, was a pretty ugly and poorly reasoned opinion, but that's not usually a justification for straight overruling when, as the Chief says, the result in *Austin* might still be justified on other and clearer grounds. No doubt Congress, if it turns to revising the law after *Citizens United*, will try to craft just such an approach.

> Justice SCALIA, with whom Justice ALITO joins, and with whom Justice THOMAS joins in part, concurring:
>
> I write separately to address Justice STEVENS's [opinion which] purports to show that today's decision is not supported by the original understanding of the First Amendment. The dissent attempts this demonstration, however, in splendid isolation from the text of the First Amendment. It never shows why "the freedom of speech" that was the right of Englishmen did not include the freedom to speak in association with other individuals, including association in the corporate form. To be sure, in 1791 (as now) corporations could pursue only the objectives set forth in their charters; but the dissent provides no evidence that their speech in the pursuit of those objectives could be censored.
>
> The lack of a textual exception for speech by corporations cannot be explained on the ground that such organizations did not exist or did not speak. To the contrary, colleges, towns and cities, religious institutions, and guilds had long been organized as corporations at common law and under the King's

> charter, and . . . the practice of incorporation only expanded in the United States. Both corporations and voluntary associations actively petitioned the Government and expressed their views in newspapers and pamphlets. For example: An antislavery Quaker corporation petitioned the First Congress, distributed pamphlets, and communicated through the press in 1790. The New York Sons of Liberty sent a circular to colonies farther south in 1766. And the Society for the Relief and Instruction of Poor Germans circulated a biweekly paper from 1755 to 1757. The dissent offers no evidence—none whatever—that the First Amendment's unqualified text was originally understood to exclude such associational speech from its protection.
>
> The dissent says that when the Framers "constitutionalized the right to free speech in the First Amendment, it was the free speech of individual Americans that they had in mind." That is no doubt true. All the provisions of the Bill of Rights set forth the rights of individual men and women—not, for example, of trees or polar bears. But the individual person's right to speak includes the right to speak in association with other individual persons. Surely the dissent does not believe that speech by the Republican Party or the Democratic Party can be censored because it is not the speech of "an individual American." It is the speech of many individual Americans, who have associated in a common cause, giving the leadership of the party the right to speak on their behalf. The association of individuals in a business corporation is no different—or at least it cannot be denied the right to speak on the simplistic ground that it is not "an individual American."
>
> The Amendment is written in terms of "speech," not speakers. Its text offers no foothold for excluding any category of speaker, from single individuals to partnerships of individuals, to unincorporated associations of individuals, to incorporated associations of individuals—and the dissent offers no evidence about the original meaning of the text to support any such exclusion. We are therefore simply left with the question whether the speech at issue in this case is "speech" covered by the First Amendment. No one says otherwise. A documentary film critical of a potential Presidential candidate is core political speech, and its nature as such does not change simply because it was funded by a corporation. Nor does the character of that funding produce any reduction whatever in the "inherent worth of the speech" and "its capacity for informing the public." Indeed, to exclude or impede corporate speech is to muzzle the principal agents of the modern free economy. We should celebrate rather than condemn the addition of this speech to the public debate.

Justice Scalia writes perhaps the most interesting and evocative opinion in the case. He clearly says that corporations cannot be excluded from the First

Amendment as speakers *simply because* they are corporations. This is a point with which all nine Justices agree, or at least with which everyone except Justice Kennedy agrees. What are the examples Justice Scalia points to? They consist exclusively of organized groups or organizations or corporations with a clear expressive purpose with which the members or owners agree. They are, in other words, speakers who combine the power of many like minded individuals to express their individual and collective views: The New York Sons of Liberty; the Society for the Relief and Instruction of Poor Germans; the antislavery Quaker corporation; religious, educational, and literary corporations; and the press. There is no talk of General Motors or Microsoft here. These groups are today's equivalent of the NRA; the NAACP; the ACLU, and so forth. They are the very kind of groups that, in corporate form, the solicitor general was trying to rescue through a clearer understanding and rationale for the truly messy *Austin* case and its successor in *McConnell.*

So why did Justice Scalia join the Kennedy opinion but concur separately as well? Perhaps it was to imply, as Chief Justice Robert's opinion did, that a decision to invalidate a categorical exclusion of corporations was correct, but that didn't mean that all corporations would be treated as individual speakers for purposes of the First Amendment. Corporations may have—as they had before *Citizens United*—speech rights of different sorts, as with commercial speech, but the degree of protection for those rights was not always the same. Even corporations' political expression may be protected, but to different degrees depending on the expressive versus pure business nature of the corporation and its members or its purely investment-oriented shareholders. The law prohibiting electioneering by corporations and unions within thirty days of an election wiped out all of those rights and painted with too broad a brush.

On the speech versus speakers point Justice Scalia also qualifies the Kennedy opinion. Justice Kennedy seems to say that what the First Amendment protects is speech, not speakers, as if one can wrest free speech from its authors and liberty from the animating constitutional meaning of the First Amendment. The problem with this is that the guarantee is of "freedom of speech," and it is unlikely that this was meant literally by the framers: speech is what is free and not the source of the words, or images, etc. Justice Scalia's view appears to be different. The purpose of the First Amendment was, he admits, the freedom of individuals in a new, free, democratic union. He says,

> The dissent says that when the Framers "constitutionalized the right to free speech in the First Amendment, it was the free speech of individual Americans

> that they had in mind." That is no doubt true. All the provisions of the Bill of Rights set forth the rights of individual men and women—not, for example, of trees or polar bears. But the individual person's right to speak includes the right to speak in association with other individual persons.

Justice Scalia's opinion was joined by Justice Alito and, on the subjects mentioned above, by Justice Thomas. That makes for a pretty tepid "Court" for Justice Kennedy's opinion. Justice Thomas, as mentioned previously, joined the Court's opinion, as well as the Roberts and Scalia concurrences, but dissented from the part of the Kennedy opinion that upheld the disclaimer and disclosure requirements. He was on pretty sound constitutional ground in doing so, based on the *McIntyre* case[6] that recognized a strong right of speakers to anonymity. He claims, rightly I think, that the Kennedy opinion must be read as overruling or seriously undermining the *McIntyre* opinion. Justice Kennedy obviously couldn't get enough votes to make the opinion a hat trick.

Justice Stevens, writing for all four of the dissenting Justices, wrote a long and impassioned dissent. We will look at just a few largely self-explanatory parts of it.

> Justice STEVENS, with whom Justice GINSBURG, Justice BREYER, and Justice SOTOMAYOR join, concurring in part and dissenting in part:
>
> In the context of election to public office, the distinction between corporate and human speakers is significant. Although they make enormous contributions to our society, corporations are not actually members of it. They cannot vote or run for office. Because they may be managed and controlled by nonresidents, their interests may conflict in fundamental respects with the interests of eligible voters. The financial resources, legal structure, and instrumental orientation of corporations raise legitimate concerns about their role in the electoral process. Our lawmakers have a compelling constitutional basis, if not also a democratic duty, to take measures designed to guard against the potentially deleterious effects of corporate spending in local and national races.
>
> The majority's approach to corporate electioneering marks a dramatic break from our past. Congress has placed special limitations on campaign spending by corporations ever since the passage of the Tillman Act in 1907. We have unanimously concluded that this "reflects a permissible assessment of the dangers posed by those entities to the electoral process," and have accepted the "legislative judgment that the special characteristics of the corporate structure require particularly careful regulation." The Court today rejects a century of history when it treats the distinction between corporate and individual cam-

paign spending as an invidious novelty born of *Austin v. Michigan Chamber of Commerce*. Relying largely on individual dissenting opinions, the majority blazes through our precedents, overruling or disavowing a body of case law.

[A critical] pillar of the Court's opinion is its assertion that "the Government cannot restrict political speech based on the speaker's . . . identity." . . . Yet in a variety of contexts, we have held that speech can be regulated differentially on account of the speaker's identity, when identity is understood in categorical or institutional terms. The Government routinely places special restrictions on the speech rights of students, prisoners, members of the Armed Forces, foreigners, and its own employees.

The election context is distinctive in many ways, and the Court, of course, is right that the First Amendment closely guards political speech. But in this context, too, the authority of legislatures to enact viewpoint-neutral regulations based on content and identity is well settled. We have, for example, allowed state-run broadcasters to exclude independent candidates from televised debates. We have upheld statutes that prohibit the distribution or display of campaign materials near a polling place. Although we have not reviewed them directly, we have never cast doubt on laws that place special restrictions on campaign spending by foreign nationals. And we have consistently approved laws that bar Government employees, but not others, from contributing to or participating in political activities. These statutes burden the political expression of one class of speakers, namely, civil servants. Yet we have sustained them on the basis of longstanding practice and Congress's reasoned judgment that certain regulations which leave "untouched full participation . . . in political decisions at the ballot box," help ensure that public officials are "sufficiently free from improper influences," and that "confidence in the system of representative Government is not . . . eroded to a disastrous extent."

The same logic applies to this case with additional force because it is the identity of corporations, rather than individuals, that the Legislature has taken into account. Not only has the distinctive potential of corporations to corrupt the electoral process long been recognized, but within the area of campaign finance, corporate spending is also "furthest from the core of political expression, since corporations' First Amendment speech and association interests are derived largely from those of their members and of the public in receiving information." Campaign finance distinctions based on corporate identity tend to be less worrisome, in other words, because the "speakers" are not natural persons, much less members of our political community, and the governmental interests are of the highest order.

The Framers . . . took it as a given that corporations could be comprehensively regulated in the service of the public welfare. Unlike our colleagues, they had little trouble distinguishing corporations from human beings, and when they constitutionalized the right to free speech in the First Amendment, it was the free speech of individual Americans that they had in mind. While individuals might join together to exercise their speech rights, business corporations, at least, were plainly not seen as facilitating such associational or expressive ends. . . . As a matter of original expectations, then, it seems absurd to think that the First Amendment prohibits legislatures from taking into account the corporate identity of a sponsor of electoral advocacy. As a matter of original meaning, it likewise seems baseless—unless one evaluates the First Amendment's "principles," or its "purpose," at such a high level of generality that the historical understandings of the Amendment cease to be a meaningful constraint on the judicial task.

It is an interesting question "who" is even speaking when a business corporation places an advertisement that endorses or attacks a particular candidate. Presumably it is not the customers or employees, who typically have no say in such matters. It cannot realistically be said to be the shareholders, who tend to be far removed from the day-to-day decisions of the firm and whose political preferences may be opaque to management. Perhaps the officers or directors of the corporation have the best claim to be the ones speaking, except their fiduciary duties generally prohibit them from using corporate funds for personal ends. Some individuals associated with the corporation must make the decision to place the ad, but the idea that these individuals are thereby fostering their self-expression or cultivating their critical faculties is fanciful. It is entirely possible that the corporation's electoral message will conflict with their personal convictions. Take away the ability to use general treasury funds for some of those ads, and no one's autonomy, dignity, or political equality has been impinged upon in the least.

The Court's central argument is that laws such as § 203 have "'deprived [the electorate] of information, knowledge and opinion vital to its function,'" and this, in turn, "interferes with the 'open marketplace' of ideas protected by the First Amendment." There are many flaws in this argument. If the overriding concern depends on the interests of the audience, surely the public's perception of the value of corporate speech should be given important weight. That perception today is the same as it was a century ago when Theodore Roosevelt delivered the speeches to Congress that, in time, led to the limited prohibition on corporate campaign expenditures that is overruled today. The distinctive threat to democratic integrity posed by corporate domination of politics was recognized at "the inception of the republic" and "has been a persistent theme in American political life" ever since. It is only certain Members of this Court, not the listeners themselves, who have agitated for

> more corporate electioneering. All of the majority's theoretical arguments turn on a proposition with undeniable surface appeal but little grounding in evidence or experience, "that there is no such thing as too much speech."
>
> I would affirm the judgment of the District Court.

Justice Stevens' dissent can speak for itself. Against the known background and arguable logical and historical faults of the Kennedy opinion for the Court, Justice Stevens's arguments are clear and direct. The dissent sounds very much like a combination of the arguments of the solicitor general and Seth Waxman, although as a justice, Stevens enjoys the freedom to speak on terms less captured by attention to precedent. Those arguing before the Court don't have, or don't feel that they have, the same luxury. Justice Stevens, moreover, makes the fundamental point—with which even Justice Scalia implicitly agrees—that the *Citizens United* case cannot be truly decided without returning to the basics. These include the text of the First Amendment, its original purpose, and its historical meaning from 1781 to 2010. If the Court's opinion is right that corporate and organizational speech is, across the board, the equivalent of individual speech, then Justice Kennedy is correct in his bold and absolutist conclusions. But the test of that question lies not in prior cases or nice distinctions or the satisfaction of "tests"—or on the fact, as Kennedy says, that corporate speech is the "voice[] that best represent[s] the most significant segments of the economy." It rests, instead, on the text of the "Freedom of Speech," its original meaning and its animating purposes, and the historical understanding of its role over time from 1791 to 2010.

Speech and the First Amendment

In our general discussion of the *Citizens United* case and the constitutional status of corporate speech, we will turn to the basics. We will begin with the text and original meaning of the First Amendment and the purposes it was to serve, and then we will move on to the historical record from the founding period to the present. We will not find, or even seek, a definitive answer to the meaning of freedom of speech, but instead we will look to perspectives and arguments that should be considered when addressing the fundamental questions that the Court in *Citizens United* largely ignored.

JUST THE TEXT: DISSECTING THE WORDS AND THEIR LOGIC

The First Amendment says "Congress shall make no law respecting an establishment of religion, or prohibiting the free exercise thereof; or abridging the freedom of speech, or of the press; or of the right of the people peaceably to assemble, and to petition the Government for a redress of grievances." What is the most natural reading of the text regarding freedom of speech?

One view is that (a) freedom of speech is a liberty, (b) that applies to the act of speaking, not simply its "speech" byproduct; and (c) that it extends only to individuals and not to a larger class of "persons" that might include corporations or organizations. This reading seems logically to flow from the last three clauses, the freedom of speech, of the press, and the right of the people to assemble and petition.

Take freedom of the press as an example. It would be awkward at best to read the freedom of the press as protecting only the product of the press—a newspaper, for example—as opposed to the persons engaged in the act of reporting and publishing. Without those people's freedom in the act of selecting, writing, and publishing, there would be little of importance left in the protection of the published article produced. The freedom attaches to the acts of people who select, write, and judge the public function and value of an article. So also would it be strange to protect the "speech" uttered by people without guaranteeing their freedom to choose whether, when, and what to say. And the third provision protects the right of the people (not corporations) to assemble and petition.

Furthermore, the whole amendment speaks clearly to liberty of individuals: freedom of believers or nonbelievers to the absence of compulsion to worship in their preferred church; freedom of believers to exercise their religious convictions; freedom for people to have and express ideas and views; freedom of those publishing news and opinion to engage in the act of publication; and freedom of people to gather in assemblies and petition for grievances.

When the parts of the First Amendment are looked at together, it appears that the First Amendment is listing the key components of the free-willed individual's liberty from government in a democratic and free society ruled by the people. The product of these liberties—religious belief and affiliation; speech; news and opinion for public use; assembly and petition for government's attention—may produce products that are valuable or silly, right or wrong, but to make the ability of individuals to act in this realm dependent on someone else's judgment of the product's value or rightness would be to destroy the liberty or freedom itself. As Justice Rehnquist put it, "[E]xtension of [First Amendment protection to corporations based on] individual freedom of conscience strains the rationale beyond the breaking point. To ascribe to such artificial entities an 'intellect' or 'mind' . . . is to confuse metaphor with reality."

There is, however, an opposing view of the text's meaning. As Justice Kennedy necessarily decided in his opinion for the Court, and as Justice Scalia said in his concurring opinion, the operative word in the First Amendment is "speech," not "speak." The speech or message itself is made free from censorship or unwarranted restriction; its source is incidental—except for trees or polar bears, sources whose speech won't count, he says.

Under this view, which I will call utilitarian, the purpose of the free-speech guarantee, and perhaps the other First Amendment guarantees as well, is to create a marketplace of ideas, to seek truth (or progress at least) through the open competition among ideas and asserted truths. The beneficiary of free speech is not primarily the speaker but the listeners or readers or viewers whose capacity for discernment will be improved and whose choices on matters of politics, policy, economics, and so forth will be wiser, thus serving the system of democratic self-government. The value of speech by corporations is its contribution to the scope of the public marketplace of speech. Corporations are, Justice Scalia has said (and was quoted in the Court's opinion by Justice Kennedy), "the voices that best represent the most significant segments of the economy."

For the utilitarian view to work, someone must decide which speech, which subjects and views, are most valuable and thus worthy of promotion—protection and encouragement. Corporations are pervasive and important institutions in today's free-market economy. To free their views from restriction, such as a prohibition of their electioneering in the critical last thirty days before an election, is to promote the introduction of new ideas and truths into the marketplace of ideas and the competition of claims to truth. Extending free speech to corporations will add to, not distort, the fund of knowledge and fact (and ignorance and folly) in a democratic society. To restrict that particular voice in the marketplace would harm the democratic process.

To argue, as the government did in the *Citizens United* case, that this new voice will distort and threaten the marketplace of ideas is to discredit the individual citizen and voter. In the words of Justice Kennedy's opinion for the Court, "When the government . . . command[s] where a person may get his or her information or what distrusted source he or she may not hear, it uses censorship to control thought. . . . The First Amendment confirms the freedom to think for ourselves."

The conflict between these two opposing but perfectly respectable views is the conflict between liberty and utility. On this difference, the text of the First Amendment, it turns out, is ambiguous. And the argument from liberty to utility is just a vicious circle from which there is no escape. For those preferring liberty, the act of speaking, not its product, is what is important; if individuals are free to speak, all the opposing truths and views will emerge. For government to see to it that useful ideas and information are available in the marketplace of ideas is paternalistic, a denial of respect for individual liberty.

The utilitarians, however, say that for the government to *restrict* the sources of ideas in the marketplace (as it has in the electioneering restriction) is also paternalistic—protecting the audience and polity from information and views that government judges likely to distort their understanding, instill ignorance, and influence their judgment. Including corporate speech in the marketplace protects liberty—the liberty of the audience of individual voters and free agents. We might hope that the text would definitively solve the question and extract us from this endless back and forth. But as it turns out there is nothing in the text that could be described as definitive. As is so often the case with the Constitution, the plain words themselves don't reveal answers.

The textual reasonableness of both readings, however, does suggest a middle ground, and perhaps a principled one. It is that both readings are correct but deal with separate aspects of speech and its freedom. The first reading, that speech is a product of the individual's act of liberty or freedom, and the liberty to formulate and express one's views, is paramount. There is ample reason to read the freedom of speech this way, as we will see in our discussion of intention and historical meaning. The scope of liberty, being individual and aimed toward protecting against government intervention in the domain of thought and belief, must be very strong, requiring the most compelling of government interests to override it, achieved in the narrowest possible way that least restricts the individual's liberty.

Yet the First Amendment is also based on the premise that with competing opinions, perspectives, and truths the capacity of the individual to participate in a democracy will be advanced. The First Amendment, in other words, has utilitarian ends as well. To serve these ends, the sum of information, opinion, and belief available to individuals is important, as is limiting impediments to types and subjects and originators contributing to the speech market. The idea is not unlike antitrust law, which prevents impediments to a free market in goods and services and the like. This conception of the First Amendment focuses on speech itself, the artifact of information, without regard to its source. But it does so only if the speech is valuable to the functioning of the market, and only to that extent. In other words, the speech-productive aim of government in imposing market controls or facilitating market expansion should be justified by the proven fact of an impediment and limited in means and purposes to curing it.

The result of this combined liberty and utility approach to speech would be analogous to the government's argument that corporate speech should not be fully protected in the way individual speech is because of the absence of a liberty foundation, yet it should be protected at a reduced level, measured by a judgment about its utility for the marketplace of speech. Individual speech would be primary and protected at the highest level; corporate speech not tied to individuals would be presumptively free but subject to reasonable, market-based government regulation. It could be an example of an alternative rationale that Chief Justice Roberts mentioned, and it might be appealing to Justice Scalia because it retains the original focus of the First Amendment on individual freedom yet gives corporations a presumed seat in the speech marketplace in recognition of the fact that speech, too, is constitutionally valuable in itself.

THE HISTORICAL BACKGROUND OF THE FIRST AMENDMENT

When the text of the Constitution is ambiguous, as it quite often is, the Supreme Court generally turns to the historical record. What did the drafters and framers intend? What did the ratifiers (people in the states) understand the language to mean? What conditions at the time of ratification might explain the animating purposes behind the language?

When James Madison introduced the first draft of the Bill of Rights, the provisions now contained in the First Amendment (then the Fourth Amendment) were clearly reflective of the First Amendment's origin in individual freedom of conscience and the correlative right of the individual to express his or her views.

> "The civil rights of none shall be abridged on account of religious belief or worship, nor shall any national religion be established, nor shall the full and equal rights of conscience be in any manner, or on any pretext, infringed.
>
> The people shall not be deprived or abridged of their right to speak, to write, or to publish their sentiments; and the freedom of the press, as one of the great bulwarks of liberty, shall be inviolable.
>
> The people shall not be restrained from peaceably assembling and consulting for their common good; nor from applying to the Legislature by petitions, or remonstrances, for redress of their grievances."[7]

The original language is suggestive, though not conclusive, evidence of the orientation of the freedom of speech toward the "people," or individuals. The assembly and petition rights were likewise attached to the "people" speaking in common cause.

Madison's proposal was taken up and was the subject of considerable discussion and debate in Congress, in the drafting committee for the Bill of Rights, and in many states; it emerged finally in the form with which we are familiar. But there is no doubt that it originated and retained through its ratification the central purpose of preserving religious freedom and freedom of conscience, the two animating values shared broadly by Americans in light of their prior struggles for independence from England. These were two values that were deeply grounded in the conditions of freedom for individuals. Corporations were not part of this picture.

The broader historical circumstances in the eighteenth century—the colonial, revolutionary, and postrevolutionary times through the Articles of Confederation, the Constitution, the Bill of Rights ratification, and the decade or so following—are not directly helpful. There was much talk of freedom of conscience and religion, freedom of the press, and the conditions of democracy that would be founded on them. There was consistent political expression by groups of like-minded people, such as the Sons of Liberty and others to which Justice Scalia refers. As he writes:

> The lack of a textual exception for speech by corporations cannot be explained on the ground that such organizations did not exist or did not speak. To the contrary, colleges, towns and cities, religious institutions, and guilds had long been organized as corporations at common law and under the King's charter, and as I have discussed, the practice of incorporation only expanded in the United States. Both corporations and voluntary associations actively petitioned the Government and expressed their views in newspapers and pamphlets. For example: an antislavery Quaker corporation petitioned the First Congress, distributed pamphlets, and communicated through the press in 1790. The New York Sons of Liberty sent a circular to colonies farther south in 1766. And the Society for the Relief and Instruction of Poor Germans circulated a biweekly paper from 1755 to 1757. The dissent offers no evidence—none whatever—that the First Amendment's unqualified text was originally understood to exclude such associational speech from its protection.

The problem, if there is one, is not with Justice Scalia's history. There is good reason to accept it as a description of expressive activity in the late eighteenth century. But it doesn't really say anything about the activities and perceived rights of *business* corporations or their predecessors; it only speaks to the joint or collective expressive activities of groups of individuals and, of course, the press, which was often then expressly partisan and quite unlike the newspaper of today. His account doesn't refer to any explicit discussion of the rights, much less the speech rights, of business organizations, whatever form they took. And it certainly doesn't suggest that corporations should be treated like individuals for purposes of freedom of speech.

Justice Scalia can, and does, suggest that there was a utilitarian flavor to the need for free expression, though this doesn't, even in his account, deprecate the dominantly libertarian message and value of individual freedom of conscience—whether that freedom is enjoyed privately or in what today we would call expressive associations. But that doesn't prove much, if anything, about speech by business organizations. At best it leaves some marginal room in the liberty of speech for future interpreters to read utility—the need for broad information and wide opinion—into the speech guarantee.

Finally, Scalia's history doesn't say anything about the role of the press, which may be seen as the means by which a utilitarian need for full information is to be assured (rather than the government). Scalia should have addressed the press. He didn't do so for the simple (but perhaps flawed) reason that the Court's opinion stated that press freedom was no different than freedom of speech. That reading simply cannot be squared with Madison's original language.

BRINGING THE FIRST AMENDMENT UP TO DATE

Justice Scalia's argument is that corporations and their ilk were not generally hated and feared, as he rhetorically accuses Justice Stevens of saying. And in any event, he says, the character of the business corporations that emerged in the middle years of the nineteenth century was very different, and public attitudes at the time of ratification shouldn't be held against the quite distinct, modern, and pervasive corporate form that we now enjoy. The point is valid. It simply has no bearing on original meaning or intention of the First Amendment.

But the point is critical to others who think about the constitutional validity of corporate freedom of speech. The constitutional text's indeterminacy means that the constitutional answer depends on whether to *extend* the First Amendment beyond its original meaning, not simply based on it. This, in turn, requires a turning away from textualism and originalism to a different question: in light of its purposes then and today, *should* the First Amendment be extended to confer freedom of speech (in its powerful form) on *business* corporations (not just ideological or religious organizations, for example) on grounds of utility, not liberty, and in light of historical and cultural values that have changed since the eighteenth century. Putting the question this way doesn't condemn it constitutionally; it simply requires a quite different, creative form of judicial interpretation, which is not unlike that employed regularly by the Court since the beginning of the nineteenth century. Today it is decried as judicial activism. Others defend it as an inevitable and necessary means of applying aspirational constitutional terms to present circumstances.

Indeed, we can say that, even for Justice Scalia, interpreting the First Amendment to grant full free-speech rights to corporations is not an exercise limited to one historical period in the eighteenth century. This is a question of *judicial* judgment in light of all that has happened since and is happening today. When the Court undertakes such an exercise in creative interpretation, however, it is not free to "do good." The Court instead has placed limits on the scope of its power by virtue of the fact that it is the unelected branch whose power is largely independent of democratic political will. That constrained inquiry is, in the words of Justice John Harlan, whether [denying corporations freedom of speech] violates basic values 'implicit in the concept of ordered liberty,'"

> built on the balance Our Nation has struck between that liberty and the demands of organized society. The balance is the balance struck by this country, having regard to what history teaches are the traditions from which it developed as well as the traditions from which it broke. That tradition is a living thing, not a series of isolated points pricked out in terms of [freedom of speech.] It is a rational continuum.[8]

The inquiry, in short, is based on reason, history, and evolving public values over the course of the nation's existence, applied to the liberty of speech by business corporations in 2010.

Whatever one thinks of the "self-discipline" Justice Harlan's approach imposes on the Supreme Court, its articulation above is perhaps the fullest and best—and the most intellectually honest—formulation of the Court's power *and duty*. It was a duty recklessly ignored by the majority opinion in *Citizens United*, based on the false premise that the free-speech issue had already been decided and the only discipline incumbent on the Court was that of citing precedent.

But the Court's failure doesn't excuse those seriously interested in the corporate speech question from doing two things: (1) recognizing that the decision may or may not be correct; depending on (2) a thoughtful assessment of what the broad landscape of history teaches us about the values and meanings of speech freedom we have today. We can't even begin to undertake such a large and searching inquiry here, but we can identify some elements of the issue on which its resolution will likely turn. I offer my list below, with only brief discussion.

1. *THE GROWTH OF CORPORATIONS.* The expansion of the corporate form over time has been sweeping. Beginning with state-chartered or licensed business corporations in the ınineteenth century, further expansion has often been driven by liability concerns and federal tax policy. Today we enjoy a wide range of options, including joint ventures, limited liability corporations, nonprofit corporations (including foundations), political action corporations, charitable corporations, and more. The vast proportion of corporations are single, or single-family, corporations, many of which are small in scale but some of which—indeed the most politically active of which—are privately owned by the very rich. The very largest corporations—three percent of the total, according to the solicitor general—tend to be business corporations that are publicly held and, often, multinational. As a rule, their involvement in politics has been limited to lobbying on behalf of their business interests and sponsoring PACs by which employees make campaign contributions to candidates.

It can fairly be said that the corporation is a pervasive and culturally settled form in which virtually the entire range of personal and group activity takes place, from the church to the interest group to politics. But its ubiquity doesn't establish a historical or cultural consensus that corporations should be treated just as individuals are in terms of speech freedom or other "liberties." All forms of corporations are very highly regulated at the state and federal levels. Restrictions on purpose, governance, management, and expression by the corporation are pervasive, especially for the nonprofit and charitable corporations and the large and publicly held business corporations. Such restrictions can be seen as evidence of regulatory concern about the corporate form, not acceptance of its status as an individual with full legal and constitutional rights. The range of regulations on the corporation's behavior would not be possible were the corporation infused with the full measure of constitutional rights possessed by individuals. This is true, specifically, with respect to liberty and expression. The "purpose" restrictions imposed on corporations limit free will and free choice, and the corporation's expression—whether, when, and what it can say—are heavily regulated by the securities laws, fair-trade laws, advertising regulations, and the like—not to mention the political campaign restrictions that were overturned in *Citizens United.*

One can argue, of course, that the ubiquity of the corporation has changed its public and cultural status, thus justifying a greater freedom for the corporation in American society. There is force to this argument, though it wouldn't necessarily apply to all corporations. Society and public attitudes have evolved; the law simply hasn't kept up and the Constitution is one source by which change can be forced. One test of this argument might be to ask whether public opinion and political values would support the dismantling of the state and federal regulatory regimes for corporations. The fact that the inclination over the past century, and indeed the inclination today in the tax, securities law, and financial sectors, for example, is toward, not away from, regulation, suggests that the answer would be no.

2. *CORPORATIONS AND POLITICS.* A similar case based on ubiquity might be made for the participation of corporations in politics. The rise of ideological groups—the ACLU, the NRA, the Tea Party movement, the AARP, and so on—has been fostered by the advantages of the corporate form and, more to the point, by the changing face of political activity at all levels of government. Collective forms of expression and political action have become a necessary ingredient of political influence, whether benign (as it generally is) or malignant. The individual voice has, in most ways, been drowned out in our political culture. And corporations, through farm alliances, the Chamber of Commerce, industry or trade associations, and other political action groups in corporate form, have become major forces in the shaping of policy in our representative form of government. To leave corporations out of the political system, or to cripple their freedom of action, is to deny reality. Through trade associations and interest groups, through pervasive lobbying activities, and even through political expression, advertisements, and action, corporations have already emerged as major political actors, even (though only occasionally to date) outside their business domains and in the unrelated ideological battles about social policy and war.

The electioneering restriction in *Citizens United* seems, from this perspective, but a grain of sand on a beach of corporate political participation. A thirty-day rest from corporate wars doesn't mean much, and in any event the remaining players in an election—the 527 political action corporations, the nonprofit and charitable corporations—will still be heard during the thirty-day period. Indeed, they will still be the dominant independent voices heard.

There is a certain denial-of-reality quality to those who object to full speech rights for corporations on matters of politics. Yet there is clearly an undeniable wellspring of cultural and political resistance to broad corporate freedom. Congress itself has tried to stem the tide—ineffectively, to be sure, but perhaps, as the Solicitor General said in oral argument, in a non-self-interested way. Representatives, senators, presidents, even state and local officials express frustration that they are trapped in a system run amok, driven by money from start to finish. Only the individual voters remain independent of the money tide, and it seems clear that they are unhappy with it: disgusted and frustrated would be a better description.

To make the argument for speech rights based on historical evolution and cultural change one must, under the Constitution at least, transcend the fact of reality and ask about the values and beliefs of those who count, the individual voters in the representative political process for whose interests the Constitution was crafted. If that is the question—as it must be—the argument for corporate freedom must fail. In an unbroken line from the founding to the Progressive Era through FDR and to Obama, the cultural values and, indeed, the collective political will have supported restrictions on corporate freedom, and especially in politics. There simply isn't any other way to interpret the forces at work in the 1974 Federal Campaign Reform Act or the McCain-Feingold reform act. Failure in these efforts to control spending, and especially corporate spending in all its forms, may say something about reality, but it says nothing about values, history, culture, and political will.

3. *CONSEQUENCES.* Finally, we can explore the consequences of the Court's decision in *Citizens United.* Here, it can be said, the jury is still out, and the cries of doom are premature, perhaps simply wrong, and certainly misdirected in important ways. The classic business corporation has necessarily, and in its own business interests, been involved in politics, especially by way of PACs and lobbying. It doesn't need the First Amendment to have its say. But the business corporation's involvement has been almost entirely business-related, and narrowly so. Will these corporations—Microsoft, Ford, and the like—now race into the broad political arena? Not, I think, unless they are forced to do so. Indeed, the recent shareholder and public uproar about Target's sponsoring an ad supporting a gay marriage opponent in a political race speaks volumes: keep to your business and stay out of election politics is the message of Target's shareholders and its politically diverse customers, who clearly care about corporations and politics. Businesses are unlikely to

undermine their business interests and their customer or client base to fulfill the political whims of management.

On this question, however, disclosure is critical. Ironically, notwithstanding what Justice Kennedy said in his opinion, by making corporations full First Amendment rights holders, *Citizens United* is likely to *undermine* disclosure—at least in the absence of overruling or seriously recasting the *McIntyre* anonymous speech case. In the 2010 midterm elections it is already clear that new corporate forms—in this case 501(c)(4) nonprofit corporations—are emerging in the wake of *Citizens United* because they afford corporations the ability to make unlimited contributions with anonymity.

Yet the controversy about *Citizens United* may also, and perhaps more importantly, be misdirected. The villain in the act, if there be one, is almost certainly not the small or the large business corporation, which tends to stick to business. It is instead the hybrid forms of corporation—the 527s, the 501(c)(4)s, the ideologically committed foundations and private corporations. These will be much more difficult to control, for as a general rule they already possessed full First Amendment rights before *Citizens United*—ironically, under *Austin* and *McConnell*. Are they the modern equivalents of the Sons of Liberty? Can some of them be satisfactorily distinguished from the others, especially given the seemingly absolutist language in *Citizens United* about speaker-based distinctions under the First Amendment?

Perhaps, instead, we *should* see them as the Sons of Liberty in our new, internet-based, mass-communication, political culture. Let them speak and waste their money; they can't control the voters, they can only persuade them. This is a central premise of the First Amendment: through many voices and many views something—hopefully something good—will emerge. This is a belief, a faith, not a fact. It is the basis for Justice Scalia's much quoted statement:

> The premise of the First Amendment is that the American people are neither sheep nor fools, and hence fully capable of considering both the substance of speech presented to them and its proximate and ultimate source. If that premise is wrong, our democracy has a much greater problem to overcome than merely the influence of amassed wealth. Given the premises of democracy, there is no such thing as too much free speech.

TOO MUCH FREE SPEECH?

In *Citizens United* the answer to the "too much free speech" question lies primarily in matters of methodology and substance. *Citizens United* is an instance of constitutional interpretation based on an almost utter lack of constitutional reasoning. Its corporate speech holding yielded an unnecessary limit on the political process with regard to issues of corporate regulation and power, campaign reform, and disclosure requirements. A tidy mess, that.

Whether the consequences of *Citizens United* are good or bad, or even largely irrelevant, is beside the point on the questions of methodology and constitutional substance. So is the sentiment that "there is no such thing as too much free speech." The sentiment, true or not, is not a substitute for historically and culturally based constitutional reasoning by the unelected and independent branch of government.

As to the practical consequences of the decision, we know that they are potentially broad and deep, ranging from campaign spending to disclosure to anonymity in speech to changes in the state and federal licensing and regulatory framework for all corporations. But it is too early to know what those consequences will be and whether they will be good, bad, or indifferent.

All we know for sure is that they will have been the result of a deeply fractured Supreme Court and a deeply flawed approach to interpreting the Constitution.

CHAPTER TWO

Government and Its Speech Forum

Pleasant Grove City v. Summum, 129 S. Ct. 1125 (2009)

A forty-five minute drive south from Salt Lake City is the city of Pleasant Grove, Utah, and within the city sits Pioneer Park—the site of a local controversy that launched a landmark expansion of the doctrine known as "government speech." A passerby would not necessarily guess at such significance. The park is somewhat hidden, and its expanse is limited, taking up only part of a small city block and totaling only a couple square acres. Its attractions are a hodgepodge of monuments and historical markers, including an old granary, a wishing well, and a privately donated Ten Commandments monument. One local editorial writer commented, "If I were going to place a public monument to anything, one of the last places I would choose to do it is in Pleasant Grove's Pioneer Park." But that did not stop a small and unconventional local religious group called Summum from arguing before the Supreme Court of the United States for the right to place its own monument next to the Ten Commandments in Pioneer Park.

In September 2003, Summum wrote Jim Danklef, the mayor of Pleasant Grove, asking to erect its own religious monument right next to a Ten Commandments monument donated by the Fraternal Order of the Eagles, a national nonprofit group with local chapters. The city denied Summum's request, noting that a donated object or donating group must have a direct history with the city of Pleasant Grove. Summum, a small, New Age religion, had no such relationship with the almost entirely Mormon Pleasant Grove. Only in August 2004, almost a year after denying the request, did the city formally adopt these requirements for private donation of a monument.

Summum is a homegrown religious and philosophical organization based in Utah. The group's main sanctuary is a twenty-six-foot-high copper-toned pyramid near downtown Salt Lake City. There, the group teaches philosophy classes, initiates newcomers, and produces "Nectar Publications," an alcoholic drink that Summum believes to contain "spiritual concepts and information." As a result, Summum's headquarters is also a licensed winery.

Summum is a form of Gnostic Christianity, although it labels itself more as a philosophy than as a religion. Its practices include meditation, lectures, and—most bizarrely—the mummification of humans and pets. But it is Summum's beliefs surrounding the biblical story of Moses that placed the group at odds with the city counsel of Pleasant Grove. Summum tells an alternate story of Moses's trip up Mount Sinai, in which Moses actually received two sets of tablets but only revealed one set to his followers, believing they were not ready for the complex principles embodied in the first set. That first set of tablets, according to Summum, contained the following Seven Aphorisms:

I. The Principle of Psychokinesis. Summum is Mind; the universe is a mental creation.

II. The Principle of Correspondence. As above, so below; as below, so above.

III. The Principle of Vibration. Nothing rests; everything moves; everything vibrates.

IV. The Principle of Opposition. Everything is dual; everything has an opposing point; everything has its pair of opposites; like and unlike are the same; opposites are identical in nature, but different in degree; extremes bond; all truths are but partial truths; all paradoxes may be reconciled.

V. The Principle of Rhythm. Everything flows out and in; everything has its season; all things rise and fall; the pendulum swing expresses itself in everything; the measure of the swing to the right is the measure of the swing to the left; rhythm compensates.

VI. The Principle of Cause and Effect. Every cause has its effect; every effect has its cause; everything happens according to Law; chance is just a name for law not recognized; there are many fields of causation, but nothing escapes the Law of Destiny.

VII. The Principle of Gender. Gender is in everything; everything has its masculine and feminine principles; Gender manifests on all levels.[1]

It was Summum's goal in Pleasant Grove to place this second set of revelations alongside the original commandments, apparently to finish the job

Moses started. In May 2005, after the city's first rejection of the display, Summum sent another request to pursue this goal in Pioneer Park, but neither the mayor nor anyone else at city hall responded. So Summum began to wage a legal battle that would climb to the Supreme Court, in the form of a contest between private speech and government speech.

Summum first sought injunctive relief in the federal district court, seeking to force the city of Pleasant Grove to allow the Seven Aphorisms monument. The city's decision, argued Summum, violated Summum's right to speak freely (build a "Seven Aphorisms" monument) in a public forum (Pioneer Park). In other words, Summum's position was that if the city of Pleasant Grove let the Fraternal Order of the Eagles donate its monument, it must let Summum donate one too. The district court was unconvinced, and denied Summum's motion for injunctive relief.

At the time Summum brought its free speech challenge, another group was challenging the presence of the Ten Commandments monument itself, arguing that it violated the Constitution's establishment clause requirement that "Congress shall make no law respecting an establishment of religion." Summum later brought its own separate lawsuit in 2010 to challenge the Ten Commandments monument on establishment clause grounds, on the theory, in effect, that if we can't have ours, they shouldn't get theirs. This establishment clause controversy becomes an important sideshow in the Supreme Court.

Summum's luck changed when it appealed its case to the United States Court of Appeals for the Tenth Circuit. The first promising sign for Summum was that the three-judge panel held that both the Ten Commandments monument and Summum's proposed Aphorisms were private speech protected by the First Amendment. The court next held that the collection of monuments and other donated installations in Pioneer Park was a "traditional public forum," where the government generally may not bar speech based on the content of the message. Pleasant Grove's blessing of the Ten Commandments on one hand, and rejection of the Aphorisms on the other constituted an impermissible content-based distinction. Pleasant Grove's only justification—that the distinction was based on a preference for historically significant installations—did not satisfy the exceedingly high "strict scrutiny" standard. As a result, the court of appeals reversed the district court and held that Pleasant Grove must allow Summum to erect its Aphorisms in Pioneer Park.

By October 2008 the Summum lawsuit was the talk of the town. In the months leading up to the Supreme Court oral argument, the mayor circulated newsletters advising Pleasant Grove citizens to "prepare yourself with the facts. Consider carefully the impression your home or business will make on the nation." National news outlets began to cover the dispute between Summum and Pleasant Grove, and local and national editorialists offered opinions from one side or another—all anticipating the monumental argument that would take place that November.

▪ ▪ ▪

Before we turn in earnest to the *Summum* case, some general background on the public forum for speech and the recently emerging government-speech doctrine is in order. We'll start at the beginning. In the early days of the Republic there was no formal judicial recognition of an individual's access to public property for expression. Indeed, there were few first amendment decisions at all. The First Amendment free speech guarantee wasn't understood to apply to states until after the Civil War and adoption of the Fourteenth Amendment, and the conclusion that the Fourteenth Amendment incorpo rated much of the Bill of Rights, including freedom of speech, wasn't firmly established until the early twentieth century.

The need for a right of access to public property for speech—specifically streets, sidewalks, and parks—was not formally recognized until the late 1930s and the 1940s. In a largely rural nation there was simply no need for such a right, as public speech took place in streets and sidewalks and parks as a matter of custom and habit. As industrialization occurred and highly populated urban areas developed, that situation changed, and with the rise of antiwar and related protests, the communist scare, and religious strife in the first half of the twentieth century, government—often municipal—efforts to restrict the activity greatly increased through blunt-edged licensing and laws against littering and disturbing the peace.

This activity gave rise to the free-speech concept of the traditional public forum in the form, originally, of an individual's right (subject to reasonable and neutral time, place, and manner restrictions) to use the public streets, sidewalks, and parks which had "time out of mind" been available for expressive activity. It wouldn't be until the 1970s and the decades thereafter that the public forum would take on a broader and even more speech-protective character with the addition of the nontraditional limited public forum, which allowed claims of access to a wide range of other public facilities and locations. The limited public forum consisted, generally, of property dedicated by government to particular uses, like schools, theaters, civic centers, and airport terminals, to mention just a few. The limited public forum doctrine allowed government to limit speech in such areas—but only if, and to the extent that, their dedication to specific purposes or types of speech was reasonably necessary and incompatible with wide open access for speech, and only then if the government did not discriminate against speech based on its ideas or points of view. A university auditorium might be reserved for classes and for speech that served the educational needs of students and faculty, for example, but within those limited purposes—say, discussion of forms of government—the university could not permit speech about democracy but prohibit speech about communism.

Finally, other areas could be declared by government to be nonpublic forums, serving programmatic purposes that were completely incompatible with any form of public speech, as long as that designation was reasonable (an inquiry that a court would undertake in the name of the First Amendment) and as long as the government did not enforce the speech limitation in a discriminatory manner, favoring ideas the government liked and disfavoring those it didn't like. My law school classroom is such a nonpublic forum, dedicated to educationally relevant talk about constitutional law among me and my students only, but it must be free of censorship (from me) of the relevant constitutional ideas students are free to express when I call on them.

With public forum analysis now consisting of the true public forum (streets, parks, sidewalks, and other nondedicated spaces), the limited public forum, and the nonpublic forum, a highly complex yet speech-protective system had been put in place. All government property was presumptively available for free speech. Streets, parks, and sidewalks would always be available for free speech. For other property, the government bore the burden of justifying any limitations it wished to place on its property and in any event could never, in any forum, treat speech differently based on government preference for one view over another.

It is against this historic background that the doctrine of government speech arose in the late twentieth century. The doctrine assured government the ability to speak (not a First Amendment right to speak) and immunity from any First Amendment claim that might be based, for example, on the point-of-view preference involved in any government view that is expressed—antismoking, pro-war, antiabortion, for example. So the limitations of public forum analysis were suspended for government speech, whether it be a government advertisement or the Congressional Record. Early cases tended to arise in the setting of particular statements by government that displaced or competed with opposite views on a question. It soon became clear, however, that the government's expressive right could not be limited to isolated instances of speech but would also necessarily involve the reservation of property or space for government speech only (and for private speech endorsed by government as expressing government's viewpoint), and the reservation of space would have a temporal component, ranging from a short period (say, a sponsored political debate) to a long and even indefinite period, like government websites. With cases involving the government editorial decisions of a public television station, advertisements for beef, dedicated government websites, and NEA-supported artists, the government speech idea grew into what I call the government speech *forum*—a time and place where no message but that of the government (or private speakers whom the government, selects to express its point of view) can be expressed.

Whether and how the claimed government speech forum would apply to monuments in a public park was the question at issue in the *Summum* case. Beneath the surface of this issue, however, were some very fundamental First Amendment questions. Our focus will be on these questions. Is First Amendment immunity for government speech constitutionally justified, and if so, why? Should government's choice of private speech qualify as government speech? Should government's speech power be extended to a government speech forum in which only approved ideas and viewpoints can be expressed?

■ ■ ■

The lawyers appearing before the Court in the *Summum* case were experienced at Supreme Court practice. Pleasant Grove City was represented by Jay A. Sekulow of Washington, D.C., Chief Counsel for the American Center for Law and Justice. The United States, which was permitted to participate in the oral argument because of the case's potential impact on federal parks and monuments, was represented by Daryl Joseffer, the deputy solicitor general in the Department of Justice. Summum was represented by Pamela Harris of Washington, D.C., the executive director of the Supreme Court Institute at the Georgetown University Law Center.

Chief Justice Roberts opened the session.

> CHIEF JUSTICE ROBERTS: We'll hear argument first this morning in Case 07-665, *Pleasant Grove City v. Summum*. Mr. Sekulow.
>
> MR. SEKULOW: Mr. Chief Justice, and may it please the Court:
>
> The Court below erred when it held that the First Amendment forces Pleasant Grove City to accept and erect on its property a private party's donated, unattended, permanent monument.
>
> The decision suffers from two constitutional defects: First, the court's conclusion that a donated Ten Commandments monu-

> ment constitutes private speech rather than Government speech is wrong. Here each of the monuments on display in Pioneer Park have been selected by the Government, are owned by the Government, controlled by the Government, and are displayed on Government property. When the Government is speaking, it is free from the traditional free speech constraints of the First Amendment.
>
> Second, the court compounded its error by further concluding that Pioneer Park is a traditional public forum for the erection of permanent, unattended monuments by private parties.

A little additional background is needed here. Recall that the government speech doctrine had evolved from a right of government to speak, to a claim that government could reserve places for government speech, like an automobile license plate with a state motto. This development presented a potential conflict with the already established public-forum doctrine and its uniform rule against viewpoint-based discrimination.

How does the government speech idea fit into the public-forum-based First Amendment analysis? Is the public park a public forum? Or is it a monument display, more like a museum? And is the city's claim in *Summum* a forum claim at all? Or is it instead a claim to set aside part of a public park as a new kind of forum—a government speech forum—in which only the ideas that government agrees with can be heard? Is the government claiming that in its reserved space it—government—has freedom of speech effectively protected by the First Amendment because the government's speech is immune from First Amendment challenge? How could such an idea be possibly squared with the liberty roots and the text of the First Amendment, which protects people from government, not government from people?

It is this drama of background and ideas and questions that will be played out in the oral arguments in the *Summum* case.

> CHIEF JUSTICE ROBERTS: Mr. Sekulow, you're really just picking your poison, aren't you? I mean, the more you say that the monument is Government speech to get out of the Free Speech Clause, the more it seems to me you're walking into a trap under the Establishment Clause. If it's Government speech, it may not present a free speech problem, but what is the Government doing supporting the Ten Commandments?

This is something of a dilemma in the case. If the government is free to speak its preferences and mind—on abortion, taxes, and even religion—how can the latter religious speech be squared with the First Amendment's prohibition of government establishment of religion, which is generally interpreted to prohibit government action that prefers one religion over others or religion over nonreligion? Is government's right or power to speak limited by the establishment clause of the First Amendment, even though the government's speech is permitted and even facilitated by the free speech clause of the same First Amendment? This is really confusing stuff, which might be dismissed as just so much pickiness if only it weren't so very, very important.

> MR. SEKULOW: Well, the Ten Commandments here was displayed in Pioneer Park to show the pioneer heritage of the community. This was a community of pioneers on a quest for religious liberty. That's why this town was established. There is no Establishment Clause claim here. Here the city stated that the reason they accepted the donation of a monument from the Fraternal Order of Eagles was to represent their pioneer heritage.

For now we can hold the establishment clause in abeyance, with just a few observations. First, the establishment clause might well preclude the government from endorsing the Ten Commandments as a religious document to be favored, but the government might, instead, display the Ten Commandments as a part of a cultural or historical exhibit as long as the display would be understood in that way and not as an endorsement of a religious belief. This distinction is tricky, and it will become important later on when the Court and lawyers discuss exactly what the city's message was in this case. The second point is that the establishment clause claim was not raised in the case. But this won't stop the Court from worrying about it in oral argument. If in the end the Court decides that there is a likelihood of an establishment clause violation that forecloses the City's speech claim, the case might be sent back to the lower courts for further evidence and full consideration of the issue.

> CHIEF JUSTICE ROBERTS: Mr. Sekulow, if somebody comes upon this monument in the park, how are they supposed to tell whether it's Government speech or private speech?
>
> MR. SEKULOW: Well, Mr. Chief Justice, [it's stated] on the face of the monument that it's presented to Pleasant Grove City in Utah County by the Fraternal Order of Eagles. As far as Government speech [is concerned], here the Government exercised control. After all, they allowed it, accepted it, and allowed it to be erected on

their property. Under Utah law, all right, title, and interest to that property transferred.

JUSTICE SOUTER: Isn't the tough issue here not so much whether there is Government speech? I will assume and I do indeed assume that there is. Isn't the tough issue here the claim that there is in fact a mixture, that it is both Government and private? And the argument for its continuing to be private speech I take it is simply the Eagles identification with the presentation and their espousal of what the monument says. How do you think we ought to deal with the mixture issue?

This issue is both simple and also very, very tricky. If it's government speech, one would think, the government must in fact "own" the speech. But as it turns out that's not always the case, as the government can speak through the private speech of others if the government endorses their speech as expressing the government's idea. At the simplest level an example might be the use of a quote from Lincoln in a speech by a public university president or the displaying of a state motto on a license plate. But it can also happen when the government—say, a public university—picks one speaker over another and does so because it prefers the ideas of the selected speaker and expresses that government preference through the act of selection. These kinds of cases do arise quite often. The hard questions involve how one determines when the government's endorsement is clear enough that people know it is the government that is speaking. That's clear enough in my constitutional law classroom, where students must answer my questions and can't talk about contract law. But it's harder with a private artist whose performance has been financially supported (endorsed) or denied funding (nonendorsed, which is a message too) because the government likes or dislikes the ideas of the artist.

Justices Souter and Ginsburg see this case as such a hard case—expressive endorsement through selection of the Ten Commandments monument, and nonendorsement through rejection of the Summum monument. It seems perfectly plain that, without more, people could see the rejection of the Summum monument as a rejection of the Summum religion.

MR. SEKULOW: Well, I think the fact that the monument originated by the Eagles as a third party doesn't in any way take away from the fact that most of the monuments in parks are donated by or originated with third parties—

JUSTICE SOUTER: They probably are, but most of [the other monuments]—and you correct me if I'm wrong here—do not contain in a prominent place in the monument itself the statement that, you know, this is the gift of or the position of or what-not of X, Y or Z, whereas this monument does.

MR. SEKULOW: Most of them, Justice Souter, do actually have statements. In fact, a perfect example would be at Gettysburg National Military Park, where a number of those monuments, most of them, are donated by or originated by third parties. They'll often say "Donated by," for instance, "the Father Corby—

JUSTICE SOUTER: We may have more cases coming.

MR. SEKULOW: I hope not.

JUSTICE SOUTER: But tell me, what is the criterion that we should use to decide what the significance of the private identification is?

MR. SEKULOW: I think the key should be the issue of control, who controls the message ultimately here. And the fact is the Statue of Liberty originated by the Franco-American Union was originated by a third party. The United States by resolution accepted it. At that point title transferred.

JUSTICE GINSBURG: If we accept that there is Government speech, I think Justice Souter's question is: Isn't this really the Government endorsement of the Eagles' message? I mean, the Eagles are all over this monument, their symbol of the eagle, and the Eagles want it to be known that this is their monument. Indeed, I think in the *Van Orden* case [a recent establishment clause case involving the Ten Commandments monument on the statehouse grounds in Texas], wasn't [the government's explanation that] Texas did this in recognition of the good work that the Eagles do in trying to prevent juvenile delinquency?

MR. SEKULOW: Right. And I think that actually points to why, once it's controlled and owned by the Government, the fact that it originated in the third party, Justice Ginsburg, changes the equation for ownership and control to the Government.

JUSTICE SOUTER: Well, if it does, it changes it, as I understand your answer, by eliminating the private aspect of the speech. So that your real answer to me is it's not a mixture.

MR. SEKULOW: It's not.

The problem with Sekulow's clear and simple solution is that holding title, without anything more, doesn't make clear to the public viewing the monument what the city's distinct message is, much less that the city actually owns it. For them, the message might as easily be a religious one, not a historical one. Should the public viewer's interpretation of the monument matter under the First Amendment? Or should the government's purpose, disclosed or not, be determinative, since the speaker is the government and as a free speaker it has the right to say what it wants whether everyone understands it or not? And what about selective government support of art, or theater? There's no pretense of government ownership in that setting.

> JUSTICE STEVENS: Assume you didn't have the policy that you do have, but it was perfectly clear that the city decided not to put up this [Summum] monument because it disagreed with the message of the monument. Whether you call it Government speech or private speech, would that be permissible?
>
> MR. SEKULOW: It wouldn't be a First Amendment free speech claim for Summum [as the city's disagreement is the city's speech, which therefore displaces Summum's free speech right to reply or equal access]. I think that's important to point out. The basis upon which they sought access, if you will, is a species of an equal access claim.
>
> JUSTICE KENNEDY: But, Justice Stevens's question is important, maybe not for your case but for other cases. Why isn't he correct that if you don't like the message then that raises a claim that the government is discriminating against speech because of its content, which it cannot do under the First Amendment when it is regulating private speech.
>
> MR. SEKULOW: Because if the Government is speaking, if it's the Government's message, they're of course allowed to engage in content-based statements. The Statue of Liberty was a statement of liberty enlightening the world. I could give a list of monuments that do that.
>
> JUSTICE KENNEDY: But it doesn't seem to me that you have to make the Government-speech argument for you to make the argument that you just made.
>
> MR. SEKULOW: No, not necessarily. Governments make determinations of what they are going to put in their parks to communicate a message. That's very different from the typical equal access case, where the Government merely opens up its facilities for a variety of viewpoints, Justice Stevens, and then cannot engage in content-based or viewpoint-based—

It is at this point in the exchange that the tautological quality of government speech becomes obvious: if the government says its discrimination is an act of speaking, then it is so, and the public forum restrictions on viewpoint discrimination by government disappear.

JUSTICE SOUTER: So if the city says, we are going to have a designated ten-acre field in which *anybody* can put up a monument, but you can't because we don't like your message, there's a First Amendment problem. But if the city hides the ball and says in effect, we will accept monuments from people who want to place them on our property if the monuments have some kind of an arguable historical connection or a connection with people with long association with the community, as long as they have that sort of criterion in mind then they can select any way they want to?

JUSTICE SCALIA: It goes to the same thing, doesn't it? I mean, whether it's the Government stating the message or whether it's the Government creating a limited public forum for the presentation of only those messages that it thinks are important, it comes to the same thing, doesn't it?

MR. SEKULOW: Well, it depends on—if it's a limited public forum, certainly limited public forums can be based on subject matter and speaker identity. Even in the designated public forum, it could be limited in that regard.

But I think that points to the confusion of what took place here. The Court in our view conflated those two issues, the issue of forum and Government speech. And while they're both separate bases upon which we believe the Tenth Circuit opinion could be reversed, the reality is that in this particular case once title passed and control vested in Pleasant Grove City, they were the owner and effectively controlled [the space in order to communicate the city's message—in other words, government speech.]

JUSTICE STEVENS: Let me ask you a question to make sure I understand your position. It would have been permissible for the city to say, "Our park is filled with monuments and we are only going to let those in who convey messages that we agree with"?

MR. SEKULOW: If the policy is that the Government's controlling those messages, it's not individual private expression, that would be permissible.

JUSTICE STEVENS: But really, in this sort of case the debate as to whether the policy justifications for the monument are a sham or are not are really irrelevant?

MR. SEKULOW: From a legal standpoint on Government speech, it's irrelevant.

This is a very bold position that Sekulow is taking. If it's government speech, nothing else really matters, and that is true for a government speech forum in which it reserves control over private speech. For example, the government's control over a website that allows only speech supporting government. Can that really be right? Can government simply designate a place or time for ideas it likes, without more, and call that a government speech forum free from First Amendment scrutiny? If there is some limit to what government can do in such situations, is it to be found in the very meaning or definition of government speech or in legislation Congress might pass to limit such power?

JUSTICE STEVENS: Even if it's a Government forum for private speech, I think it's the same thing. You're defining—you define the forum to include only those—the forum is putting up monuments. You just put up those monuments that agree with the message.

JUSTICE KENNEDY: And the same question Justice Stevens had, just to tack onto his question here, your answer was: Oh, well, the Government owns it. Suppose the Government says: We will accept ownership only if we agree with the message. That just puts his question. I think the ownership argument is not an answer to the Justice's question.

MR. SEKULOW: It's not ownership, Justice Kennedy, in and of itself. Ownership is an indicator, a factor for control, but it is control of the message. When the Government implanted that monument donated by the Fraternal Order of Eagles, they were sending a message. It was not a message of "I am the lord thy God"—

JUSTICE SOUTER: Nothing could be a more obvious control of the message than the criterion that says we will decide in determining to accept it or not, we will decide on the basis of whether we agree with the message. That is control with a vengeance.

MR. SEKULOW: The difference is—the difference between each of those cases and the case here is the Fraternal Order of Eagles surrendered control of their message and their speech. In the typical equal access case, Justice Stevens, they do not.

JUSTICE SOUTER: Well, they—they do in the example Justice Kennedy just raised and the example that I just raised. The Eagles come along say: Here's the monument; take it; it's all yours.

MR. SEKULOW: Which happened here.

JUSTICE SOUTER: And the—the Government says: Okay, we'll take the Eagles monument. We will not on identical terms take the Summum monument because we disagree with the message. At the point they make the decision they don't own anything. What they are doing is controlling, in your words, and they are controlling on the basis of agreement with the message. Why isn't that a First Amendment violation?

MR. SEKULOW: If the Government is the speaker, they are certainly entitled to do that. If they are not, that would be a very different scenario.

JUSTICE SOUTER: It wouldn't be a speaker on your view until it takes control of the monument.

MR. SEKULOW: No; the speech selection itself is an independent basis under *Forbes, Finley,* and *American Library Association* to bring these kind of—

These three cases involved government acceptance or rejection of a private message based on government's disagreement with it when the government acts in the capacity of an editor of a public television station (*Forbes*), a patron of the arts (*Finley*), and a librarian. The Court has said that these are speech acts by the government and thus immune from First Amendment scrutiny.

These and other similar cases involving government selection of private speech as part of government expression have gotten confused in the oral argument with the separate public forum doctrine, which may allow some government selectivity about subject matter of speech (in my class, constitutional law, not contract law) but don't involve selectivity based on government's mere dislike of the ideas contained in the speech. Such specific idea-based choices about speech that is permitted is *only* allowed if the selection decision is an act of government speech—in other words, an effort by government to communicate its own ideas through selective adoption or endorsement of others' speech.

The so-called public-forum doctrines are a constitutional mess in many ways, yet the forum concept is important in two ways to the Court's treatment of the *Summum* case. First, with the recognition that government can speak through selection of private speech of others, the government speech doctrine and the government's resulting immunity from First Amendment challenge has been expanded from a right to speak its mind just like anyone else, to a right to reserve space and time in which only approved private speech will be allowed—a government speech forum, if you will. In this forum the government's actions are a mix of speaking combined with a heavy dose of *regulation* of private speakers who would like access to the government's space but are denied a place because the government disfavors their ideas. The kinds of settings in which this forum-based government speech occurs are numerous—including educational settings, information sites, and the full range of government websites—and, in this case, even space that was formerly a public park, the "from time immemorial" place for speech, which will occupy the Court when Pamela Harris, representing Summum, takes the podium shortly.

JUSTICE SOUTER: But those are cases in which, to begin with, the Government is engaging in a process of, in effect, sponsoring speech. And here we have not, I think, reached the point in which the public park is to be analogized either with a publication or a magazine or grants to the arts.

MR. SEKULOW: I think, when it comes to the issue of selecting monuments for its park, it's very similar to a museum curator or the arts.

CHIEF JUSTICE ROBERTS: Thank you, Mr. Sekulow.

Hmm. The mayor of Pleasant Grove City as a museum curator! That's an image.

Sekulow did a good job. He had a theory and he stuck to it. It may be a pretty frightening theory of government power to many people, but even so he defended it clearly and well. He stuck the Court with the logic and practical consequences of the Court's own prior decisions. He thus avoided explaining why and on what constitutional basis the government must have such vast power. That is a public-forum and individual-speech-freedom question, which Mr. Sekulow was able to cordon off as irrelevant to government speech. Things got pretty confusing at the end when the forum analysis was introduced, but the confusion was largely the Court's, not Sekulow's.

Following Sekulow was Daryl Joseffer, a deputy solicitor general for the United States. The United States filed a brief in the case supporting Pleasant Grove City, and he was allowed some of Sekulow's time to present the United States' view. As we will see, he takes a very strong and tough position favoring the government speech view, and he is literally barraged with challenges and questions from some of the Justices.

CHIEF JUSTICE ROBERTS: Mr. Joseffer.

MR. JOSEFFER: Mr. Chief Justice, and may it please the Court:

Of course the Government can select the content and viewpoint of monuments on the National Mall and in other public parks across the country. The Vietnam Veterans Memorial did not open us up to a Viet Cong memorial. When the Martin Luther King Memorial is completed on the mall, it will not have to be offset by a monument to the man who shot Dr. King.

JUSTICE ALITO: Can't there be a situation where the Government does create a monument that is a limited public forum? Let's take the example that you just gave, the Vietnam War Memorial. I presume the Government could not refuse to have the names of certain deceased soldiers on that monument because it disagreed with certain ideas that they had espoused at one point or another.

This is a very good and very tough question. It forces Joseffer to take a strong and extreme position right out of the gate—something I'm sure he would have preferred not to do.

MR. JOSEFFER: Well, when it is Government speech, we can have a Washington Monument and a Jefferson Memorial without an Adams one. I mean, we do get to decide [whom] we want to memorialize on the mall because it's Government speech.

But there are also two legal theories here. The first is that this is Government speech. The second is that even if it [were] private speech, this would be one of those unusual contexts like public broadcasting, museums, libraries, where normal forum principles do not apply because the Government is acting as a curator and value judgments are, therefore, both inevitable and appropriate.

The second theory really isn't different, it is just government speaking through selection of private speech and thus having complete control over the government's forum free from First Amendment scrutiny. The justices, however, aren't interested in neat theory at this point. They want to get down to brass tacks and find out just how far the Government's view of the case extends.

JUSTICE STEVENS: Suppose the Government in the Vietnam Memorial decided not to put up the names of any homosexual soldiers. Would that be permissible?

MR. JOSEFFER: Yes. When the Government is speaking, it can choose [whom] to memorialize and [whom] not. As a matter of the Free Speech Clause, there are no limits on the Government's ability to speak freely. Under the Equal Protection Clause, the Establishment

Clause, perhaps the Due Process Clause, there might be thought to be independent checks on the Government's speech. But the Free Speech Clause, whatever else it does, does not prevent the Government from speaking freely.

Another tough answer to a tough question. The answer is statist in the extreme. Joseffer acknowledges that the government's power to speak is not a liberty or a right under the First Amendment, but instead a power inherent in government which immunizes government from any First Amendment scrutiny for what it does: displace others' speech; discriminate against disfavored ideas; exclude others from a speech forum based on their ideas. If that's not the functional equivalent of a right of free speech, I don't know what would be. At least it's a remarkably strong immunity. Other limits like equal protection might apply, but it's really hard to imagine how that could be the case, for the Court's articulation of the government speech power allows it to discriminate against ideas and speakers with complete impunity, which in normal circumstances would flatly violate equal protection.

All of this raises very big questions that seem, in part, to worry some of the justices . . . except, perhaps, Justice Scalia.

JUSTICE SCALIA: It seems to me the Government could disfavor homosexuality just as it could disfavor abortion, just as it can disfavor a number of other things that in many States people are free to do. The Government can disfavor all of it, can't it?

MR. JOSEFFER: The Government would be powerless to do anything if it cannot first formulate and then express its own viewpoints.

JUSTICE ALITO: Why is that the answer to the question? Why isn't the answer to the question that monuments generally are not a forum? There is a fundamental difference between the speaker's corner in the park where anybody can speak and a permanent monument that takes up space, presumably limited public space. And if you have the unusual situation where you are have a monument that is really analogous to a forum, then the forum analysis would be applicable. But to apply it to something like the Washington Monument or the Jefferson Memorial is ridiculous.

MR. JOSEFFER: When the Government is acting as a curator as in the museum context, normal forum principles do not apply.

In *Forbes*, for example, this Court held that when the Government acts as a public broadcaster it normally can engage in viewpoint discrimination, including making a decision about who will participate in candidate debates. And the same point applies here to monuments, I think, for a combination of three reasons.

First, the Government has an overwhelming interest as a property owner in not being saddled with structures it does not want; second, the limits on the availability of public space you refer to; and, third, the Government's sovereign interest in using monuments on its own property to tell its own story, as the Federal Government has done here on the Mall.

It's similar to, for example, a sculpture garden where the Government can choose what sculptures to put in the sculpture garden without necessarily having some overriding theme or overriding reason.

If I could give two examples of that, in Meridian Hill Park here in Northwest D.C., between 15th and 16th streets, the Government chose to accept and place a variety of privately donated structures that have no evident connection to one another. They cover people as diverse as Joan of Arc, President Buchanan—

JUSTICE BREYER: But suppose they only accept Democrats who are sculptors, and they reject all the Republicans? Are you saying the First Amendment would not stop that?

MR. JOSEFFER: The Free Speech Clause on its own force does not prevent the Government from speaking freely. But as a matter of rational basis review under the Fifth and Fourteenth Amendments, it is hard to see how the Government would have a legitimate governmental interest in pure partisan activity.

But the Free Speech Clause, what it does is that it limits the extent to which the Government can regulate other people's speech.

In other words, government has no free speech right. But when it speaks it is immune from First Amendment challenge by other persons who do have free speech rights. One of the reasons the First Amendment speech guarantee does not restrict government's own speech is that the First Amendment only limits government regulation (prohibition, restriction, etc.) of other people's speech.

JUSTICE KENNEDY: Well, under the Equal Protection Clause would—if you wrote an Equal Protection Clause opinion, you would end up saying it's content-based. That's the First Amendment.

MR. JOSEFFER: If it's Government speech, though—

JUSTICE KENNEDY: I don't think that you can avoid the hard part by saying, "Oh, other amendments of the Constitution might apply." The heart of the question is whether the Government may discriminate based on content, and that's a First Amendment question.

MR. JOSEFFER: But when the Government is speaking or when the Government is acting as a curator as with a museum or a sculpture garden or a library or here, the Government is absolutely entitled to make both content and viewpoint-based distinctions. It's the same as the Government putting a painting in a Government museum.

JUSTICE SOUTER: I see your point, but the trouble with that as an argument here is that the private part of the speech is just as much chiseled in stone as the public part. So it's not going to go away at the end of the day, and there isn't any way that the Government in effect can engage in the gesture of saying all private speech is treated the same way, whatever way that might be. So we've got a more difficult problem here. What you are, in effect, saying is yes, you can find instances of Government speech in which there is clearly a private identification consistent with it, but the only appropriate analysis is the analysis for government speech. You can't have it both ways, you've got to pick one or the other; and it is the Government aspect which controls the First Amendment purposes. That, I take it, is your answer?

MR. JOSEFFER: Yes.

JUSTICE SOUTER: There is nothing unusual about it, but we haven't had this kind of a challenge before. So I guess it still rests on you to say why we should submerge the private part to the Government part. There may be a very good reason, but I want to know what your reason is.

MR. JOSEFFER: It's simply that once the Government takes control of something, says this is our speech, then it's the Government speaking.

CHIEF JUSTICE ROBERTS: Thank you, counsel.

Joseffer's contribution to the argument was that he made the very broad claim of government speech power on behalf of the United States government, not just the mayor of Pleasant Grove City. He upped the stakes in a big way. He also agreed with Sekulow's strong definition of the government's speech power and held the line on that issue without wavering. It is a tough line to hold given its great breadth. We will see the other side in the case taking an equally tough line, though a more limited one that has the advantage of strong First Amendment tradition. The case has all of the makings of a great oral argument.

CHIEF JUSTICE ROBERTS: Ms. Harris.

MS. HARRIS: Mr. Chief Justice, may it please the Court:

The city here gave the Eagles access to its public park for a display about the Ten Commandments, and it denied Summum access for a display about the tenets of its faith. That's a violation of the core free

> speech principle that the Government may not favor one message over another in a public forum. The Eagles display here is not Government speech. The city had nothing to do with the Ten Commandments Monument.

This is a very clear, strong statement: the park and its monuments are not government speech; they are instead a public forum reserved for speech by individuals. The city's original acceptance of the Eagles' monument and its later rejection of Summum's monument were point-of-view-based restrictions of others' speech which the First Amendment has from the beginning strictly forbidden. The clear and straightforward statement of Summum's argument seems to unsettle Justice Scalia a bit.

> JUSTICE SCALIA: You say in a public forum. I mean, that sort of begs the question. I mean, that—that encapsulates your—your—encapsulates your answer. Has the city allowed anybody to put up a monument there willy-nilly? I mean, a public forum, as you know, we can have parades in the park, we can have protest. Anybody can do it, so long as you get a license and you're not interfering with some other group. That's a public forum. Has this city said anybody can put up a monument in this park?
>
> MS. HARRIS: Justice Scalia, there is a very serious factual question in this case about whether the city ever had a bona fide selection policy for this park. But putting that to one side for a moment, a public park is a public forum. A monument in a park may be a mode of communication for that forum—

Harris is simply challenging the Supreme Court with its own words. The Court has repeatedly said "from time out of mind" that public parks are public forums in which debate and disagreement can take place and in which government cannot prefer its favored ideas over others. Indeed, this is one of the truly foundational ideas under the First Amendment, for if people have freedom to speak but nowhere to do so, the freedom would be meaningless. To assure a place for free speech, the parks, streets, and sidewalks must be free. Regulations of the time, place, and manner of speech in parks can be enforced by the government, but not selectively based on the content or specific ideas expressed in the speech. There is no question that Pleasant Grove City accepted the Ten Commandments monument because it was agreeable—and, maybe, because it was historically significant—and the city rejected the Summum monument because it was disagreeable. It expressed views that the city found objectionable.

JUSTICE SCALIA: It's a public forum for some things. Is it a public forum for everything? It may be a public forum for processions, for parades. But is it a public forum for anybody constructing a monument?

MS. HARRIS: If you look at the question that way, Justice Scalia, it might be said that a public park is not a forum for sound trucks, it's not a forum for sleep-ins, it's not a forum for news racks. What that means is that there is no unfettered right to engage in those forms of communication. But if the Government allows it all—

JUSTICE KENNEDY: Those are time, place, and manner regulations, with which we are all familiar. But my concern is that this case is an example of the tyranny of labels. Because it's a public forum, as Justice Scalia indicated, for parades, for protests, which are limited temporally, it just seems wooden and rigid to all of a sudden say, well, it's a public forum for something that will last 30 years for which there is only limited space. It just doesn't make common sense.

Well . . . what about a city-erected permanent sign that says "Marriage should be restricted to a man and a woman"? Is it a rigid tyranny of labels to treat that differently than the Washington Monument?

MS. HARRIS: And that is exactly why, Justice Kennedy, the city, any city, is permitted to make a decision that it will close its public parks to all unattended displays. The Court has said that.

CHIEF JUSTICE ROBERTS: How far do you push that? I mean, what about the hypotheticals on the other side? I mean, you have a Statue of Liberty; do we have to have a statue of despotism? Or do we have to put any president who wants to be on Mount Rushmore? How do you answer those?

MS. HARRIS: Of course not, is how I answer that, Mr. Chief Justice. Any city has available to it two very straightforward options for dealing with this question if by some happenstance they do have a monument on public land that is not now a Government monument. The first thing they can do is adopt any existing monuments as Government speech.

Harris has to deal with the Statue of Liberty, the Washington Monument, and a host of other examples. She does so by saying that the government can have its monument and exclude others, but only if it is speaking as the government and expressing a clear idea it holds. This is a necessary concession (and a correct one, too). It has the effect of shifting the question from public forum and government discrimination against offensive ideas to the central question in the case: What does it take for government to convert a monument into its own speech, which enjoys immunity from the public-forum limits under the First Amendment? She is prepared to draw the line between government speech and government regulation of speech (the public-forum analysis), and to draw it clearly and rigorously. For her, it is not acceptable for government to simply declare any act—such as placement of a monument—to be an instance of government speech whenever it wants to do so. If that were possible, freedom of individual speech could be seriously eroded.

JUSTICE SOUTER: How does government [adopt an act or speech as its own]? You mentioned that frequently in your brief, and I'm not sure what formality you have in mind when you say "adopt."

MS. HARRIS: Governments can adopt speech as their own in different ways, Justice Souter. The way the national Government does it under the Antiquities Act of 1906 is they formally designate preexisting structures as a monument of the United States or a memorial of the United States. And that, by the way, Mr. Chief Justice, is the response to the Statue of Liberty problem. In 1924 it was so designated.

CHIEF JUSTICE ROBERTS: So, it's frozen into time. Everything up until now is okay, but anything going forward is not?

MS. HARRIS: I'm not sure I understand.

CHIEF JUSTICE ROBERTS: Well, I thought you said the Government can accept what's there and say that's our speech. But you're challenging the ability to do that going forward.

MS. HARRIS: No. No, Your Honor. If the Government accepts what's there—what is there now and says that's ours, then they can say we have closed this forum to private speech, these parks are available only to Governmental displays.

JUSTICE SCALIA: Mr. Sekulow says that some of these monuments, notably those in the Civil War battlefields, do show who the donors are. Now is that Government speech or private speech?

MS. HARRIS: It depends. If they were privately formulated and handed off to the Government as a completed object, they are only Government speech if the Government has since then converted them by adopting them.

JUSTICE SCALIA: Now that the Government converted them, it passes a law saying, what, we—we adopt this?

MS. HARRIS: That has happened.

JUSTICE SCALIA: Isn't it enough that the Government accepts ownership of it and places it on the Government's property? Isn't that a manifestation of the Government's adoption of it?

MS. HARRIS: Let me answer both of your questions, Justice Scalia. The way it does that even if a monument makes clear that it was privately formulated, a Government can still adopt it as its own speech.

JUSTICE SOUTER: So this case—your claim would disappear if this town in Utah had passed an ordinance saying we adopt the Ten Commandments Monument?

MS. HARRIS: It would, Justice Souter. We would no longer have an equal access right going forward—

JUSTICE SOUTER: But if that's all that's involved here, we're engaging in almost a silly exercise in formality.

MS. HARRIS: Absolutely not, Justice Souter. And the reason we know it's not a formality is because the city here refuses to do it. If it were just a formality, they would check the box. They won't do it—

JUSTICE SOUTER: If we tell them you have got to take the monument down if they don't do it, don't you think they are going to pass that pretty quick?

MS. HARRIS: I don't think they are, Justice Souter. And I think it would be partly a concern about establishment clause exposure, which we already heard about today. I think that there are substantive reasons why they might not want to adopt one version of the Ten Commandments as the city's own speech. As it happens, the version of the Ten Commandments on the Eagles monument isn't even the Mormon version of the Ten Commandments. That might raise sensitivities in this town. And whenever the Government adopts one version of the Exodus account, that is not only legally sensitive but politically sensitive as well.

This is quite a nice and important point. For government to adopt one version of the Ten Commandments and reject another would, in fact, violate the nonestablishment guarantee. The city might instead adopt the Eagles' Ten Commandment monument in order to express a different message, but that message would have to be clear to all who see the monument because it would not be the religious message people would otherwise understand the monument to express. If that message were historical it would have to be made clear by some form of visible sign. For some reason that doesn't seem to be an option the city is willing to accept—perhaps for political reasons.

JUSTICE SCALIA: It depends on what you mean by adopting one version. If it's adopting the version by saying these Ten Commandments are the word of God, that's one thing. If it's adopting it by just saying this is a version of the Ten Commandments that has had a very significant place in the history of the American people—I wouldn't care what version it was if that's all they're doing. Nor would the Mormons in Utah, I think.

MS. HARRIS: Well, those are very different for establishment clause purposes, Justice Scalia. But the only way the Government can be adopting anything in this context is by saying through the act of selection we have adopted it. And the problem with that is that the Government is not allowed to select which private speech it wishes to present to the public in a public park. It can do that. It can do that in museums. It can do it in libraries. It can do it—

This is a very important question and answer by Harris. The government can adopt the Eagles' monument and make its message very clear. This it has not done. But Harris also argues that the government cannot do that in a park—a public forum open for individual speech of all kinds and all messages. Allowing government to place an expressive monument in the middle of a public forum without cordoning the monument off as a monument devoted to the government's speech and no longer available as a public park would greatly expand government's power of speech at the clear cost of space for public expression and debate. It could eat up the public forum.

Harris's argument proves unsettling to the Court, as it reveals the almost unlimitable power of government speech that displaces private free expression.

JUSTICE ALITO: Let me give you this example. Just by chance yesterday I was taking a walk in a little neighborhood park, and I saw that there was a monument—a small monument, donated, and it says right on there donated by a private neighborhood association to commemorate a number of people who were killed in the 9-11 attack on the Pentagon. And now if I searched the town records or the county record and I don't find any resolution saying they adopted this monument as their monument, does that mean that if I would like to put up a monument in the park to commemorate loved ones who died, or people [whom] I respect, I have a First Amendment right to do that?

MS. HARRIS: No, Your Honor, and really for three separate reasons. First of all, it may be that the Government did adopt the monument—even privately donated monuments often involve a great deal of Government involvement at the front end, when they are created. Government often works in partnership with private donors to create the content of that monument.

JUSTICE ALITO: Well, what if the situation is a neighborhood association prepared this; they said we'd like to display it in the park; and the county or the town says fine, go ahead and do it?

MS. HARRIS: Even under those more usual circumstances there would be two things the city could do to keep you out of their park. As I said, they could adopt the monument that is there. The other thing any city can do is adopt some kind of a content-neutral ban, or a content-neutral limit, on the number of private displays it wants to have in its park.

JUSTICE SCALIA: Ms. Harris, we need a clear rule here. We can't expect the courts or the cities for that matter to investigate in every case what the degree of the Government's involvement in the monument and its message—and what is the degree, 50 percent, 45 percent, 36 years? I mean, are we going to make up a percentage? That's not the way threshold constitutional questions ought to be resolved or resolvable. We need a clear rule that the cities can rely on.

MS. HARRIS: I agree that we need a clear rule, and if clarity is important here the easiest way for the Government to make clear that it has adopted a privately formulated message as its own is to adopt it clearly and publicly. It can put up a plaque; it can designate it a city monument.

Apart from owning and adopting the monument, the government may also have to attach a plaque or some kind of sign indicating its adoption of the message, and if the message isn't obvious, stating what the government message is. Otherwise people will not know whether the government is speaking and what it is saying. Justice Scalia dislikes the detailed rules of adoption that Harris suggests. He makes the perfectly reasonable point that the presence of the monument, for example, in a public park makes all of that obvious. Surely that will often be the case.

But in the Pleasant Grove City case his generalization doesn't hold. The city won't take title and adopt the Ten Commandments monument and its religious and moral messages, but it's perfectly happy to place the monument in the park knowing that people will interpret it as a city endorsement of the obvious message. With Mt. Rushmore and the Washington Monument the government's endorsement and ownership may be clear enough without more, but with Ten Commandments monuments in parks and in front of courthouses, the same can't be said, and if it is said, the cities involved will often disavow any government adoption. Harris's point, in other words, is well taken, for the problems don't arise with the Statue of Liberty or the Lincoln Memorial, but with crèches at Christmas and Ten Commandments monuments which, thanks to the Eagles, dot the nation's public landscapes—indeed, often the lawns leading to courthouse steps.

JUSTICE SCALIA: Is there an historical basis for that, or did you just make it up? You think it would be a good idea? I mean, if that had been the practice over the past 200 years for all of these monuments that, you know, are strewn across the landscape, then I'd say yes, that's probably what the difference is.

But I'm not aware that there is any such requirement and any such practice on the part of Government. You're creating a new world. It may be a very nice world but it happens not to be the world under which our Constitution has subjected this country.

MS. HARRIS: If this is uncommon, that is because usually the Government *does* reserve monuments for governmental speech, monuments that it helps to create or monuments that it is happy to endorse after the fact. If this case is unusual, it's because Pleasant Grove has done an unusual thing here by allowing a private party to erect a permanent monument in its park, even though it is not willing to endorse the content of that monument.

And I do want to say that although clear rules are necessary, whatever the particular details of how a monument came to be on public land, there are these two clear safe harbors for any city facing that problem. Adopt it now or enact a content-neutral limit on the number of monuments in the park; and we think the city could do that on a going-forward basis. It could say we have no room—for aesthetic reasons, for space constraint reasons—

JUSTICE GINSBURG: Can we go back to your basic premise that this is a public forum, in any and all instances; and certainly in the speech area, demonstration area, from time immemorial public parks have been places where people can speak their minds. But I don't know of any tradition that says people can come to the park with monuments and put them up if they will, so long as they meet the time, place, and manner restrictions that a park may impose. So you're making an assumption that from time immemorial, monuments, just like speeches, can be presented by anyone who wants to.

MS. HARRIS: No, Justice Ginsburg. Monuments are different from speeches and because monuments are different, the Court has held that unlike oratory, a city can decide to close its parks entirely to all private unattended displays. It could not say, "We've heard enough speeches; no more speeches." It can say no private—

JUSTICE SOUTER: If that is so, what is the point of using the public forum analysis at all?

MS. HARRIS: Because here the city has not done that. The city has not made the decision that it will bar all private unattended displays.

JUSTICE SOUTER: That may mean that you have the foundation for a speech discrimination argument but that would not be the answer if we were dealing with a traditional public forum in the sense that the Court's cases have used the term. So it seems to me that your use of public forum is just by kind of remote analogy here, and I'm not sure that it's helping you or would help us if we used it as criterion for decision.

MS. HARRIS: Oh, I think it may be helpful, Justice Souter, because once we know that we are talking about a public forum, we know that access cannot be limited on a content basis.

JUSTICE KENNEDY: Well, you can stick with it as long as you want. But suppose that we were to say that we were unconvinced by the comparison between speeches and parades on the one hand and monuments on the other, so we did not apply the public forum analogy. Would that be the end of your case?

MS. HARRIS: Oh, no, Justice Kennedy. Even outside a public forum, in any context—even in a museum or library—in any context in which the Government is regulating private speech, it may not act in a way that is designed to suppress one particularly disfavored message or view; and we think that's what happened here.

CHIEF JUSTICE ROBERTS: Well, but it does all the time. Cigarette companies don't get equal time because the Government says the Surgeon General has determined it is bad for your health. It always suppresses alternative viewpoints.

MS. HARRIS: When the Government is speaking for itself, then the Government does have a right to prefer certain viewpoints over others, but here the city has consistently refused to adopt the content of this monument as its own, and it is still disclaiming endorsement of that monument. The justification for that Government speech exception is that sometimes, as the United States has said, the Government is entitled to speak in its own voice to promote its own messages, its own policies. But it says it's not doing that here.

JUSTICE SCALIA: You will say just the opposite when you come back here to challenge the Ten Commandments monument on Establishment Clause grounds. You will say something like this: Anybody who comes into this park and seeing this monument owned by the Government, on Government land, will think that the Government is endorsing this message. That's what you will say. Now why would it be true there, but it's not true here? Would anybody think that on public land owned by the Government the Government disagrees with this message?

MS. HARRIS: Justice Scalia, for one thing, if this case were being litigated under the Establishment Clause, it wouldn't be critical whether the monument were actually Government speech, because the Establishment Clause can be implicated by the Government's interaction with private speech as well. That said, I do not think it's the case that anybody who came across this monument would know that the Government is speaking.

The monument says it is presented by the Eagles. It has the Eagles emblem. The mayor himself testified in his deposition that he thought the monument was owned by the Eagles, because it is the Eagles and not the city that maintains that monument. I think there is a very real question about what people would think here, and if those perceptions are important, the easy way to clarify it is for the city to step up and adopt the monument as Government speech, which it won't do here.

Harris is correct. The establishment clause question doesn't turn on authorship of a message or ownership of a monument. It turns instead, as the Supreme Court has made perfectly clear, on whether to an average individual viewer it appears that the government is endorsing a religious message, whatever its ownership. And as the Court has suggested on more than one occasion, the way a government can help avoid an establishment-clause violation is to disavow any such message or to present it in a way that does not lead the viewer to the conclusion that government is endorsing it. Often a sign will do that trick, too.

This case, however, involves a claim of government speech by the city, a claim of government avowal, not of disavowal. If the government intends to speak a message, why would it try to hide its authorship?

JUSTICE SOUTER: There is no pervasive understanding or nonpervasive one, I would have thought, in the United States that anyone who wants to display a message in granite in a public park can put it there. No one assumes that. Everyone assumes that, if the granite monument is there, the city or whatever has said, yes, we approve it, put it there.

MS. HARRIS: Everybody may assume that, and they would be right. The city in this case did say, yes, we approve that monument and not that one. So you can put yours up, and you can't. That doesn't solve the First Amendment problem. If all we have is that the city has permitted one private speaker to erect a monument, there is no constitutional or judicially manageable line between that and just the ordinary thing the Government always does when it grants preferred access to a public forum, which is to say you're in, you're out. If that's enough for adoption, then there are no more First Amendment violations through lack of equal access.

JUSTICE SOUTER: Yes, but even on your own criterion, if the city passes a resolution saying we adopt this, you're still going to be faced with precisely the content discrimination problem that you're arguing about here.

MS. HARRIS: But because it's adopted it as its own message, then we think the Government is speaking. And when the Government is speaking, it is entitled to make content and viewpoint distinctions, but in order to do that, it has to step up and speak itself. That's the justification for the Government speech doctrine.

Frankly, the Justices seem confused here, and Harris is reminding them about the law that they have created, which distinguishes government speech from government regulation, and immunizes only the former. For example, if the government permits some speech, or signs, in a public park, but not others because it doesn't like what they say, the government is almost certainly *regulating* speech in an unconstitutional manner. The only way to avoid that conclusion is for the government to claim that it is *speaking* for itself through the first choice, and thus doesn't have to permit the contrary view to be expressed. This is obviously tricky business in a public park, which is why Harris argues that the government's speech intentions and its message must be clear to all—as government speech.

JUSTICE SOUTER: You're basically just arguing for a clear statement rule. There is an affirmative Government act of some indication of approval when it says, yes, you can put the monument here. And what you're arguing for is, well, we want a clearer statement, we want it to say, yes, we really adopt it, it's ours from the heart. And that seems to be the difference between your position and the position that acceptance of the monument is enough.

MS. HARRIS: I would formulate it only slightly differently, which is not so much a clear statement but that those are really two different things, approving it for access and adopting the message as the Government's own.

JUSTICE ALITO: And when Government adopts it, can it at that time specify what it understands the statement to be?

MS. HARRIS: I think it can, Justice Alito. Now that the Government is speaking, now this is the Government's own message, and it can tailor its adoption to make clear what message it's adopting. And in answer to some of Justice Scalia's questions, I think the Government here could put up a plaque in front of the Eagles' monument that says "Monument of the City of Pleasant Grove and dedicated to the role that the Ten Commandments play in secular law." It can do that.

JUSTICE SCALIA: Suppose the resolution of adoption by the City Council just says, "The City Council agrees that this monument of the Eagle Association expresses an idea worthy of the public's attention." Is that enough?

MS. HARRIS: No. I think that the ordinance has to do one more thing, which is to say, "This is a monument of the City of Pleasant Grove, we adopt the content of the monument," not just "we approve it." "We are giving it preferential access, and here is why."

JUSTICE SOUTER: You want a signing statement as well as a signature?

(Laughter.)

MS. HARRIS: Like that.

Harris is sticking to her guns that the government has to be clear about when it is speaking. For her this is not just a logical byproduct of the government speech doctrine itself; it is also an essential *constitutional* means by which government speech claims can be limited or judged because the doctrine has the potential to greatly reduce the amount of government property on which individual free speech has traditionally occurred.

CHIEF JUSTICE ROBERTS: Given the focus on public perception, does it depend on the content of the speech? In other words, if you came across a monument and it said, "The Eagles are a lot better than every other organization, you should give money to the Eagles," someone is going to walk by that and say, "Well, that's probably not the City, that's probably the Eagles." But the Eagles, you know, for all the good they do, did not come up with the Ten Commandments, and somebody is going to look at that and say, "That's probably the City." They are not going to look at that and immediately say, "That's what the Eagles believe."

MS. HARRIS: Well, I think it's actually trickier than that, more complicated than that, Your Honor. Again, given this monument, I think there will be questions about whether this is the speech of the Eagles. And I actually think that, given all the legal sensitivities around a Ten Commandments monument, your average citizen, when they see a religious monument in a park, may well think that may be private speech because the Government usually can't endorse or at least sometimes can't endorse religious speech. So I actually think these questions are very complicated. And, again, if you want to be clear about who's speaking, there's an easy way to do that, which is for the Government straightforwardly and clearly to adopt this speech as its own.

JUSTICE SCALIA: What if it's just a statue of George Washington? What kind of a resolution does the city council adopt? "We endorse everything George Washington ever said"?

MS. HARRIS: No. No. Again, and in my answer to Justice Alito, they can adopt any resolution they want so long as they adopt that statue as a city memorial.

JUSTICE SCALIA: That's right, and I think they would adopt a resolution that says, "We think George Washington is worthy of respect and emulation on the part of our citizens." If it could say that, why couldn't it say the same thing about the Ten Commandments? "We think the Ten Commandments are worthy of respect and"—and I wouldn't say "emulation"—I would say "respect and reverence by our citizens." Would that be enough?

MS. HARRIS: If the City says what you just said, "We are adopting this monument insofar" and however it wants to finish that sentence, that is fine.

JUSTICE SCALIA: You don't think that's fairly implied by the mere fact that it is there in Pleasant Grove's park and that Pleasant Grove City

Council has allowed it to be constructed there? Don't you think that's implicit?

MS. HARRIS: No, I don't, Your Honor. I think that all that implies is that Pleasant Grove has decided this speech is worthy of display in this public park based on its content. And that is the decision the City can't make. If it were just a formality, if it were simple, and "it's all the same, who cares?" then I think that Pleasant Grove would be here saying something different, which is, "We adopt. We adopt. We'll check that box." There are substantive reasons why it doesn't—

JUSTICE SCALIA: Maybe the City doesn't know what you mean by "We adopt," just as I don't know what you mean by "We adopt."

MS. HARRIS: Well, whether or not the City knows what we mean, we know from the City's brief that what it's saying is that the Government speech here is only in the act of selection. Selection. It's not about the content of that monument. That's not enough to make a Government speech, and the City is not permitted to speak through selection, and—

JUSTICE SOUTER: The difference it seems to me between you and your friends on the other side is [that] you want this clear statement.

MS. HARRIS: Well, I do think that the city is a bit on the horns of a dilemma because it wants to have it both ways. It wants to be able to say this speech is governmental for purposes of blocking equal access rights; but not so governmental that it's a big Establishment Clause problem. So yes, I think there is a dilemma here for the city.

Thank you, Your Honors.

CHIEF JUSTICE ROBERTS: Thank you, counsel.

The case is submitted.

▪ ▪ ▪

The oral argument in the *Summum* case was of the highest possible caliber. The lawyers' positions were clear and coherent, they explained them well, and the questions and answers were direct and certainly very helpful to the justices, who had to wrestle with a very hard case with broad implications. The stakes are high for the First Amendment.

It is thus a bit surprising that when the justices issued the opinion in the case, they were largely of one mind. In the contest between government speech and the public forum, government speech won. The decision was announced on February 25, 2009, about four months after the oral argument and well in advance of the end of the term when the most contentious cases tend to be announced. Every justice except Justice Souter joined Justice Alito's opinion for the Court; Justice Souter concurred in the result but not the reasoning of the Alito opinion. There were no dissenting opinions.

> Justice *ALITO* delivered the opinion of the Court.
>
> No prior decision of this Court has addressed the application of the Free Speech Clause to a government entity's acceptance of privately donated, permanent monuments for installation in a public park, and the parties disagree sharply about the line of precedents that governs this situation. [Was the City] engaging in [its] own expressive conduct? Or were they providing a forum for private speech?
>
> If [the City was] engaging in [its] own expressive conduct, then the Free Speech Clause has no application. The Free Speech Clause restricts government regulation of private speech; it does not regulate government speech.
>
> Indeed, it is not easy to imagine how government could function if it lacked this freedom. "If every citizen were to have a right to insist that no one paid by public funds express a view with which he disagreed, debate over issues of great concern to the public would be limited to those in the private sector, and the process of government as we know it radically transformed."

The two paragraphs immediately above are surprisingly, indeed troublingly, strong and absolute. If the government's action is speech (or expressive, an even broader term), "the Free Speech Clause has *no* application." None, zippo, nunca . . . Can that be right? Why shouldn't the free-speech clause be seen as protecting individual speech when the government exceeds its limits of speaking? Mustn't there be some limits, lest the government simply declare all public property expressive and wipe out free speech in any public place? And wouldn't those limits have something to do with speech freedom? Yet the opinion says (surely an unintended overstatement) that the free speech clause "does not regulate government speech." Justice Alito uses that freighted word, "freedom." Is government speech a "freedom?" Is it thinkable that the government enjoys a *freedom from the people* in a democracy?

> A government entity may exercise this same freedom to express its views when it receives assistance from private sources for the purpose of delivering a government-controlled message.
>
> There may be situations in which it is difficult to tell whether a government entity is speaking on its own behalf or is providing a forum for private speech, but this case does not present such a situation. Permanent monuments displayed on public property typically represent government speech.

> Governments have long used monuments to speak to the public. Since ancient times, kings, emperors, and other rulers have erected statues of themselves to remind their subjects of their authority and power. Triumphal arches, columns, and other monuments have been built to commemorate military victories and sacrifices and other events of civic importance. A monument, by definition, is a structure that is designed as a means of expression.

I think I would have left out the part about kings and rulers and reminding "their subjects" of their authority and power. Ditto for the military victories and sacrifices. It all seems disturbingly statist. I don't think of the government as my ruler—and certainly not in the way I would think of Stalin were I a Russian during his reign. And even for our American heroes, like Washington and Jefferson, we also get to know, thanks to freedom of speech, about their failings, sins, and hypocrisies.

> When a government entity arranges for the construction of a monument, it does so because it wishes to convey some thought or instill some feeling in those who see the structure. Just as government-commissioned and government-financed monuments speak for the government, so do privately financed and donated monuments that the government accepts and displays to the public on government land. It certainly is not common for property owners to open up their property for the installation of permanent monuments that convey a message with which they do not wish to be associated. And because property owners typically do not permit the construction of such monuments on their land, persons who observe donated monuments routinely—and reasonably—interpret them as conveying some message on the property owner's behalf. In this context, there is little chance that observers will fail to appreciate the identity of the speaker. This is true whether the monument is located on private property or on public property, such as national, state, or city park land.

This proposition is far from beyond dispute. What about sculpture on public land? Do we assume that the government adopts it as its own expression? I think not. Artists may simply have been allowed to put up their art as a matter of practice. The art may have been approved by a private selection committee, but the government—city council, parks commission—may well dislike it very much, or even doubt that it is art.

> We think it is fair to say that throughout our Nation's history, the general government practice with respect to donated monuments has been one of selective receptivity. A great many of the monuments that adorn the Nation's

public parks were financed with private funds or donated by private parties. Sites managed by the National Park Service contain thousands of privately designed or funded commemorative objects, including the Statue of Liberty, the Marine Corps War Memorial (the Iwo Jima monument), and the Vietnam Veterans Memorial. States and cities likewise have received thousands of donated monuments.

In this case, it is clear that the monuments in Pleasant Grove's Pioneer Park represent government speech. Although many of the monuments were not designed or built by the City and were donated in completed form by private entities, the City decided to accept those donations and to display them in the Park. Respondent does not claim that the City ever opened up the Park for the placement of whatever permanent monuments might be offered by private donors. Rather, the City has "effectively controlled" the messages sent by the monuments in the Park by exercising "final approval authority" over their selection. The City has selected those monuments that it wants to display for the purpose of presenting the image of the City that it wishes to project to all who frequent the Park; it has taken ownership of most of the monuments in the Park, including the Ten Commandments monument that is the focus of respondent's concern; and the City has now expressly set forth the criteria it will use in making future selections.

[Summum] voices the legitimate concern that the government speech doctrine not be used as a subterfuge for favoring certain private speakers over others based on viewpoint. [Its] suggested solution is to require a government entity accepting a privately donated monument to go through a formal process of adopting a resolution publicly embracing "the message" that the monument conveys.

We see no reason for imposing a requirement of this sort. The parks of this country contain thousands of donated monuments that government entities have used for their own expressive purposes, usually without producing the sort of formal documentation that respondent now says is required to escape Free Speech Clause restrictions. Requiring all of these jurisdictions to go back and proclaim formally that they adopt all of these monuments as their own expressive vehicles would be a pointless exercise that the Constitution does not mandate.

In this case, for example, although respondent argues that Pleasant Grove City has not adequately "controll[ed] the message" of the Ten Commandments monument, the City took ownership of that monument and put it on permanent display in a park that it owns and manages and that is linked to the City's identity. All rights previously possessed by the monument's donor have been relinquished. The City's actions provided a more dramatic form of adoption than the sort of formal endorsement that respondent would demand, unmistakably signifying to all Park visitors that the City intends the monument to speak on its behalf.

What respondent demands, however, is that the City "adopt" or "embrace" "the message" that it associates with the monument. Respondent seems to think that a monument can convey only one "message"—which is, presumably, the message intended by the donor—and that, if a government entity that accepts a monument for placement on its property does not formally embrace *that* message, then the government has not engaged in expressive conduct.

This argument fundamentally misunderstands the way monuments convey meaning. The meaning conveyed by a monument is generally not a simple one like "Beef. It's What's for Dinner." Even when a monument features the written word, the monument may be intended to be interpreted, and may in fact be interpreted by different observers, in a variety of ways. What, for example, is "the message" of the Greco-Roman mosaic of the word "Imagine" that was donated to New York City's Central Park in memory of John Lennon? These text-based monuments are almost certain to evoke different thoughts and sentiments in the minds of different observers, and the effect of monuments that do not contain text is likely to be even more variable.

Contrary to respondent's apparent belief, it frequently is not possible to identify a single "message" that is conveyed by an object or structure, and consequently, the thoughts or sentiments expressed by a government entity that accepts and displays such an object may be quite different from those of either its creator or its donor. By accepting a privately donated monument and placing it on city property, a city engages in expressive conduct, but the intended and perceived significance of that conduct may not coincide with the thinking of the monument's donor or creator. Indeed, when a privately donated memorial is funded by many small donations, the donors themselves may differ in their interpretation of the monument's significance. By accepting such a monument, a government entity does not necessarily endorse the specific meaning that any particular donor sees in the monument.

The forum doctrine has been applied in situations in which government-owned property or a government program was capable of accommodating a large number of public speakers without defeating the essential function of the land or the program. For example, a park can accommodate many speakers and, over time, many parades and demonstrations. A public university's student activity fund can provide money for many campus activities. A public university's buildings may offer meeting space for hundreds of student groups.

By contrast, public parks can accommodate only a limited number of permanent monuments. Public parks have been used, "'time out of mind, . . .

for purposes of assembly, communicating thoughts between citizens, and discussing public questions,'" but "one would be hard pressed to find a 'long tradition' of allowing people to permanently occupy public space with any manner of monuments."

If government entities must maintain viewpoint neutrality in their selection of donated monuments, they must either "brace themselves for an influx of clutter" or face the pressure to remove longstanding and cherished monuments. Every jurisdiction that has accepted a donated war memorial may be asked to provide equal treatment for a donated monument questioning the cause for which the veterans fought. New York City, having accepted a donated statue of one heroic dog (Balto, the sled dog who brought medicine to Nome, Alaska, during a diphtheria epidemic) may be pressed to accept monuments for other dogs who are claimed to be equally worthy of commemoration. The obvious truth of the matter is that if public parks were considered to be traditional public forums for the purpose of erecting privately donated monuments, most parks would have little choice but to refuse all such donations. And where the application of forum analysis would lead almost inexorably to closing of the forum, it is obvious that forum analysis is out of place.

In sum, we hold that the City's decision to accept certain privately donated monuments while rejecting respondent's is best viewed as a form of government speech. As a result, the City's decision is not subject to the Free Speech Clause, and the Court of Appeals erred in holding otherwise. We therefore reverse.

It is so ordered.

There is, if I may speak openly here, all sorts of mischief in this straightforward and almost bland-sounding opinion. It is mischief about government power, government nontransparency, government discretion to declare what its acts are—expressive or not.

Government has been given an unbridled power (if we take the opinion literally) to jeopardize the public forum in America. Government of course is the owner of its land and spaces and things. Property owners usually have complete control over uses of their land. So might the government, were it not for the principle, "time out of mind," that streets and parks are public property and public forums for speech and liberty. And indeed, under long settled "public forum" doctrine the Supreme Court has also said that there are limits on the government's ability to close off speech from all forms of government property—not absolute limits, but First Amendment limits that foreclose government from closing property to speech and then allowing an exception for speech and ideas it favors.

In my government-controlled classroom I can limit speech to the subject of constitutional law that is being discussed, but I can't prohibit conservative views and allow only liberal ones. Government can prohibit speech that disrupts pedestrian movement on sidewalks, but it cannot prohibit all speech activities whether they disrupt movement or not. These public forum rules have been strong medicine and are often nettlesome for government to obey, but they have helped make possible a form of free expression that nurtures democracy and freedom.

After Justice Alito's opinion, however, those public-forum rules have been completely replaced for any government action deemed "expressive" by a power not subject to the free speech clause, as the Court puts it. Why would the Supreme Court so undermine the public-forum idea, which has served as the foundation of individual public speech in this country? The government's property, after all, is really my—our—property.

> Justice *STEVENS*, with whom Justice *GINSBURG* joins, concurring:
>
> To date, our decisions relying on the recently minted government speech doctrine to uphold government action have been few and, in my view, of doubtful merit. The Court's opinion in this case signals no expansion of that doctrine. . . . [E]ven if the Free Speech Clause neither restricts nor protects government speech, government speakers are bound by the Constitution's other proscriptions, including those supplied by the Establishment and Equal Protection Clauses. Together with the checks imposed by our democratic processes, these constitutional safeguards ensure that the effect of today's decision will be limited.

Justice Stevens's opinion is interesting though a bit obscure. He would prefer a decision that would straightforwardly treat Pleasant Grove City's acceptance of the Ten Commandment monument as an endorsement of its message. He dislikes Justice Alito's opinion which vests complete authority in the city to assign expressive meaning, including meaning that is open-ended and dependent on the views of those who see the monument. If government speaks, it says something and shouldn't be able later to hide in the ambiguities of meaning.

Stevens also says that the immunity from First Amendment challenge should not be absolute. Other grounds, such as the reasonableness of the government's decision to create its own speech forum, could still apply, and the establishment clause of the First Amendment would also be a limit—perhaps also the petition clause. What if government's message on a monument were hate speech? Should there be no limit? More notably, the government's expressive action might violate the equal-protection guarantee. It might also violate a law of Congress that limits government's speech, or even a right of privacy or reputation. Should such limits, or others, be imposed?

For Stevens, in short, the opinion can be read as implying too much government power.

> Justice *SOUTER*, concurring in the judgment:
>
> I agree with the Court that the Ten Commandments monument is government speech, that is, an expression of a government's position on the moral and religious issues raised by the subject of the monument. And although the government should lose when the character of the speech is at issue and its governmental nature has not been made clear, I also agree with the Court that the city need not satisfy the particular formality urged by Summum as a condition of recognizing that the expression here falls within the public category. I have qualms, however, about accepting the position that public monuments are government speech categorically.

Justice Souter prefers a "go slow" approach: limit the scope of decisions; don't unnecessarily venture opinions on issues that have yet to arrive at the Court. He points, especially, to the establishment clause issues as complex and premature for resolution. Justice Stevens, who is skeptical about the government speech doctrine itself, would agree about the need for caution.

▪ ▪ ▪

So we end up with an opinion in *Summum* that has unanimous support from the justices but not unanimous enthusiasm or appetite for clarity. The Court seems to have settled on the "government speech" doctrine and its essential rationale and characteristics, even when its effect is to create a government speech *forum*, not just to allow the government to speak its mind as everyone else does. And it has done so *unanimously*. What are we to make of the First Amendment government speech doctrine and its oxymoronic quality—a limitation placed on private speech in order to protect the government's freedom to speak?

From the government speech doctrine's very beginning the Supreme Court seems to have concluded that the government's expression could not be incorporated into the speech-protective public-forum analysis. Government speech involved, necessarily, point of view discrimination (as any speech does) and the government's ability to speak could not be cabined by any judicial inquiry into reasonableness. When government chooses to speak, it must be free to do so whenever and however it wishes, the Court says, for government speech to its publics is essential in a democracy in order that people know what and why the government is doing in order to form their own opinions and express their support or opposition. The government must be able to provide information to people about laws that are passed and programs that are offered. It would be strange and counterproductive, for example, for government to have a website with information about Social Security benefits and eligibility yet permit speech by individuals about any subject on the website, or even speech in opposition to Social Security.

But what about the Social Security site which includes an opportunity for people to extol the value of Social Security but prohibits any criticism of the program? Should the government's speech power go that far without some First Amendment scrutiny? In *Summum* Harris's argument was that it shouldn't go that far, and that public forum analysis was perfectly suited to keep it from going that far. The government speech forum, in other words, is not needed for government speech. Government can and must speak, but there is no need for a new government speech doctrine in order for government to exercise a power it clearly possesses in the constitutional scheme of things. The utility of the government speech doctrine, in other words, is simply and only to permit government to foreclose competing ideas in *its*, the government's, place of speaking, in effect reserving the podium to itself and its friends. Sometimes, as with the first—the informational Social Security website mentioned above—government can and must do so. But not with the second.

Harris argues that the First Amendment is needed in order to keep the first separate from the second, and that public-forum analysis would be up to the task. All that would be required is that Pleasant Grove City state clearly what city-sponsored message the monument has been accepted to express. If the message would otherwise be ambiguous, the city can do what is necessary (perhaps an explanatory sign) to prevent confusion. With this, she argues, the monument will be an instance of government speech, and a court can judge whether the message is consistent with the overall monument display or, instead, if it should be understood as an instance alone of the city's view. If the message is historically metaphorical—the beliefs and values and culture of those who settled the area—it can be judged on its own and in relation to other monuments in the park. If the monument were selected by the city to express its endorsement of the biblical version of religious truth, that will be clear too; forum analysis would not prevent the city from doing so, though other parts of the Constitution or laws might. But if the religious message were on a monument in a monument park devoted to history, it would be obvious that the monument didn't belong there. It would instead be seen as a pretextual means of expressing favored but not disfavored ideas. This is the work that could be and would be done by public-forum analysis, for even in a nonpublic forum government may not discriminate against and for speech based on its point of view.

So why did the Court shy away from forum analysis and instead escape the First Amendment entirely through the government speech analysis? The answer seems to be that from the beginning government speech took the form of speech by private individuals that was selected as a means of communicating the government's message, and even the nonpublic forum couldn't provide for that kind of quasi-regulatory government action. The first government speech case, *Rust v. Sullivan*, upheld a restriction on abortion speech by doctors and healthcare providers working at government-funded family-planning clinics. The doctors and healthcare providers were not employees of the government but were instead deemed "agents" of the government's prolife policy who could not, in that capacity, "provide counseling concerning the use of abortion as a method of family planning or provide referrals for abortion as a method of family planning." Another relatively early case involved the National Endowment for the Arts, which conditioned grants to artists on the art's conformity with "standards of decency and respect for the diverse beliefs and values of the American public." These indecency restrictions were not viewed as regulations of private speech of the artists, but as criteria imposed by the government in its expressive capacity as a patron of the arts making its own judgments about the art it chooses to support. The artists granted or denied NEA support were neither employees nor agents of the government, but purely private actors whose work would be supported (or not) based on the quality and content of the art they produced. NEA support would be a loose form of a government-patronage forum in which government tastes are fostered and expressed in the art world, and the artists' private speech is wrested from them without their consent and transformed into a government message. As content-based restrictions on private speech, the funding restrictions would almost certainly have violated the First Amendment without the government speech/patronage idea.

The selection and use of private speech to communicate a government message thus made it impossible to use the public forum doctrine as an analytical device to enable yet contain government speech. And with the development over time of a government speech forum—a time and space or place reserved for government speech, such as a website or monuments in a park—the content-based restrictions imposed by government made even a semblance of the nonpublic forum, which prohibits content-based restrictions of speech, impossible.

Yet understanding why the government speech idea and its accompanying First Amendment immunity arose separately from the public forum analysis doesn't entirely explain why the doctrine has taken the expansive scope it now enjoys. The broad, indeed absolute, immunity of government speech action from free-speech challenge means that there is no limitation whatever on government conduct and discrimination in its forum. And while public-forum doctrine enforces a reasonableness and incompatibility standard on government's decision to create a limited or nonpublic forum, there is no comparable First Amendment scrutiny of the government's decision to speak or to create a forum for its views. Finally, there is no requirement that the government state the views it is expressing, much less expressly acknowledge them, and thus there is no foundation upon which any standard of forbidden discrimination might be based.

We see all of these features in the *Summum* case: monument space in a park as a government speech forum; no specification of the message Pleasant Grove spoke; a mere assertion that the monument selection and refusal decisions were expressive in nature. Why should the government's power to speak be so broad?

The principal answer to this question is that speech by the government is essential to our democracy. We live in a country premised on the individual's control, through the vote or the power of our own speech to others about government, through challenges to administrative action in the federal, state, and local bureaucracies, and through our right to petition government and to take to the streets, sidewalks, and parks in protest to its actions. To do these things we need information from the government. What policies is it supporting, what reasons justify government actions, what consequences will befall us? To hold government and its agencies and employees accountable we need to hear from them.

On a more practical level we must receive information and advice and instructions from the government. Ours is a society in which government is pervasive, from traffic laws (and tickets) to taxes to volumes and volumes of laws and regulations about our cars, our kids, our pets, our businesses, our environment, our product safety, our agriculture practices, our property, and on and on and on. It is government that must provide us our tax returns and the instructions for preparing them, our zoning restrictions, our rights to safe workplaces and nondiscrimination, our schools, and on and on.

The government also speaks for us and to us in our public schools, on our TVs, in our news. It speaks about our values as a society, our role in the world, our history and our patriotic beliefs. It provides much of our health-care in public and government-subsidized private hospitals. It safeguards our religions and religious freedoms. And it is limited by our freedoms in what it can do to us as individuals—especially those freedoms set out as specific limits on government action in the Bill of Rights. In these and countless other respects government must have the ability to speak; indeed, government has the *duty* to speak. As Alexander Meiklejohn, perhaps the most important thinker about freedom of expression, said:

> The principle of freedom of speech . . . is not a Law of Nature or of reason in the abstract. It is a deduction from the basic American agreement that public issues shall be decided by universal suffrage. . . . [J]ust so far as, at any point, the citizens who are to decide an issue are denied acquaintance with information and opinion . . . which is relevant to that issue, just so far the result must be ill-conceived.[2]

So government must be able to speak. It must even be able to construct monuments that acknowledge sacrifices, commend accomplishment, inspire the best in us.

But government speech is not all good. It can deceive us. It can corrupt our values. It can inspire hate. One need only look to Hitler's Germany or Mussolini's Italy to see examples of the power of government expression to misshape a society. Our society has its own examples, too: whites-only water fountains and entrances to public buildings; the excess exuberance of communist baiting by Congress in the twentieth century. And more to the point in the *Summum* case, government can foment fear and hate as well as preference and endorsement on the subject of religion. In the late nineteenth century the Mormons were objects of hate and fear, partly at the hand of government. Today it is Muslims. Government can endorse religion with the Ten Commandments monuments; it can criticize, even defile, a religion by selecting it out as a loony artifice, as with Summum, perhaps.

Can we simply trust government to do the reasonable, informative, true, and constructive thing when it speaks? Can we trust it to be neutral and fair-minded in its government speech forums, whether in parks or schools or on government-controlled websites? Can we trust it to be clear and transparent and to openly profess that it, the government, is fostering the idea being expressed? We might rely on the Supreme Court and the establishment clause to place limits on government speech that touches on religion, but it is unclear from *Summum* whether the Establishment Clause will be interpreted in a way that would place a significant limit on government speech. The Supreme Court has in recent years become more solicitous of government's endorsing religiosity and accommodating to (in other words, preferring) religion in general and religions in particular. The favored religions all tend to be the conventional and domesticated ones—the Old Order Amish; the Native American Church; and of course Christianity.

The Constitution itself tells us not to trust government. The idea of limited powers, of divided power among and within the executive, legislative, and judicial branches, of federalism, and of course the Bill of Rights, all suggest an attitude of healthy skepticism about, and external controls on, government power, including the power of speech and persuasion and distortion of the individual's marketplace of ideas.

So how can government speech be controlled? Some have suggested, as indeed Ms. Harris argued, that government speech and its specific message be made clear to all who see or hear it. This would make the government face up to its message and would allow those who receive it to judge it by its authorship and to detect and respond to its abuses. There is much to be said for this prescription, including the fact that it seems perfectly logical and benign. There are two problems with it, however.

The first problem is that the Supreme Court in *Summum* and in its previous cases seems to have rejected such a limit for two reasons: (a) it would unduly constrain government with technical requirements, and (b) messages have many meanings, and those meanings change over time. The first reason, in my mind, is laughable; bureaucracy is pervasive, so why shouldn't the government experience some? More important, clear and enforceable rules and boundaries are essential for the protection of speech from government infringement. The second reason is mere makeweight. The fact that meanings can be multiple and change over time has nothing to do with government being clear about its own message.

The second problem is that government doesn't always speak itself. It instead chooses private messages to support, as with NEA funding or private monuments or who gets to be in the parade. The chosen private speakers—decent artists, the Eagles, the float with a crèche in a Christmas parade, those who drive a car with a state motto—may not even know that they are being used to shape a government message; indeed, as with the driver, they may not intend even to speak. Can we force the private messengers to wear a collar saying that they are speaking for the government, too? One solution to this problem, of course, is to limit (or even prohibit) government speaking through the private speech of others. This may not be an altogether bad idea, at least when the private speaker has not consented to be used for government's expression of its own idea, and when the government has the practical option of speaking for itself. Indeed, the great expansion of the government speech forum, a development that enlarges government control of the private speech marketplace by reserving time and space for its favored messages only, has resulted from situations in which the government is speaking through others. But how would the limitation work? We probably wouldn't want to eliminate all public parades, or government literary prizes, or government mottos on license plates.

Transparency, explicitness about the government's message, and a rule closely scrutinizing (but not eliminating) government speech through the speech of others are useful limits and antidotes to government speech. But they are procedural devices. They don't go to the substance of government speech—the ethnic slur, the feeding on fear, the calculated shaping of religious and other opinion. Dealing with these problems of substance is the heart of the difficulty with government speech and the central problem that has been left unaddressed to this day. Alexander Meiklejohn tells us that "The principle of freedom of speech . . . is not a Law of Nature or of reason in the abstract. It is a deduction from the basic American agreement that public issues shall be decided by universal suffrage." When government's speech is aimed at participating in public discussion, its aims should be focused on the needs of a free and self-governing public. Much government speech consists of providing information and guidance for citizens dealing with government programs. But when government's *public* speech consists of engagement in public dialogue, government must be transparent, open, truthful, and reasoned in its speech. That way, at least, people will know what the government is doing and can use democratic political means to nip it in the bud.

TOO MUCH FREE SPEECH . . . AND TOO LITTLE?

Justice Alito said in his *Summum* opinion that "when a government entity arranges for the construction of a monument, it does so because it wishes to convey some thought or instill some feeling in those who see the structure." My concern with the statement is not with government conveying a thought, a cognitive message, through a monument. Transparency and clarity of message can take care of that aspect of the government's speech. But we should be much more concerned about government "instilling some feeling" in those who see the government's speech, whether it be a monument, or an ad, or an image, or a work of art. Feelings transcend reason and cognition. Images that convey them are appeals to emotion. Plato thought art was dangerous, for its meaning and its power could not be limited and its force could not be squared with a reasoned marketplace of ideas and opinion. To be sure, emotion plays a role in public discussion and debate. Religious faith does too. But they shouldn't play a role in the hands of government. In this sense Justice Alito was simply flat wrong, and dangerously so.

A Platonic limitation on government speech (reason, not emotion) would surely be hard to manage, though it nicely comports with the dialectic assumptions underlying the First Amendment. There may be other possibilities for substantive constraint. And it may well be that substantive limits simply can't be enforced, and that limits on scope of government speech can only be enforced through democratic channels.

But the question demands serious thought, for the Supreme Court has unleashed a dangerous power through the government speech doctrine. And the Constitution, after all, assumes that we control government, not the other way around. That, it seems, is a message lost on the Supreme Court when it decided to protect, in the name of the First Amendment, the government's right to speak free from interference from individuals, from us. Where were the textualists and originalists when that happened?

III Forms of Speech

What, exactly, is this thing we call speech? Is it expression with a cognitive meaning or message, say an argument or analysis or fact? Or is it also a metaphor of meaning, sensual, aesthetic, constructed by an audience; or a social practice or ritual; or a bird's song or wind whispering through the pines?

In the two cases we will discuss below, the Supreme Court wrestled with these very questions. The first is the *Hurley* case, which involves the annual St. Patrick's Day Parade in Boston. Is a parade "speech" under the First Amendment, and if so, what is the message or meaning, who is the speaker, and, indeed, need there *be* a speaker at all? In the second case, *Boy Scouts v. Dale*, the Supreme Court wrestles with an equally profound First Amendment question: what if someone chooses not to speak but the resulting silence is given meaning by others? Can that be speech? What is the speech? And can the nonspeaker claim the resulting message or image or metaphor as his or her own for purposes of the First Amendment? Does the First Amendment protect all instances, or artifacts, of "speech," whatever their origin? Justice Scalia seems to say "yes," free speech extends to everyone and everything . . . except for polar bears.

The *Hurley* and *Dale* cases have important implications for the constitutional protection of artistic and aesthetic expression, subjects on which I have written in the context of those cases. Our discussion of the cases here, however, will address a more fundamental First Amendment speech issue that affects all of free speech jurisprudence. How broad and deep does the constitutional term "speech" range, and with what consequences? Are the roles of speaker, speech and message dispensable, even irrelevant, under the First Amendment? And where do polar bears fit in?

CHAPTER THREE

Expressive Conduct Unleashed

Hurley v. Irish-American Gay, Lesbian and Bisexual Group of Boston, 515 U.S. 557 (1995)[1]

With the *Hurley* case we pursue the questions of speech and its source, nature, and meaning under the First Amendment. What if speech might exist even in the absence of a creator and an expressive object? Can constitutionally recognized speech emerge "out of thin air?" Indeed, with aesthetic expression, might not much expression emerge from thin air?

An example may help. Dada is a form of art that consists of the ridiculous, the purposefully incomprehensible, and the totally deconstructed. An early Dada stage performance involved "skits enacted by (African) masked figures dressed in colorful costumes" who accompanied themselves with drums, pot covers, and frying pans as they recited poems that sounded like this:

> gadji beri bumba
> glandridi lauli lonni cadori
> gadjama bim beri glassala
> glandridi glassala tuffin I zimbrabim
> blassa galassasa tuffin I zimbrabim

"The noise from the stage was deafening. There was bedlam in the hallway. The performers behaved like new recruits simulating mental illness before a medical commission."[2]

We might say, in this example of Dada, that the expression has speakers and creators and many individual and collective objects or performances, but the meaning or message, cognitive or aesthetic, is largely of the audience's construction.

Is this very uncommon way in which we might think of speech when we think of aesthetic or metaphorical expression necessary to a full appreciation all of the forms that freedom of speech might take? If so, we will have crossed a threshold, perhaps, in our conception of freedom. But the new threshold will prove treacherous. How can the concept of speech out of thin air be limited? Everyone sees meaning in objects, events, memories, acts. Must everything, at least for the meaning giver/receiver (often one and the same), become speech: the storm, the blade of grass, the warm bath? Might the feeling of comfort and security and peace evoked by the warm bath on a cold day be described as aesthetic and, thus, expressive? Are all acts of discrimination directed at others potentially "speech" acts that we who would see them as metaphors should be free to preserve from government prohibition or regulation?

It is to these questions that the profoundly important, yet often frustrating, *Hurley* case will be considered in the following story. The case presents a great story, but we must also keep our eye trained on the issues: What is the nature of the expression in *Hurley*? How does it occur? Is it distinct in any useful ways from cognitive political or cultural speech, not in subject necessarily, but in process, form, skill? Are the costs—even to the First Amendment freedoms themselves—simply too great to cross the cognitive/aesthetic line without an author because there can be no principled and practical limit that can be enforced to stop us from tumbling down the slippery slope?

The *Hurley* case involves the exclusion of an objectionable group with an objectionable view—pro-gay—from the longstanding annual St Patrick's Day Parade in Boston, and the Massachusetts law that deemed the exclusion illegal discrimination. Is a parade speech? Is a parade an event in the nature of metaphor and viewer construction rather than linear transmission of a message from a known, intending speaker to an audience that comprehends what the speaker means? Is the selecting of parade participants in the construction of the parade distinguishably expressive from the rejection of one or more participants? Is an orchestra director's selection of instrumentalists for a performance an act of free speech? What if the director deselects a violinist, not on grounds that he is a poor violinist, but on grounds that he is black and the aesthetics of racial diversity is not a message the director wishes to convey?

▪ ▪ ▪

The South Boston Allied War Veterans Council is a private association of representatives of veterans groups that for many, many years have organized and conducted the annual St. Patrick's Day–Evacuation Day Parade in Boston.[3] In the early 1990s, the parade was firmly in the hands of the Veterans Council and its Chief Marshal, John Hurley. For as long as he could remember, he has been known widely and affectionately in South Boston as "Wacko" Hurley, or better yet, as Wacko. "Some people find it hard to say. They say 'John,' but that goes right by me. There's a lot of Johns. Sometimes you might be in a bar and someone says, 'Hey Wacko!' and everyone gets nervous. Like 'here we go.'"[4] He obviously cherishes the name.

Hurley's work with the parade began many years back, in 1953, some six years after he returned from WWII, where he served in the Navy. The Allied War Veterans Council was then a smallish group, and while the parade had been around for many years, it had not then grown to the size and stature it attained by the 1990s. By 1964, at the young age of thirty-three, Wacko Hurley was elected Chief Marshal, and he never looked back.

As Chief Marshal, Hurley organized the parade, issued invitations for groups to participate, acted upon applications by new participating groups and, in the case of controversy or uncertainty, took a questionable application to the full council, which made a decision with everyone having one vote. Hurley's job was to put the whole parade together, from start to finish.

By the early 1990s the parade had many groups and floats and an audience of as many as one hundred thousand people. It had three themes, as Hurley would later testify: traditional family roles and values; honoring St. Patrick; and being Irish. But it was not a parade to make one or even three specific points; it was rather an amalgam of participants and celebrations that were consistent with tradition in the parade and not discordant with the three themes—or what might be better described as values. And the council and Hurley were firmly in charge of the themes.

It was in 1992 that the trouble started. It began with an application by the Irish-American Gay-Lesbian and Bisexual Pride Committee of Boston [later to become the Irish-American Gay, Lesbian and Bisexual Group of Boston (GLIB)] to march in the parade. GLIB members wanted to march as a group behind their banner, which took varying forms over the course of the controversy but in the end simply carried the group's name as a symbol of pride and presence in the community of South Boston. As GLIB put it, its members wished to "march in the parade as a way to express pride in their Irish heritage as openly gay, lesbian, and bisexual individuals, to demonstrate that there are such men and women among those so descended, and to express solidarity with like individuals who sought to march in New York's St. Patrick's Day Parade."[5]

It didn't take long for the council to consider and reject the application; nor did it take much time for controversy to flow in Boston and, soon, on a national level. Accusations swirled; local politics took center stage; and ultimately the matter went to court in Massachusetts. GLIB claimed that because its members were gay and its identity pro-gay, its participation had been rejected in violation of Massachusetts's nondiscrimination law. The Allied War Veterans Council, in other words, was simply homophobic and in rejecting GLIB's application the council had denied GLIB's right to free speech in the marketplace of ideas—the parade.

During the roughly three-year period from 1992 to 1995 lawsuits were filed and defended by all of the parties involved in the controversy: the Allied War Veterans Council; GLIB; the transportation department; the city; and the mayor, to name some. The litigation engaged the often-repeated attention of every level of the Massachusetts state and federal courts, including ultimately the United States Supreme Court. The Allied War Veterans Council lost virtually every battle until the very end. They were ordered by the Massachusetts courts to allow GLIB to march in the parade (they obeyed, and then the next year cancelled their parade instead of submitting to GLIB's inclusion). A great deal of legal talent became engaged in the fight, mostly on GLIB's side, and often without any or much cost.

The council, however, had to pay its own legal fees and costs and hire its own attorney. This they did in the person of Chester Darling, a solo practitioner in Boston with a small practice. Along the way he had help, but it was he who carried the load from start to finish. It would not be until June 19, 1995, that the case would effectively end with a unanimous decision by the Supreme Court. It was a decision that in many ways went to the heart of our ongoing inquiry: Exactly what form did the speech take; who was doing the speaking for constitutional purposes; what were they saying; and should it really matter if no one was speaking, as long as expression emerged "from thin air"?

■ ■ ■

The Supreme Court that heard oral argument in the *Hurley* case in April 1995 was not much different in ideological composition from the Court that would decide the *Citizens United* case in 2010. The chief justice was William Rehnquist, and with him on the more conservative side of the Court were Justices Antonin Scalia, Clarence Thomas, Sandra Day O'Connor, and Anthony Kennedy. On the liberal side were Justices John Paul Stevens, David Souter, Ruth Bader Ginsburg and Stephen Breyer. The lawyers who would argue the case were Chester Darling, a local lawyer in his own one-man firm in Boston, who had handled the case from beginning to end, and John Ward of Boston, who represented GLIB. Ward was relatively new to the case and practiced with an established firm in Boston.

The oral argument was active, engaging, even exciting, according to those fortunate enough to get a seat in the Supreme Court's courtroom. People literally sat on the edges of their seats.

■ ■ ■

CHIEF JUSTICE REHNQUIST: We'll hear argument first this morning in Number 94-749, *John J. Hurley and the South Boston Allied War Veterans Council v. the Irish-American Gay, Lesbian and Bisexual Group of Boston*. Mr. Darling.

MR. DARLING: Mr. Chief Justice, and may it please the Court: The central issue in this case is whether Government can mandate the expression of messages and viewpoints in a privately organized parade over the objections of the private organizers.

The Veterans Council clearly stated what the expressive purpose of their parades [was]. They announced during trial and prior to their application for a parade permit that they wished to celebrate their traditional religious and social values.

QUESTION:[6] What is the evidence to show that the purpose of this parade was to express any viewpoint?

MR. DARLING: The parade is inherently expressive.

QUESTION: Well, do you want us to make a finding, then, that a parade is *per se* an expressive activity?

MR. DARLING: Yes, I do, Your Honor.

There is a long and deep history here, going back at least to the Court's decisions upholding the right to parade and march in the civil rights era. In those cases the Court severely restricted the government's ability to condition approval of parades on anything other than speech-neutral criteria such as traffic safety, crowd control, and the like. Mr. Darling's point is that those cases would be in jeopardy if the government in Massachusetts could require the veterans to admit a gay rights group to the parade when the veterans did not want to express a gay rights view in or through the parade. As we will see, the legal and factual issues surrounding this basic claim by the veterans are complex, but the nub of the idea is not, and it's Darling's obligation to keep that clear. What would the Court have done in the 1960s had the KKK asked to participate (in robes or with a KKK banner) in a civil rights march led by Dr. King? Is the march an expressive event protected by the First Amendment?

Would the KKK's participation itself be expressive, and thus undermine the marchers' point?

Of course, one can argue that the civil rights marches had a clear theme, indeed a clear message, too: racial equality. This message would have been specifically negated by KKK participation. The veterans' parade message was more ambiguous, less cognitive, more aesthetic. GLIB's participation also may have negated part of the theme the Allied War Veterans Council claimed to have in mind for the parade, but with the veterans' parade it is less clear that the theme and message the council sought to communicate had any real relationship to the message actually disseminated and received by those attending the parade.

> QUESTION: Mr. Darling, you've answered, I guess, two questions, and I want to make sure that you stand by the answer in each one, and I want you to comment again on the relevance of each one. First, I think you told Justice Kennedy not only that the parade was expressive in its nature—I guess all parades are in your view—but that that was crucial to your case. You also said that the particular message, the viewpoint, if you will, was generally a celebration of religious and social values of Irish Catholics. Is that viewpoint crucial, the existence of that viewpoint as the expression conveyed by the parade, crucial to your case?
>
> MR. DARLING: I would think not, Justice Souter.
>
> QUESTION: May I just interrupt you and get to another point? You're saying that your viewpoint is essential to your case, and I take it you're saying it's not essential to your case that your parade have any viewpoint at all.
>
> MR. DARLING: That's correct.
>
> QUESTION: But is it essential to your case that the parade be expressive?
>
> MR. DARLING: No, it's not. As far as I'm concerned, if my clients march down a street on a permit that's issued by the City of Boston, whether it's a moving assembly or a group of persons, there will be some people that will make a determination that my clients or that group of people are expressing something.

This view of parades as expressive will need, and get, much more attention in the argument. The point, however, is worth underlining here. Darling is saying that the expressiveness of a parade—its character as speech protected by the First Amendment—inheres in the parade itself, through the interpretation given the parade event by those who see it. As we will see, this is a pretty dramatic view of speech, but it is the strongest (though not the only) view upon which Darling can stand, and he will do his very best to hold the ground.

QUESTION: But let's assume that in fact they are expressing nothing, so that the parade stands on the same footing, let's say, as a public restaurant, would the result be the same in this case?

MR. DARLING: If it was a permitted activity and there was no expression involved, probably not, Justice.

QUESTION: Okay.

QUESTION: Well, I'm not sure. I take it that the whole position of the respondents [GLIB] is that they want to proclaim a message. And it seems that your answer would be that even if your parade is nonexpressive in its history and in its tradition, that you have the right to keep it that way.

MR. DARLING: We have a judgment that made a finding that it was impossible to discern any specific expressive purpose in my client's First Amendment activity, but this Court has access to the exhibits, and particularly a video tape that demonstrates without question that my clients are engaging in a First Amendment activity with viewpoints and political messages and celebrating their religious values. The judge, the trial judge, acknowledged and identified those very values my clients are expressing.

Darling is doing his best to limit the scope of the very broad claim of protected expression he has stated, and rightly so. He's saying that it is the *parade* that is expressive—of *what* it is expressive is in part a function of the audience. A permitted restaurant isn't expressive, as such. Would a group of protestors entering the restaurant to challenge one of its policies—themselves expressing their view—somehow convert the restaurant's ordinary business into expression because of the protest? Darling would rather not go there. His position is that a parade—and especially his clients' parade—is *itself inherently expressive*, and its protection under the First Amendment doesn't depend on what GLIB had in mind.

QUESTION: Well, just hypothetically, let's assume, following Justice Souter's line of questioning, that this parade was like a picnic or something that had no expressive purpose whatsoever. That may be wrong. Let's assume [it] hypothetically. It seems to me that you still have an argument, and maybe you don't think you do. I should think you still have an argument that even if it is neutral in its custom and in its format, you have the right to say that it cannot be used for some other person's message.

MR. DARLING: Well, I'm sorry if I misspoke, Justice Scalia, but the fact is that no group of people nor any individual can be compelled to speak on behalf of the State or be the courier for the State's message [here, a message of diversity].

QUESTION: Mr. Darling, I understood your brief to say this is your parade and you can do with it what you will, somebody else can do what they will with their parade. That's the essence of your argument. It's your parade to make it do whatever you want it to do.

MR. DARLING: That's correct. My clients define the scope and content of the parade. They vote to include and exclude people and groups with messages that they approve of in their parade that are consistent with the overall theme, a celebration of the patron saint of the Archdiocese of Boston, St. Patrick.

QUESTION: Are there any limitations on that?

MR. DARLING: Yes. The limitations are adjudged on a case-by-case and a group-by-group manner by the veterans. They vote to include and exclude groups, and they vote on the basis of their own personal feelings. Not just Mr. Hurley but the vote of 60 people made the determination to exclude the respondent in this case.

QUESTION: Mr. Darling, I thought you said you couldn't do whatever you wanted with a parade. I thought you conceded that you could not exclude gays, lesbians, and bisexuals from marching in the parade if they want to march, so long as they are not trying to convey a message which you do not want conveyed.

MR. DARLING: That's correct, Justice Scalia. The fact that my clients do not have a litmus test so far as sexual orientation is concerned for participation in the parade is very clear from the record. My clients have excluded messages, not the people. The—

QUESTION: What is the message in this case? How would you state the message that GLIB is trying to convey?

MR. DARLING: GLIB had three purposes that were found as expressive during the trial. They were enumerated by the court as first to express its members' pride in their dual identities, second to demonstrate to the Irish-American and the gay, lesbian, and bisexual communities the diversity within those respective communities, and [third] to show support for the Irish-American gay, lesbian, and bisexual men and women in New York City who were seeking to participate in the New York St. Patrick's Day parade. They sought to demonstrate and proclaim their diversity on the basis of their sexual orientation in the parade. They also had a political message to support the people that were excluded from the St. Patrick's Day parade in New York.

My clients have messages that they really don't have to explain. They merely have to display them. They—

QUESTION: The message is, it's great to be Irish.

MR. DARLING: That's one of them, Justice Souter.

QUESTION: That's enough, isn't it?

(Laughter.)

MR. DARLING: One of them. I cannot emphasize enough the fact that for thirty-two years I've been explaining the basis for my client's speech, and being asked why they wish to express their religious values, what relationship do the Joey's clowns have to St. Patrick, all of the most absurd questions I've heard in my modest career.

What this case revolves around is messages. My clients have their messages. They may be old-fashioned, or they may be traditional messages.

QUESTION: Well, what you're saying, I gather, Mr. Darling, is it isn't just a message it's great to be Irish, but that it's great to be Roman Catholic, too.

MR. DARLING: Your Honor, Mr. Chief Justice, the messages contained in my client's parade are numerous and powerful messages. They include an anti-abortion group. Now, that group had been excluded for several years because they wished to display signs and pictures, and shout to the crowd, the spectators, and hand out literature as they passed down the street.

QUESTION: Well, could you answer my question more directly? Is the Roman Catholic religion a part of your message?

MR. DARLING: It certainly is, Mr. Chief Justice. The Ancient Order of Hibernians have been an integral part of the veterans parade for many years. They declined to participate in the parade because of the forced inclusion of [GLIB] in the '92 and '93 parades. My clients wanted that religious component in their parade, the Ancient Order of Hibernians. Because of the forced inclusion of the viewpoint by the courts, the Hibernians did not participate. My client's speech was diminished.

QUESTION: Why do they let the Baptists join the parade if it's a Catholic parade?

MR. DARLING: Well, it's part of their cultural expression, Justice Stevens. They're ecumenical in their Irish—

QUESTION: Up to a point.

(Laughter.)

QUESTION: Well, as I recall, the district court found that St. Patrick would not have excluded the homosexuals, lesbians, and bisexuals, isn't that right, something to that effect. His mission was not just to the straights, or something of that sort.

(Laughter.)

QUESTION: Is that a finding of the district court, or the lower court here?

MR. DARLING: I believe that was a homily that was added at the end of the judgment in the superior court decision, but clearly the fact that homosexuals and bisexuals and lesbians have marched in my client's parade for years is of no great consequence to my clients, that a gay city councilor who is openly gay who marched, and that appears in the record, and he was not disturbed. And Mr. Hurley did not have him excused from the parade, as he did in '93, when the court ordered my clients to include GLIB with their sexual orientation message, and Mr. Hurley ordered the exclusion of a truck with an antigay message on it, and assisted by the police they were thrown out of the parade.

My clients do not care about the sexual orientation or the religious background or the ethnic composition of anyone in their parade. They select groups that are consistent with what they perceive to be their version of a celebration of St. Patrick in their neighborhood, and it has some neighborhood features, and that's why the Baptist Bible trolley is invited, and that's why a number of local organizations are invited.

QUESTION: So what are we supposed to do—I take it that you concede, or do you not, that if your groups want to—your group cannot discriminate on the basis of race, can it?

MR. DARLING: Justice Breyer, my clients, if they wish to discriminate on the basis of their speech, in their speech they can, but as far as discriminating independently of their speech, that is conduct, and—

Here is where we start sinking into a morass (an instructive one, ultimately) and the questioning gets tedious, yet also challenging. The underlying problem is the slippery slope. Can a person who refuses to hire someone because he or she is black claim that it wasn't race that accounts for the decision but rather the unwillingness to express a message of approval of equality? To go so far would convert all illegal acts, potentially, into speech. Darling does not want to get into this area. He wants to stand on the clearer ground of saying that the veterans were clearly speaking through the parade; gays were not prohibited from participating; it was just the message of GLIB that undermined the Veterans' message and thus would deny the veterans' freedom of speech. He quite willingly says that of course discrimination—acts of discrimination—are not speech, but acts that government can clearly regulate. He would like for that statement to be enough for the moment, given that in his view the parade was speech and therefore the line to be drawn between acts of discrimination and discriminatory speech need not even arise in the case. But he knows better, because he litigated the case from the very beginning, and he is aware of the fact that the Massachusetts courts made some strange fact findings about why GLIB was excluded and whether the parade was speech. Fact findings in trial courts are usually binding on appellate courts, including the Supreme Court, whose business is law, not fact. But if the Supreme Court is bound by a finding that the veterans were not expressing anything in the parade, and, more important, if it is bound by the finding that the GLIB march and marchers were excluded because they were gay, not because of the effect their participation would have on the veterans' speech, Darling is in very, very deep trouble.

He knows it.

QUESTION: I take it that there's a finding that the parade normally includes everybody, and however they didn't include these people not because they weren't proud to be Irish—they were—but because they didn't like their sexual orientation. Now, are you saying that you do have a right to exclude because of the sexual orientation, or are you saying that wasn't why they were excluded, and if it's the latter, what do we do about the fact-finding?

MR. DARLING: I'm suggesting that the finding of discrimination, Justice Breyer, was made inappropriately on the very basis of the words you have just read. The trial judge equated the sexual orientation with messages and values. In my book, if you combine a message and a value you've got a viewpoint, not a sexual orientation.

QUESTION: But what are we supposed to do, because what we have is that sentence of the supreme judicial court, which I take it is a finding. Are we supposed to say–look into the record and say they're wrong? Are we supposed to remand it for a further factual finding? Are we supposed to take it as a fact? What do you suggest we do?

MR. DARLING: I would suggest, Your Honor, that the Court review the entire record, because I would be very distressed if my clients' rights of free speech were abridged on the basis of one judge's opinion of what message and viewpoint combined to mean.

QUESTION: But one judge always finds the facts. Where the trial judge makes the finding that Justice Breyer has asked about, he says the defendant's final position was that GLIB would be excluded "because of its values and its message, i.e., its members' sexual orientation." That seems to conflate two different concepts. It's quite a confusing finding.

MR. DARLING: Mr. Hurley and the Veterans Council knew nothing about this group when they first approached the Veterans Council to march in their parade. They had no name. They had three people that were forming a group that wanted to march, so naturally, when they finally sent in an application, which is reflected in the exhibits, that described themselves as a social club, they did not have enough information about the group and they were also hearing information in the community about the three participants that wanted to organize the group.

After they found out what the messages of the group were, they took a vote, and they voted to exclude any group with any sexual theme from their parade. They're entitled to do that. They're entitled to define the parade in any form and shape that they wish. That was not pretextual.

If my clients were marching with a group of people that did not have the signs and the messages that are reflected in this record, then there would be no dispute. The fact that the sign, the proclamations on the sign, and their announced messages [were included, means that] my clients can reject [it]. They can include and exclude any messages they wish to.

I reserve the balance of my time if there are no further questions.

Darling has acquitted himself quite well. He knows the case, knows the record, knows the problems, and has a clear, direct, and forceful theory from which he argues. He holds his ground and tries mightily to stay away from the treacherous shoals of the state courts' fact findings on whether the veterans were engaged in speech through the planning, organizing, and executing of the parade; or whether they were just parade planners who intended no message or expression of any note; or whether they were simply engaged in hidden discrimination against gays. Darling says the parade is an inherently expressive event, and that the planning, organizing, and executing of the parade is a creative act entitled to respect as speech because of the themes it pursues through the parade and because of the meanings the spectators draw from it. This is good but, as we will see, far from firm ground to stand on.

But what if, as the Massachusetts courts implied, the Veterans were just parade planners who intended no message—or more specifically whose "in the air" cultural message was very diffuse and noncognitive? Just a "feeling good today in our nation and community" message? Should that be protected speech? Must speech have *a*, or a fairly coherent, message? Or is asking that much ignoring the sensuous and aesthetic and emotional properties of speech?

And what if the veterans' parade is protected, but very diffuse, speech, and it is now competing against GLIB's competing claim to be able to express its own, more specific, more cognitive and pointed view? Why in such a case should the veterans prevail over a better-defined claim of right to expression? Because the Veterans did all of the work?

And then, finally, there was that nasty fact finding, to which we will soon return. What if the veterans' parade doesn't count at all as speech, for whatever reason (nothing there; too general; not intended to express)? Then, of course, the veterans would have no shelter in the First Amendment because their rejection of GLIB would look just like a discriminatory act.

In the alternative, the veterans could argue that the government forced them to include GLIB under the nondiscrimination law, and by doing so to carry GLIB's message. That would be a case of compelled speech by the veterans. This argument is there, but Darling doesn't emphasize it. Why? Because it rests the veterans' claim on the speech intentions and activities of GLIB: only if GLIB were speaking a clear message would the Veterans be able to say that the government had required the veterans to carry it; and even then only if the spectators saw GLIB's message as being endorsed by the veterans. Who would believe that?

As we will see in the second half of the oral argument, this is indeed messy, fascinating, and really fundamental stuff the Court and the lawyers are getting into. Do the participants also realize that lots more is at stake—like the constitutional protection for art? Think about a Picasso painting—what he put there, what we see there, what meaning those who would protest might assign to it.

CHIEF JUSTICE REHNQUIST: Mr. Ward, we'll hear from you.

MR. WARD: Mr. Chief Justice, and may it please the Court: This is a case about discrimination. The finding of the trial judge in this case was that the council excluded the members of GLIB on the basis of their sexual orientation, that they excluded them for who they were, not what they said.

QUESTION: Well, I assume you concede that your clients wanted to be in the parade because they wanted to proclaim a message.

MR. WARD: Well, I think the term "message" as it's been used in this case really is more confusing than illuminating, Justice Kennedy. My clients wanted to be included in the parade. They wanted to be included in what the trial judge found to be an open recreational event. The trial judge found that they had been discriminated against. He ordered that they be included on the same basis as everybody else. Everybody else self-identified.

QUESTION: Do you think it's a fair conclusion from this record that GLIB had no interest in proclaiming their message in this event?

MR. WARD: I think that there is a difference between who someone is and what their message is. They did not come in with a sign saying "Gay is Good."

Ward must be careful here. Is he saying that there is no message in self-identifying? What about gays who come out of the closet? Isn't that all about message? The question here is whether there was expression protected by the First Amendment as speech. The Court is bound and determined to plumb the depths of this question—to get as close to the heart of the matter as possible.

QUESTION: To get back to the question of why GLIB wanted to be in the parade, they didn't want to be there to recreate, as was found by the Massachusetts Supreme Court. GLIB's purposes are to express its members' pride in their dual identities as Irish or Irish-American, to demonstrate to the Irish-American community and to the Gay,

Lesbian, and Bisexual community the diversity within those—and to show support. All of those are expressive activities. They were there to express something, weren't they?

MR. WARD: Justice Scalia, I think that when Linda Brown went to school in Little Rock, her going in there was expressing something. For purposes of the discrimination statute, the expression is incidental. When a discriminator excludes someone, that also under some circumstances sends a very powerful message. The—I think that the point here, Justice Scalia, is that one—under the antidiscrimination laws one cannot be penalized for merely self-identifying any more than the—when a discriminator excludes—

Ward is getting himself led into a pointless squabble here, and it doesn't supply the makings of a clear argument. Unless explicit, cognitive (logical, not emotional or sensuous) declarative statements are the only things that count at speech (which they aren't, according to the Supreme Court—witness flag burning), the fact is that self-identification can, in some circumstances, constitute speech and the expression of a message. The hard questions lie below the surface: when, why, how, who?

QUESTION: Why is that? This isn't a matter of penalizing. It's a matter of not wanting to convey the expressions, the demonstrations, and the showings of support that this group wanted to make in that particular parade. If Massachusetts antidiscrimination law results in forcing parade organizers to allow people with signs and placards that are inconsistent with what the parade says its message is, then it's a problem under the First Amendment, isn't it?

MR. WARD: I'm saying that didn't happen, and I'm saying it for two reasons, Mr. Chief Justice. First of all, there was a State finding also that this was an open recreational event, that there really was—

QUESTION: Well, let's pose it in a different context. Suppose there's a Ringling Brothers Barnum and Bailey Circus in town and they have a parade, and an animal rights group wants to join the parade with their signs that say [that] animals shouldn't be used as they are in circuses. Now, do you think they have a right under a public accommodation law to join that parade?

MR. WARD: Justice O'Connor, I see a very clear distinction between viewpoint discrimination and discrimination against people simply for being who they are.

QUESTION: Yes, but a Barnum and Bailey parade doesn't have any viewpoint other than just, gee, the circus is in town and everybody come.

(Laughter.)

MR. WARD: What the council is doing is that they're reading a message into the mere presence of a group that's protected under the Massachusetts statute. Discriminators always do that. That's what discrimination—

QUESTION: They're not reading into it. The group said that they wanted to express their pride in their dual identities as Irish and homosexuals. The parade organizers do not believe, whether you agree with it or not, that being homosexual is something to be proud of, and therefore [they] do not want that idea to be expressed in their parade. Why is that not simply saying you don't have to have expressed what you do not want to have expressed?

MR. WARD: Because whatever the group had as its expressive notion when it formed, all it said in the parade is, we are Irish-American lesbians, gay men and bisexuals.

The exchanges remain tendentious, but there is an important point lurking under the surface. It is the slippery slope argument. If speech isn't objectively (or by intention) ascertainable, can't virtually all acts be converted into speech, like the act of job discrimination? Ward will work hard on emphasizing the slipperiness of the slope, in the hopes of getting the Court, when it sees the bottom, to scurry quickly back to the top and draw a clear line. The speech act must be objectively ascertainable by evidence; the message must be clear and coherent (and therefore, perhaps, cognitive). Otherwise, no speech protection. If that's unsatisfactory, the person who wants to speak can simply be clearer about what they are doing and what they want to say. That's not too hard, is it?

Well . . . maybe it's not too hard for a hard-core proponent of a view. But politicians sure have difficulty with it. And artists? Musicians? Is that kind of clarity even possible, or desirable?

QUESTION: But the point—suppose that were true. You know the case of *Wooley v. Maynard*—the New Hampshire . . . [vehicle] license [plate] that said 'Live Free or Die' [which the driver had illegally covered up because he disagreed with it, and believing that other drivers would think he supported war]?

MR. WARD: Right.

QUESTION: The driver of that car was not engaged in expression. He didn't think about it. But the point was that once somebody told him he had to express a message, the Court found that this was State interference, and that this was State-mandated expression, which is contrary to the First Amendment. And the point is that even if the parade were not expressive earlier, and I doubt that, I should think the organizers could say we don't want it turned into an expressive activity, and that this case is much easier than a . . . license [plate motto] case.

MR. WARD: I think, Justice Kennedy, that GLIB is like the numbers, it's not like the sign. In other words, what the council was doing is what discriminators always do. They're conflating identity with some message that they read into it, and—

The justices are getting frustrated, especially with Ward's continual sliding and ducking around the questions and issues. He needs to get off this ground, for it isn't helping his case, and more important, it doesn't have the quality of an affirmative argument. The negation of everything is just negation.

QUESTION: Well, can we just get one thing established? You would agree that if the reason for the exclusion of your clients was solely because of their message—solely because of their message—that the exclusion would be within the First Amendment rights of the organizers of a private parade?

MR. WARD: I would agree that the council is free to discriminate on the basis of viewpoint. If my clients came in with a sign saying, "Gay is Good," they could keep it out. However, that's not what happened here. The finding—

QUESTION: Mr. Ward, there is a statement I think in the court of first instance and in the supreme judicial court of three purposes. They sound like they're expressive. The last one was support for the New York group that was seeking to march in the parade there. Now, would you review those three and tell me why each of them is not conveying a message?

MR. WARD: I don't disagree that each of those purposes is expressive, Justice Ginsburg. My point is that none of those messages was stated in anything that GLIB said in the parade. They simply carried a sign.

QUESTION: Well, none of the parade's messages were [explicit], either, and we're talking about that which is kind of reasonably implicit and reasonably conveyed throughout. Are you taking the position that unless you literally have a sign with a declarative statement on it that the rule does not apply?

Ward is now invited to make the slippery slope argument, or at least tell the Court where it can draw the line. We have some lines: intention of the speaker; objective facts of express speech; cognitive messages. What about emotion? And most important for Ward, *why* is self-identification a good line to draw?

MR. WARD: I'm taking the position that when all other groups in the parade are allowed to simply self-identify, that the act of my client in simply self-identifying, which is all they did, is not the expression of an antithetical message in that sense.

QUESTION: So I guess you're saying that in the absence of an express declarative statement, none of these three purposes to which Justice Ginsburg has alluded and the Massachusetts courts found as your expressive point, is in fact a point being expressed at all.

MR. WARD: I'm saying no, they certainly *did not find* any expression in the parade.

Now Ward turns to the fact finding. It is perhaps his strongest tactic, though it really has nothing to do with the issues. And when the Court gets down to examining the "fact" found—the veterans were not speaking, they were just discriminating against gays—the justices likely don't believe it any more than Ward would if asked in confidence. It would also be pretty ugly for Ward to win the case on the basis of an ambiguous and, frankly, unwise, offhanded footnote in a state court judge's decision, leaving the First Amendment issues hanging.

But there is something to Ward's tactic, even if we might not applaud it. Appellate courts, like the Supreme Court, are generally bound by fact findings made in the trial court, which has the advantage of seeing the witness and judging credibility, for example. But there are some exceptions to this rule, and fact findings on which First Amendment rights turn are among them. There the Supreme Court can dig into the record more searchingly and is not bound by the lower court's fact findings.

QUESTION: Well, what did your group's sign say?

MR. WARD: It said simply, Mr. Chief Justice, "Irish-American, Gay, Lesbian and Bisexual Group of Boston," which is the identity of who these people were. It did not say, repeal the sodomy laws. It did not say, we question your traditional values. It did not say anything of that kind.

QUESTION: That is enough to show that you are proud of that fact, which is what their object is to express their pride in those dual identities. That's all you need to show that pride, is to hang it up in a sign. How else does one show pride in a certain thing?

MR. WARD: In the same sense that a black person marching in the parade, I take it, would be proud of his or her identity.

QUESTION: That's right, and if that person held up a sign and said, black unity, that would be an expression of pride in blackness.

MR. WARD: Except that generally speaking, lesbians, gay men, and bisexual people are not immediately evident to the—

Oops! If gays are not evident, then they have to send a message. But does black skin do that? To whom, when, why, how? Is it enough if it sends the message to just one person? These are questions of line drawing that can't be escaped. But the Court seems to want no part of Ward's answer—be explicit. Is his answer too simplistic?

The justices try mightily to probe this fundamental question.

QUESTION: Exactly. I mean, the point at issue is whether there's an expression of anything in their mere marching with a sign saying what they are, and it seems to me you must acknowledge that it is–there is an expression of pride in what they are.

MR. WARD: I would call it self-identifying, just as a Star of David, just as—

QUESTION: So long as you mean, by self-identifying, pride. I'll accept that.

(Laughter.)

QUESTION: May I ask you a question, Mr. Ward? It's really remarkable in this case, it seems to me, that both of you seem to agree on the applicable law. They agree they can't exclude you because of who you are, and you agree they can exclude you if you're sending a message. So the real question is, how do you decide which it is, and the point, the question is, for me at least, do you answer that question by looking at your motive, their interpretation of what you look like, or the reasonable neutral person's interpretation of the sign? What is the standard?

MR. WARD: I think it's objective facts. It's an objective question. You look at two things. You look at what kind of event the council has created, what the court found was an open recreational event, and then you look at the impact of the inclusion of the unwanted group on that event.

This Court's cases have suggested that if a group [the parade organizer] is so organized around a discernible specific expressive purpose that the mere inclusion of the unwanted group would seriously disable them from their expressive purposes, then perhaps the group wins. In this case—

QUESTION: Well, I don't know that 'seriously disable' is found in any of our cases. I think quite the contrary, that if you have an expressive purpose, you're entitled to maintain the purity of that expression. Newspapers, for instance, can't be required to print retraction articles.

MR. WARD: Exactly. However, what the trial judge found and what the supreme judicial court affirmed was that the relationship of the council to this event was that of standing basically indifferent to the messages, that that's what really happened.

Ward is testing his credibility. The fact is that notwithstanding the "finding" of the veterans' discrimination against gays (if finding is the right term for a confused comment in a footnote), there is absolutely no affirmative evidence to support the finding that the Veterans excluded GLIB or anyone else because they were gay. Did they? Who knows. But the responsibility to pin this matter down rests with GLIB's lawyers at the trial level, and they either dropped the ball or couldn't prove it and now want to engineer the fact back into the case through a judge's loose language.

QUESTION: Mr. Ward, can I ask another question, following up on my preceding question? If it's an objective test, and say objectively the neutral observer would say yes, there's an expression going on here, but nevertheless the evidence was very clear that the real motive was that they didn't want you to march with them, which is what [the court] found, that real motive would really not be controlling under the objective test, would it?

MR. WARD: Well, it controls as to the finding of discrimination.

QUESTION: Yes, but it would be permissible discrimination if the objective observer would think that there's a message there they don't like. Now, maybe they would have excluded you whether or not there was a message, but maybe they can get away with it if there's a message.

QUESTION: Could they exclude the Ku Klux Klan on the basis of the uniforms they wear, or the sheets and so forth?

MR. WARD: Anything they want to, sure.

QUESTION: But why is that different from self-identification?

MR. WARD: Because that goes to the essence, otherwise you would give a discriminator an objector's veto. Every time somebody came along and self-identified they'd say, we don't object to you. We object to your Jewish surname, or to your Star of David, or to some other feature.

QUESTION: Well, the trial court said the veteran's position is paradoxical. [It said that] a proper celebration of St. Patrick's and Evacuation Day requires diversity and inclusiveness. I suggest that for a State entity, which is the court, to tell a private speaker how to celebrate St. Patrick's Day is antithetical to First Amendment principles.

MR. WARD: Your Honor, I think that what the trial justice was doing was characterizing their position, not dictating it to them. In the end, this is a case about discrimination. The finding of the two courts below, well-supported in the record, was that the reason, the real reason that GLIB was kept out was its members' sexual orientation and not any message, because there was no message in that sense, and for that reason the judgment of the supreme judicial court should be affirmed.

And with that, Mr. Ward closes his argument. He had a very tough argument to make. He held his ground. But it was not good ground to hold. He needed to, but did not, effectively craft an argument that there is a limit on the slippery slope and that it can be managed and principled. And the Veterans Council fell below it, and thus should have no Free Speech protection; or should have less than the more explicit speech by GLIB. He needs to argue, for example, that antidiscrimination laws could be crippled if a black applicant could be rejected because of what his blackness—or perhaps his Afro haircut—says, not because he is black.

Darling now returns for his few reserved minutes, and he hits hard right out of the gate—on the facts.

MR. DARLING: Again, I would urge, Mr. Chief Justice and Your Honors, that any review of the record will reflect that there is absolutely no evidence of discrimination on the basis of sexual orientation by my clients in this record–in the whole enterprise.

My clients discriminated against messages. Historically they have. They included the NAACP, they excluded the KKK, they excluded an anti-gay group, and they wished to exclude a group—

QUESTION: Mr. Darling, would you comment directly on your opponent's argument that the particular signs they were going to carry [constitute nothing more] than what he describes as self-identification?

MR. DARLING: It's a message, it's an identification, it's a proclamation, and it is a message that my clients did not deem appropriate to include in their expression of their version of a celebration of a St. Patrick's Day parade, however they designed it.

QUESTION: Suppose that their actual reason was that the sign calls attention to a fact that makes the parade watchers feel uncomfortable. Is that a justification?

An interesting question indeed. Is the communication of feelings, or the inducement of feelings in others, speech? An artist would certainly say so. And so does Darling. But what about the contested field of hate speech, where the feelings are made "harm" and the speech is prohibited in order to avoid the harm? In such cases is the explanation for greater government power to regulate that the epithet, for example, isn't speech? Or that it is speech but the harm outweighs it? Both answers can be found in the cases. Are the feelings of disgust expressed by Jesse Helms (and many others) at indecent art really any different? And how do we judge those feelings of hurt and disgust to be any different or less creditable than the black student who is addressed by an epithet? Both are indecent and disrespectful of American values.

Discomfort, the Court has long told us, is the very nature of speech if it is free. And art? It is about feelings, perceptions, skills, whether in relation to the beautiful and sublime or the ugly and shocking, most artists would say. And they have a point. How about Dante's Inferno?

Not art?

Oh my, what a mess we seem to be in.

QUESTION: Suppose that what happens is that that just makes them feel uncomfortable, since it's public, and they don't like it. Now, where does that stand under First Amendment law?

MR. DARLING: My clients can exclude it. They can exclude any message in any parade that they deem inappropriate.

CHIEF JUSTICE REHNQUIST: Thank you, Mr. Darling. The case is submitted.

■ ■ ■

The Court's opinion came out at the end of the term. That was not surprising, for the case was very important and very complex and highly political, too. What was surprising, however, was the Court's unanimity, not just in result but also in reasoning. The Court begins with the brave and broad, even stirring, sentiment that parades are inherently expressive. From that point on the case is over and Darling, having lost in virtually every lower court over three years of litigation, gets his full victory, as do the war veterans.

But we know the case is not so simple as that. We know that speech is a many-faceted thing, and parades aren't all that count. We know about the slippery slope, and the absolute need to fix a point to stop our slide. We know about the many problems raised by concepts like cognition versus emotion; sensuality; beauty and ugliness; attribution of expression to conduct; intention; audience interpretation, and on and on. And we know that we need to think very carefully about art and the aesthetic. We will do so once we have digested what the Court, speaking through Justice Souter, is saying.

SOUTER, J., delivered the opinion for a unanimous Court:

If there were no reason for a group of people to march from here to there except to reach a destination, they could make the trip without expressing any message beyond the fact of the march itself. Some people might call such a procession a parade, but it would not be much of one. Real "[p]arades are public dramas of social relations, and in them performers define who can be a social actor and what subjects and ideas are available for communication and consideration." Hence, we use the word "parade" to indicate marchers who are making some sort of collective point, not just to each other but to bystanders along the way. Indeed, a parade's dependence on watchers is so extreme that nowadays, as with Bishop Berkeley's celebrated tree, "if a parade or demonstration receives no media coverage, it may as well not have happened." Parades are thus a form of expression, not just motion, and the inherent expressiveness of marching to make a point explains our cases involving protest marches.

The protected expression that inheres in a parade is not limited to its banners and songs, however, for the Constitution looks beyond written or spoken words as mediums of expression. Noting that "[s]ymbolism is a primitive but effective way of communicating ideas," our cases have recognized that the First Amendment shields such acts as saluting a flag (and refusing to do so), wearing an armband to protest a war, displaying a red flag, and even "[m]arching, walking or parading" in uniforms displaying the swastika. As some of these examples show, a narrow, succinctly articulable message is not a condition of constitutional protection, which if confined to expressions conveying a "particularized message," would never reach the unquestionably shielded painting of Jackson Pollock, music of Arnold Schöenberg, or Jabberwocky verse of Lewis Carroll.

Not many marches, then, are beyond the realm of expressive parades, and the South Boston celebration is not one of them. Spectators line the streets; people march in costumes and uniforms, carrying flags and banners with all sorts of messages (*e.g.*, "England get out of Ireland," "Say no to drugs"); marching bands and pipers play; floats are pulled along; and the whole show is broadcast over Boston television. To be sure, we agree with the state courts that in spite of excluding some applicants, the Council is rather lenient in admitting participants. But a private speaker does not forfeit constitutional protection simply by combining multifarious voices, or by failing to edit their themes to isolate an exact message as the exclusive subject matter of the speech. Nor, under our precedent, does First Amendment protection require a speaker to generate, as an original matter, each item featured in the communication. Cable operators, for example, are engaged in protected speech activities even when they only select programming originally produced by others. For that matter, the presentation of an edited compilation of speech generated by other persons is a staple of most newspapers' opinion pages, which, of course, fall squarely within the core of First Amendment security, as does even the simple selection of a paid noncommercial advertisement for inclusion in a daily paper. The selection of contingents to make a parade is entitled to similar protection.

Respondents' participation as a unit in the parade was equally expressive. GLIB was formed for the very purpose of marching in it, as the trial court found, in order to celebrate its members' identity as openly gay, lesbian, and bisexual descendants of the Irish immigrants, to show that there are such individuals in the community, and to support the like men and women who sought to march in the New York parade. The organization distributed a fact sheet describing the members' intentions, and the record otherwise corroborates the expressive nature of GLIB's participation. In 1993, members of GLIB marched behind a shamrock-strewn banner with the simple inscription "Irish American Gay, Lesbian and Bisexual Group of Boston." GLIB understandably seeks to communicate its ideas as part of the existing parade, rather than staging one of its own.

■ ■ ■

In the case before us the Massachusetts law has been applied in a peculiar way. Its enforcement does not address any dispute about the participation of openly gay, lesbian, or bisexual individuals in various units admitted to the parade. Petitioners disclaim any intent to exclude homosexuals as such, and no individual member of GLIB claims to have been excluded from parading as a member of any group that the Council has approved to march. Instead, the disagreement goes to the admission of GLIB as its own parade unit carrying its own banner. Since every participating unit affects the message conveyed by the private organizers, the state courts' application of the statute produced an order essentially requiring petitioners to alter the expressive content of their parade.

"Since *all* speech inherently involves choices of what to say and what to leave unsaid," one important manifestation of the principle of free speech is that one who chooses to speak may also decide "what not to say."

Petitioners' claim to the benefit of this principle of autonomy to control one's own speech is as sound as the South Boston parade is expressive. Rather like a composer, the Council selects the expressive units of the parade from potential participants, and though the score may not produce a particularized message, each contingent's expression in the Council's eyes comports with what merits celebration on that day. Even if this view gives the Council credit for a more considered judgment than it actively made, the Council clearly decided to exclude a message it did not like from the communication it chose to make, and that is enough to invoke its right as a private speaker to shape its expression by speaking on one subject while remaining silent on another. The message it disfavored is not difficult to identify. Although GLIB's point (like the Council's) is not wholly articulate, a contingent marching behind the organization's banner would at least bear witness to the fact that some Irish are gay, lesbian, or bisexual, and the presence of the organized marchers would suggest their view that people of their sexual orientations have as much claim to unqualified social acceptance as heterosexuals and indeed as members of parade units organized around other identifying characteristics. The parade's organizers may not believe these facts about Irish sexuality to be so, or they may object to unqualified social acceptance of gays and lesbians or have some other reason for wishing to keep GLIB's message out of the parade. But whatever the reason, it boils down to the choice of a speaker not to propound a particular point of view, and that choice is presumed to lie beyond the government's power to control.

It is so ordered.

Mr. Darling, the solo practitioner from Boston who had litigated the case from beginning to end, losing at almost every turn (though not because of any failing as a lawyer), had finally won the case at the nation's highest court, and he had done so with a unanimous decision. His is a truly remarkable story.

The Court's opinion is in many ways an equally remarkable one: long, scholarly, yet bristling with ambiguity at its foundation. Justice Souter concluded for the Court that because the parade was private, the only party that could claim free speech rights was the Allied War Veterans Council. The council's job was to construct the parade, a job accomplished by decisions to include and exclude participants, but not to alter or shape the message, if any, that the participants' marching carried. It was a thematic parade, reflecting Irish Pride, the sacrifice of Irish Veterans, the Catholic Church, and the family values of the South Boston community. The themes were broad and, frankly, ambiguous, which is not to say that the council did not shape the parade around its sense of those themes. But the parade's message was at best broad and evocative. It was not like a freedom march led by Dr. King in the South, or a pro-choice or antiabortion parade or march around the Supreme Court. Yet the council's parade, the Court says, was something more than, perhaps, a Macy's parade in which discriminating values and images are hardly the point.

Perhaps the simplest and most fitting description of the parade's message is that it was aesthetic—as well as artistic in its construction of floats, colors, marchers, and the like. Its message lies in evoking feelings and images and interpretations in the audience that are generally consistent with the values (family, pride) evoked by aesthetic and artistic representations. As Justice Souter says, "[r]eal 'parades are public drama of social relations, and in them performers define who can be a social actor and what subjects and ideas are available for communication and consideration.'" If this is so, then we have a clearer understanding of what the speech or expression protected by the First Amendment was, and the limited role the council played in shaping it. We must know this, for if the parade has no message—no specific (or cognitive) statements or claims, and no evocative (aesthetic) themes—around which the selection choices of the council can be seen as expressive ones, there is no basis for the council's First Amendment claim, and there would be no damage to free speech from a requirement, imposed by the Massachusetts law and the lower courts, that GLIB be allowed in the parade.

If the Boston parade was a means of communicating an aesthetic message, then we can know two very important things about the role of the council as "speaker" and the form in which the "communication of a message" occurred through the parade and its participants. First, we know that the council's speech acts—inclusion and exclusion of participants—did not involve the construction of a cognitive message, but instead they served to construct an aesthetic message. They served more like decisions about the palette and form of a painting, than decisions about the object to be represented. Second, we understand that the identity of the specific message being communicated lay in the minds and imaginations of the spectators, not the council and not the individual participants. Much like art, the council and the participants constructed the representation of the parade, and the viewers provided the re-representation of its meaning and message through their individual acts of creativity. There was no specific message of the parade; there were countless messages interpretively constructed from the parade. The council hoped that those messages would be generally similar, at least at the thematic level of pride and family and community values, but it could no more assure that outcome than a novelist can assure that his or her readers will draw the same meaning from the novel as the author holds in his own imagination.

Armed with this understanding of the parade, we can explore the most important question raised by the case: what is the nature of the process of communication upon which the Court rested the protection of the First Amendment and how can it be squared with the text, history, and traditions of "freedom of speech?" Answering this question is essential, for we know that aesthetic and artistic expression do not fit the traditional mold of speech protected by the First Amendment: the speaker on a street corner soapbox trying to convince an audience to his way of thinking about a social or political issue. The traditional speaker, unlike the council in *Hurley* or the poet or painter, is one with a specific, cognitive message who intends to communicate that message to an identifiable audience, who will receive and understand that specific message, whether they agree with it or not.

In order to undertake this inquiry, we will look at four illustrative and very different conceptions of what communication involves and how it works. The theories are reflected in the work of J. L. Austin, E. D. Hirsch, John Peters, and James Carey. Our discussion will help reveal what the Supreme Court interprets speech to mean, and then to judge the basis for the Court's interpretation of the First Amendment.

Speech Acts

J. L. Austin's speech act theory introduced a category of language called the "performative."[7] Performative statements are acts, in and of themselves. When results or consequences are brought about *by* saying something, then the speaker can be said to use language in the performative sense. The performative statement is qualitatively distinct from a statement that simply reports facts. The latter type of statement, once heard, may change someone's course of action subsequently, but when a performative statement is issued and understood, certain effects immediately obtain. For example, if one articulates a descriptive statement of fact, such as "it is forty degrees outside,"[8] the receiver of that statement may rely on that information and, thus, choose to put on a coat. But that consequence is not a *necessary* response or effect of the utterance. The doing of the act is not achieved by the speech.

Statements with a greater degree of illocutionary force, and hence, performative quality, include statements such as, "I promise to pay you five dollars in exchange for your hat." Assuming this statement is uttered in the appropriate context, it constitutes a promise and enacts a legally actionable contract.

While there is no such thing as a "pure" performative[9]—there are only uses of language with more or less illocutionary force according to the speech situations in which the expression is uttered—the idea of the performative says something important about the nature of language: that sometimes speech and act are so intertwined as to be inextricably intertwined. Put simply, some speech is more powerful—not in its tone or decibels, but in its impact on an audience—and thus may deserve greater respect as communication when it competes with other, less performative, expression.

In *Hurley*, Justice Souter could have used Austin's theory to support the conclusion that (GLIB) was entitled to little or no constitutional protection. Because the explicitly performative statement has a high degree of force and consequence, it might be said that the individual paraders marching in procession generated no noticeable illocutionary force, and thus no speech. The pride, entertainment value, or any other values communicated by the *parade* were not generated by, or intrinsic to, a single marching entity. To the extent that the individual parade units engaged in communication with no (or little) illocutionary force, their speech acts approach the legal realm of nonexpressive "conduct," which raises no First Amendment issues. The Court could then conclude that the council's speech selections qualify as conduct attended by substantial (or greater) illocutionary force—like "coming out," perhaps.

In this way, Austin's theory could have supported the Court's conclusion that the Allied War Veteran's Council has the right to combine multifarious voices and/or edit their themes according to its private dictates and without regard to speech interests of GLIB, because the council's decisions to include and exclude marchers "spoke" within the meaning of the First Amendment. The council's composition of the parade, which included its particular speech selection judgments, can qualify as a speech act with great, indeed primary, illocutionary force . . . not unlike an orchestra director's selection of instruments and musicians to play a score. Because the council's announcement of GLIB's disqualification performs the very act that it states and immediately effects the exclusion of GLIB, the council's judgment carries great weight, and the council's speech act can therefore be privileged above GLIB's alleged speech interest.

Justice Souter's opinion, however, did not employ speech act theory. The opinion viewed the parade as a form of robust expression, not conduct. It characterized parades in general as "public drama[s] of social relations" that make a "*collective* point."[10] It held that parades constitute "a form of expression, not just motion."[11] Characterized this way, the parade itself constitutes speech. The parade itself thus becomes the focus of the Court's analysis rather than the council's speech-selection judgment (which Austin's theory would have directed the Court to examine as an instance of performative speech).

While the Court's insight about parades may be right, the Court's initial premise—that marching is inherently expressive—would seem to concede the argument that the council's selection judgments do not uniquely cause a collective point to be made; indeed, even absent a permit-granting process—for example, if the parade were run by the city and everyone could participate—a collective, multifarious message could still be extrapolated from combining the multiple paraders' voices. In other words, the council's decisions are not productive of the thematic message communicated ultimately—that overarching message can't be known in advance. Functionally, all the council can do is control that which is *not* said. It only controls the silences. Under Austin's theory, act and speech are not inextricably intertwined in the council's (de)selection act, so the council's speech selection judgment has little illocutionary force; its process of denying permits looks more like pure conduct than speech, and should not receive First Amendment protection.

If the Court did in fact believe that act and speech were inextricably intertwined in the council's (de)selection act, no evidence of this fact exists in the opinion. Nothing mentioned by the Court would provide support for the conclusion that the council's speech act (in other words, the selection process) qualifies as an explicitly performative statement, and, as such, trumps the historically sedimented meaning that inheres in (most forms of) marching as a kind of expressive conduct. If a parade's message is social, dramatic, and thematic, arising from an entrenched historical appreciation for the cultural significance of marching, it seems unlikely that the council's intended message—be it vague or specific—could consist of anything more than its own mental construct, bearing no real significance to the parade. It makes little sense that the council should get credit under Austin's view as the preeminent speaker just because it takes individual paraders' messages and allegedly transforms them, by virtue of granting or denying a permit, into some *later-constructed* collective point.

Ultimately, the Court's decision positioned the council as the preeminent message organizer not by virtue of the illocutionary force inherent in speech selection judgments—like civil rights marches—but rather by default. The Court impliedly held that the marchers' specific messages were constitutive of the *council's* message and thus subordinate to it. The council thus received ownership over all the marchers' speech, just like a symphony owns the individual performances—or, perhaps, like the painter owns the painting and its compositional choices even though it takes on a meaning and life of its own once displayed.

Author Intent

E. D. Hirsch established the author's intent as the prevailing normative guideline for evaluating the interpretation of (literary) texts.[12] He defined authorial intent as the author or speaker's intended message, an orientation that assumes an identifiable message *and* a singularly or arguably *best* interpretation of a text. Hirsch chose this rubric because, he argued, one must be able to stabilize meaning and then judge it according to systematically reliable principles. Doing so enables the possibility of assessment. Put differently, Hirsch's theory grounded the possibility of determinate meaning in a human's preexisting determinate will to share a largely cognitive message (and trapped the meaning of the message there).

Under Hirsch's theory, the threshold question in *Hurley* must be whether the council intended to speak an identifiable message. The council did, of course, organize the parade and select the participants. But to trump GLIB's interests, the council must, at the very least, intend to express some message or express its own disagreement with one (like GLIB's). The fact that a parade is inherently expressive cannot, without more, bootstrap the council into the category of "speaker" under Hirsch's theory. Without more by way of intent and message, the parade is an event, not speech, and the council is an actor, not a speaker.

The *Hurley* Court conferred speakership upon the council because (a) the council was a private organizer; (b) a speaker is not required to generate, as an original matter, each item featured in the communication (in other words, republishers may be entitled to First Amendment protection when they only select speech originally produced by others); and (c) the selection of contingents to make a parade is an act of authorship intended to create a collective message.

The Court begins from the premise that parades and marching constitute speech and implicitly addresses the question of intent:

> To be sure, we agree with the state courts that in spite of excluding some applicants, the Council is rather lenient in admitting participants. But a private speaker does not forfeit constitutional protection simply by combining multifarious voices, or by failing to edit their themes to isolate an exact message as the exclusive subject matter of the speech. Nor . . . does First Amendment protection require a speaker to generate, as an original matter, each item featured in the communication. [Similar to a cable operator or newspaper editor,] [t]he selection of contingents to make a parade is entitled to First Amendment protection.[13]

In answering GLIB's argument that speakers receive First Amendment protection only when their communication contains identifiable messages, the Court elides the question of intent and simply reasserts that speech-selection judgments have been protected under First Amendment precedent. It does not explain why this is so. It simply draws an analogy among cable operators, newspapers, and parade organizers. But later in the opinion, the Court concludes that the council, in fact, is much different from a cable operator, resting its conclusion not on intent but on audience perception:

> Respondents contend . . . that the admission of GLIB to the parade would not threaten the core principle of speaker autonomy because the Council, like a cable operator, is merely "a conduit" for the speech of participants in the parade "rather than itself a speaker." But this metaphor is not apt here, because GLIB's participation would *likely be perceived* as having resulted from the Council's customary determination about a unit admitted to the parade, that its message was worthy of presentation and quite possibly of support as well.[14]

The Court concludes that the council's claim is about autonomy more than anything else. Again skirting the question of why the council deserves speaker status, the Court likens the council to a composer:

> Petitioners' claim to the benefit of this principle of autonomy to control one's own speech is as sound as the South Boston parade is expressive. Rather like a composer, the Council selects the expressive units of the parade from the potential participants, and though the score may not produce a particularized message, each contingent's expression in the Council's eyes comports

> with what merits celebration on that day. . . . The Council clearly decided to invoke its right as a private speaker to shape its expression by speaking on one subject while remaining silent on another. . . . [I]t boils down to the choice of a speaker not to propound a particular point of view.[15]

The metaphorical alignment between a composer and the council, however, fails to provide a reason why the council's speech-selection judgment is specific enough to cancel out other potential speakers and forms of speech under Hirsch's view. At best, the composer metaphor imports an uncritical assumption into the *Hurley* equation: that the council necessarily must have had an intent to speak because a composer always has an intent to compose music. The confusion stems, perhaps, from a failure to appreciate the differences between cognitive speech and sensual artistic expression, where intent and message are dramatically different.

In short, the Court implies that intention inherently resides in parades (not speakers) even without the possibility of stabilized meaning. The opinion offers no doctrinal reason grounded in intent that explains why, for the purposes of the First Amendment, the council deserves credit as a speaker.

Communication as Dissemination

John Peters discusses a model of communication that views communicative activity through the metaphor of a one-way *broadcast* to which there exists a general access.[16] This communication-as-dissemination model is indifferent to its receivers, which is not to say that receivers are of no relevance. It means that all receivers are equally desirable, and the model relinquishes any investment in (or control over) the meanings that highly diverse audiences may assign to the message. The theory never maintains that audiences receive messages uniformly. Whereas Austin's model locates the creation of meaning within the text itself (as interpreted within a certain context), and Hirsch calibrates the evaluation of meaning using the construct of author intent, the Peters model locates meaning-making primarily within audiences themselves. The degree of intelligibility and, thus, the significance of a message is determined by conditions of possibility in which the relevant audience (or audiences) circulates; as well, the model does not presume that any given message will, in fact, get taken up by those on whom it falls. Ultimately, the dissemination model values the sheer "expenditure" of seeds of communication, because that activity distributes, or plants, the roots for engagement in democratic practices.

Whether the medium is newspaper advertisements, radio broadcasts, price tags, or art, the Court and Peters agree that dissemination of information is a crucial prerequisite to fertile democracy. If we apply Peters's theory to *Hurley*, however, it becomes evident that the value of dissemination itself was not determinative of the Court's decision.

Under the communication-as-dissemination model, the parade arguably constitutes a technology of dissemination because listeners or receivers enjoy a general access to the unidirectional message(s) aired. Viewers of the parade need only stand on the street, or perhaps watch the parade on television. Parades are a medium whose historically politicized form and typically public appearance tend to advertise the views expressed. The disseminator's purpose or intention is not the message's source of meaning; neither of these needs to be pinned down for speech or a speaker to qualify as a technology of dissemination. That being said, two potential speakers exist in *Hurley*: the individual marchers or entities participating in the parade (GLIB), and the composer (organizer) of the parade (the council).

If the parade itself qualifies as First Amendment speech under Peters's theory, it seems likely that the individual marchers or entities participating in the parade ought to be protected as speakers, if only because one cannot have a parade without paraders. In that sense, the human body functions as a technology of dissemination, and ought to be protected vigorously even though it presents an instance of 'organic' technology. An intended message is not needed to qualify the marchers as a technology of dissemination, only the foreknowledge, perhaps, that their acts will be perceived as communicating some kind of message.

Under the dissemination model, speech-selection decisions in general, like those of the council, might rise to the level of protected speech—even though selection necessarily involves the exclusion of some speech—since selection decisions are a necessary precondition to any forum or medium that must edit the amount of content carried due to spatial constraints or the constraints of a competitive marketplace. In reality, however, the Supreme Court adopted a much different approach and did not base its opinion strictly on ideas of dissemination. The Supreme Court argued in *Hurley* that parades, unlike cable lines, operate as *more than* "conduits" for the dissemination of information, which suggests that the Court views the parade as more than a mere technology of dissemination, but as an aesthetic expression, perhaps. Rather than derive the First Amendment privilege of a parade purely from its capacity to function as a technology of dissemination, the Court articulated two different grounds for protecting the parade as expression. First, unlike a cable transmission, which involves no substantive message contributed by the cable operator's channel-carriage decisions, a parade constitutes speech because it makes a point, or communicates a new message tailored by the council's selection choices. Second, the Court emphasized that the parade deserved protection because it did not threaten the very survival of certain speakers. GLIB could hold its own parade.

The Court's attempt to distinguish the council from cable operators and newspapers makes little sense, considering its reliance on an analogy among the three earlier in the opinion, where it reasoned that the council exercised editorial judgment similar to that of a cable operator and/or a newspaper editor. In order to argue that the *parade* constitutes speech, the Court has to say that the council is totally *different* from the cable operator or newspaper editor. Yet, in order to argue that the council's *speech-selection judgment* constitutes protected speech, the Court has to say that the council is *highly similar* to the cable operator or newspaper editor. As such, the Court refuses to characterize the parade as a technology of dissemination, yet likens the parade to those figures (newspaper editors or cable operators) who receive First Amendment protection due, in large part, to their position as critical disseminators of communication.

Communication as Culture

The key feature of James Carey's communication theory is its cultural perspective. Carey contends that, historically, Americans conceived of communication "in the idea of transmission: communication is a process whereby messages are transmitted and distributed in space for the control of distance and people."[17] But in Carey's view, to reduce communication to a mode of transmission is unduly and artificially to narrow the realm of activity that can be said to have communicative significance, and to deceive oneself into believing that humans communicate only for the purpose of sharing information or getting things done. That is to say, the transmission model treats communication like an instrument—a tool for getting things done.

Carey claims instead that "media of communication are not merely instruments of will and purpose but definite forms of life: organisms, so to say, that reproduce in miniature the contradictions in our thought, action, and social relations,"[18] including those contradictions housed within the symbol of the First Amendment itself. In defining communication as "culture," Carey widens the very definition of what qualifies as communication beyond notions of intent or purpose. Instead, he contends that "communication is a symbolic process whereby reality is produced, maintained, repaired, and transformed."[19]

Thus, Carey's model, unlike Hirsch's model, accepts the premise that meaning is socially constructed. Though humans trade in the currency of words,

> words are not the names for things but . . . things are the signs of words. Reality is not given, not humanly existent, independent of language and toward which language stands as a pale refraction. Rather, reality is brought into existence, is produced, by communication—by, in short, the construction, apprehension, and utilization of symbolic forms. Reality, while not a mere function of symbolic forms, is produced by terministic systems—or by humans who produce such systems—that focus its existence in specific terms.[20]

In other words, humans can identify semi-stabilized meaning—shared meaning—through ritualized communication practices, but stabilized meanings and their structures of reference gain force through human, ritualistic repetition, and they act back on us with the power of "truth" in a manner that is always culturally and historically informed.

Carey's shift from a transmission model to a cultural one entails several implications. First, because humans live in a symbolically mediated and constructed reality, communication is valuable for different reasons than might be assumed under, say, Peters's dissemination model. Communication becomes "the primary phenomena of experience," and warrants more (and different) attention than it receives historically. It includes not only "relations of property, production, and trade—an economic order,"[21] but more important, "the sharing of aesthetic experience, religious ideas, personal values and sentiments, and intellectual notions—a ritual order."[22] Aesthetics and speech are inseparably linked.

Second, Carey's shift means that thought is "predominantly public and social. It occurs primarily on blackboards, in dances, and in recited poems. The capacity of private thought is a derived and secondary talent, one that appears biographically later in the person and historically later in the species. Thought is public because it depends on a publicly available stock of symbols."[23] Thus, Carey troubles the notion, and the very possibility, of a private speaker. Third, because thought is a priori derived from a publicly shared stock of symbols, "problems of communication are linked to problems of community."[24] Because our *habits* of communication entail a participatory process necessarily derived from the republic, communicative practices are both sources of and resources for maintaining and changing the democratic order.

In short, a cultural, ritualistic theory of communication values expressive activity for the kind of comment it makes about the relationships between culture and society, or between expressive forms. It values the ways in which "experience is worked into understanding and then disseminated and celebrated."[25]

Carey's theory opens up two distinct understandings in *Hurley*. The first is that, if the paraders as a whole effect a collective expression that captures, in miniature, the council's idyllic ritual order, then the parade ought to function as a political comment on the council's beliefs about the status of social relations. The council, as conductor, is an entity that holds certain ideas; the parade is the dramatic embodiment of the idealized ritual order that the council imagines. Ostensibly, the council's ideal world would exclude GLIB as outside the boundaries of a virtuous civic life. Irrespective of the fact that many people today would find this message reprehensible, the council possesses the permit for the entire parade, which is one historically common procedure for entering into and participating in the (re)construction of social structures. Since, for Carey, symbolic enactment is something in which all humans engage, his model of communication might dictate that civic participation in the form of parading or marching is inherently ritualistic, symbolic, and therefore inherently human. For these reasons, it ought to qualify as speech under the First Amendment. Hence, forcing a privately organized parade to grant a permit to objectionable messages presumptively usurps a basic right. This is, of course, what the Court ultimately decided.

While this view explains why the parade itself ought to be protected as First Amendment speech, it provides little ground for characterizing the parade as the *council's* speech. Because the origin of communication takes on a radically "public" character in Carey's theory (and Carey does not explain whether one can ever "own" words), it is difficult for the council to find much basis for asserting preeminent speaker status. The council may hold a permit to conduct the parade, but that does not provide us with a First Amendment–based rationale as to why the council should be granted dominion over other communicators. Carey's broad definition of communication would likely encompass the council's speech-selection judgments as inherently expressive, but it would undoubtedly extend the same to the parade itself and to the individual marching units.

In a competition for primary speaker status between the council and GLIB, Carey's theory might actually favor GLIB. To the extent that the council's conception of itself as *the* speaker is grounded in a transmission model—that is, as the council claimed, it sought to control the transmission of traditional religious and social values and people's ability to express sexual themes—Carey's theory might reject the council's post hoc rationalization as less important than the individual marchers' ability to engage in expression. If meaning in a public parade is indeterminate—only later constructed by audiences—there seems little First Amendment justification for privileging the council's exclusion of GLIB. Communication is the name Carey extends to experiencing, disseminating, and celebrating phenomena, not the name for the practice "of controlling space and people."[26]

Moreover, under Carey's view, meaning is socially constructed and constitutive of reality. This premise has a couple of implications, each of which favors GLIB. First, in order to make an educated guess about the council's claim that GLIB's marching would be seen as an endorsement by the council or would cause a different message to be communicated, the Court would have to consider the sociopolitical context in which the audiences viewed the parade; they would also have to engage in a cultural analysis to determine whether GLIB's participation in the annual parade would arguably hold symbolic significance for the relevant community. This would necessarily entail a study of popular reactions to, or anxieties expressed after, GLIB's participation in the parade the previous year. The Court might need to consider cultural artifacts, such as newspaper stories, transcripts from town-hall debates, or other cultural clues, and then perform a rhetorical, cultural analysis to decipher whether GLIB's participation really had the anticipated effects that the council claimed it would (in other words, misattribution and dampening of the council's proffered traditional values). Given the variety of audience reactions to any single message—particularly cultural dramas unaccompanied by explicit, preexisting statements of intent or purpose—such an analysis would not be one the council could reliably prove. It is extraordinarily difficult to predict causation or audience reaction. What neither the government nor the council can regulate under a cultural theory of communication, such as Carey's, is audience response.

Carey's radically "public" theory of communication suggests that communication is always public because it relies on a publicly shared stock of symbols. Private thought is a derived and secondary capability. This distinction inserts something of a gap between public performances, like parades, and the private thoughts that follow (for example, a bystander's impressions of GLIB's participation or the significance and meaning of the parade), and it suggests that the relationships between the two are decidedly *not* governed by the council's intentions, but rather by the ritual order(s) prevalent in the observers' minds. If Carey is right, then the state courts may have been correct when they declared the council's speech itself to be a "public" site, subject to the Massachusetts public accommodation law prohibiting discrimination against homosexuals. Of course, this is a radical departure from the traditional view of speakers under First Amendment jurisprudence, and it unravels many of our fundamental assumptions about the feasibility of owning speech. And it has troubling implications for the rights of artists and the public role of art.

The Court ultimately held that the council's parade could not be declared "public." Doing so would have shocking results, according to the Court:

> Under this approach, any contingent of protected individuals with a message would have the right to participate in petitioners' speech, so that the communication produced by the private organizers would be shaped by all those protected by the law who wished to join in with some expressive demonstration of their own. But this use of the State's power violates the fundamental rule of protection under the First Amendment, that a speaker has the autonomy to choose the content of *[its] own message.*[27]

Thus the Court departs from Carey's theory, and instead justifies its decision by naming the council the preeminent speaker and the parade the private expressive instrument of the council.

Speaking out of Thin Air

The First Amendment was born within a political image that presumed the existence of an individual human speaker, standing on a street corner soapbox (in other words, in a public forum), speaking his or her mind to those who choose to listen. The First Amendment's protections have long been tethered to that explicitly verbal, vocal conception of speech, and to its concomitant public-address mode of delivery.

Hurley changes that in dramatic ways. The Court's theory of communication is new yet ambiguous. The decision in *Hurley* does not fit nicely into any single view of communication. Indeed, the Court at various points seems to rely on all versions of communication discussed here. It agrees with Austin that certain kinds of acts, including parades and marching, have undeniable communicative force and are therefore inherently expressive speech acts. The Court also seems to argue, as Hirsch would, that intent or purpose is relevant to discerning the meaning of the message behind a speech selection judgment. At other times, the *Hurley* opinion also relies heavily on audience construction of a message, as Peters's dissemination model would, to determine the value of the disseminated expression at issue. Finally, the opinion also resonates with Carey's idea that communication is cultural and ritualistic. But all four theories cannot coexist—at least not coherently.

More important, some versions of the Court's communication theories are radically at odds with the traditional assumptions of the First Amendment: that speaking is an intentional act; that messages are a function of a speaker, a meaning, and an intent; and that speech is a liberty of the speaker, not the audience. *Hurley*'s result resonates only momentarily with the assumptions about intention and stable meaning that underlie Hirsch's conceptions; the same can be said for the notion of illocutionary force articulated by Austin or for Peters's view of communication as dissemination. *Hurley* is perhaps most easily squared with Carey's view of communication as culture. The Court's language is clearly most sympathetic with Carey's cultural and constructed conception of communication.

While *Hurley* in this sense may be an attractive melange of communication theory to some, it may serve poorly as a basis for law. Carey or Peters may be quite right about how communicative phenomena work, and quite content with the idea that meaning is a social phenomenon. But their models may be deeply flawed once institutionalized in the legal realm as a basis for *First Amendment speech*, sedimented in precedent and enforced by the formal powers of the government.

Too Much Free Speech?

The larger implications of these models, as law, may give pause because the Court's reasoning subordinated the speech interests of the people literally speaking and performing (the paraders) to the council's speech interest in an arguably unidentifiable message, unaccompanied by a clear speaker. Justice Souter's reasoning, like Carey's, thus threatens to cast off, for First Amendment purposes, much of the protection the law traditionally grants to individual speakers or, for that matter, individual artists. The Court effectively looses meaning "out of thin air," tethering the determination of constitutional rights to the vagaries of audience perception. Even if audience interpretation is that crucial to determining the meaning and effect of a message within a given cultural matrix, it would be a mistake to further consolidate that power by immortalizing—in positive law—the interpretation of a speakerless expressive act. To decipher this genre of "speech act," one must always rely on context, which means the *legal* result will shift as frequently as the *speech situation* does. Another way of saying this is that the answer to the definitional question—whether a speech selection judgment will qualify as "speech" within the First Amendment—will shift as often as the speech situation does.

The implications of viewing free speech as disseminated cultural metaphors and images are vast. Such a view would privilege as free speech the inadvertent as well as—indeed perhaps more than—the advertent. It would formally disconnect speakers from speech. It would also countenance an active role by government in judging and managing speech in light of its social and democratic value and benefits. Carey's theory of communication as culture would convert into speech a broad range of acts now deemed conduct, and vice versa.

Yet with art and the aesthetic, all of this seems much truer and much more fitting. The aesthetic has no single speaker. It need have no predetermined, or even intended, message. Its expressive significance lies in its capacity to enable an audience, over time, to transcend the text or image or movements, supplying new shape and meaning. Its speaker is, indeed, the interpreter, the audience. It must be able to speak for itself, and its meaning must often come out of thin air. Aesthetic expression is the opposite in most ways of the paradigm of a speaker intentionally expressing his or her own view to an audience that receives the speaker's message, not its own.

In light of *Hurley* and its implications for First Amendment protection of art and aesthetic expression, the prevalence and complexities of what speech is cannot be ignored. Should the complicated and new forms of speech growing out of new or different performative and technological conditions be allowed to override or distort the hallmark speech situation that first animated the right of free speech? Though the realities of contemporary speech complicate the idyllic picture of a single orator delivering a political speech, shouldn't the rights of the intentional, *speaking* individual be afforded the greatest degree of privilege under the First Amendment? Even if the cost of doing so is limiting the First Amendment's protection for art and aesthetic expression?

Or should the Supreme Court limit the application of the *Hurley* conception of First Amendment speech *just to artistic expression*? Perhaps so. But that takes us back to where we began: What is speech and how do we define it?

For First Amendment purposes, that is a question of text, history, and purpose, not just "communication." On those scores the answer seems clear, at least for one committed to abiding by the original intention of the Constitution—indeed, even for those willing to look at history and evolving social practices in relation to free speech: parades are not speech protected by the First Amendment, nor are expressive meanings that emerge from thin air.

It seems most likely—indeed almost certainly the case—that while parades were social and often celebratory occasions in the late eighteenth century, they were not thought of as acts of free speech. Parades were often regulated and often sponsored by government itself. They were instances of free speech and expression, but the free speech came from the participants who held signs or banners, who built floats, who played music, who entertained. In *Hurley*, this would mean that GLIB was the speaker, if there were one for purposes of the First Amendment, which applies only to government action. To see the parade organizer as the speaker is to override the direct and clear speech of individuals and groups in the parade. At least this would be so in the case of a parade wherein meaning is metaphorical or cultural, and where the "speech" acts of the organizer are hidden from view.

Why, then, would the Court undertake such a dramatic and ambiguously broad expansion of the meaning of speech in *Hurley*? One possibility is because the issue of artistic expression is lying just below the surface. Art, being itself metaphorical and often deeply ambiguous in meaning, must be protected by the First Amendment. Or so the majority of the Court believed. But that conclusion is far from clear under the First Amendment, and in any event it is possible, some would argue (including me), to set art aside as a limited category of aesthetic expression entitled to constitutional protection, thus avoiding the truly large implications of protecting all purely emotional and aesthetic expression (in other words, yielding no cognitive meaning) as free speech as well: the burning cross, a building's architecture; a car's design; a person's clothing.

The answer may be that the Court, and Justice Souter particularly, saw that in today's world of technological communication the visual and the visceral have come to play an increasingly inseparable role in communication, itself, and in speech in particular. Medium is, as Marshall McLuhan said, often the—or a central part of the—message. The speech guarantee was born in an oral and print culture. It must grow up in a visual and technological culture. Adjustment is necessary.

Yet one can argue that it's one thing to protect the aesthetic when it is related to expression of a cognitive message from a source and with a common meaning. It is an entirely different thing to protect the aesthetic when it has no clear source and no reasonably understood message.

CHAPTER FOUR

Speech out of Thin Air

Boy Scouts of America v. Dale, 530 U.S. 640 (2000)

Since age eight, James Dale had been a Scout in his home town of Monmouth, New Jersey. He began scouting as a Cub Scout, then advanced to Boy Scouts. By 1988, when he finished as a youth Scout on his eighteenth birthday, he had earned twenty-five merit badges and had become an Eagle Scout, one of the highest honors in Scouting. The next year he applied for and was accepted as an assistant scoutmaster of Troop 73 in Monmouth. About six months later he left for college at Rutgers University in New Jersey; he also remained an assistant scoutmaster for Troop 73. James Dale had been an exemplary Scout and was a fine assistant scoutmaster.

He was also gay. He was gay as a Boy Scout and as an assistant scoutmaster. He had not been open about it, and it didn't affect his stellar performance as a Boy Scout or his performance as an assistant scoutmaster. "I think what the scouting program teaches is self-reliance and leadership," Dale said. "Giving your best to society. Leaving things better than you found them. Standing up for what's right. That's one of the tragic ironies of this whole story—that when they found out that I was gay, suddenly I wasn't good enough anymore." Dale had found the Boy Scouts "much less homophobic than the norm of society. I think the Boy Scouts allows for the human factor a lot more than other organizations. It was a more supportive environment."[1]

Dale "came out" at 19, when he was attending Rutgers. He had met many other gay students—students who, like him, were positive role models—and he became comfortable with the idea of being publicly known to be gay. In his second year at Rutgers he became involved with the lesbian and gay organization at the university and shortly thereafter he was elected by the Lesbian and Gay Alliance to fill the open position of president. He became active in the gay community. "It was [in] the summer between my sophomore and junior years that I was speaking at a conference for social workers. Shortly thereafter a newspaper article ran [in the *New Jersey Star Ledger*]."[2] The story was about the seminar and Dale. A photograph of Dale was prominently displayed, with the caption "Co-President of the Rutgers University Lesbian/Gay Alliance."[3]

"About a week later I got a letter from the Boy Scouts that said I no longer meet its standards for leadership. I didn't even know what it was about. So I sent them a letter, and then I got a second letter back from them, and that said avowed homosexuals are not permitted in the Boy Scouts of America. When I heard that I felt really devastated and betrayed. This is a program that I spent my weekends and time after school focusing on, helping out at nursing homes and cleaning parks. I had given so much to the program so freely and happily."[4]

Dale sought to appeal the decision, but to no avail. He was dismissed from his position as assistant scoutmaster, and his adult membership in the Scouts was revoked. Left with no further recourse within Scouting, he sued, claiming that the Scouts' decision was illegal under the terms of the New Jersey public accommodations law, which prohibited discrimination on the basis of "affectional or sexual orientation" in any "place of public accommodation," which included the Boy Scouts. Dale's lawsuit was brought in the New Jersey courts, where he lost at the trial court level but ultimately prevailed in the New Jersey Supreme Court.

The Boy Scouts then appealed the case to the United States Supreme Court. In order to get to the Supreme Court the Scouts had to argue that the New Jersey law could not constitutionally be applied to the Boy Scouts. The Scouts rested just such a claim on its First Amendment right of free speech, on the theory that a legal requirement that "avowed" or open homosexuals be free to serve as scoutmasters would interfere with the Scouting organization's ability to express its own message that homosexuality was not "morally straight" or "clean," as the terms are used in the Scout Oath and the Scout Law.

If the Scouts' free speech and associational speech (in other words, by and on behalf of the members of an organization or association) claims sound confusing, that's because they are confusing. The Scouts' claim rested on James Dale's "coming out" and the publicity that attended his speech to the social workers' conference. The public knowledge, and the Scouts' knowledge, of Dale's homosexuality had the effect, the Scouts would argue, of making the Scouts appear to approve of homosexuality. Without the publicity given

Dale by the *New Jersey Star Ledger*, it is possible that no one on Monmouth and in Troop 73 would have known of Dale's homosexuality and therefore the Scouts wouldn't have had a pro-gay sentiment attached to them by Dale's presence as an assistant scoutmaster.

As we will see, this is a peculiar speech claim, and a peculiar First Amendment theory. It is a claim, in effect, that the Scouts are being forced to speak an unwanted message by the New Jersey law's requirement that they continue to employ Dale as an assistant scoutmaster, given that Dale has publicly (whether willingly or not) become known to be gay and associated with gay rights. It doesn't matter whether James Dale wanted or sought the publicity; it only matters that he got it. Because the Scouts don't have to be actually, physically, speaking to anyone, young Scouts or the public at large, to make their own free-speech claim, and because Dale doesn't himself have to intend to speak or even say anything about the Scouts, the argument before the Supreme Court will reflect a good deal of confusion on the part of the justices. Exactly what is the speech that the First Amendment protects? And exactly who is doing the speaking—if anyone? We know what the message of the "speech" is: the Boy Scouts are pro-gay. We just have to figure out where it is coming from.

If the speech comes from no one, but simply emerges from the circumstances, we might call the pro-gay message asserted by the Scouts to be nothing more than an artifact—something that has no knowable source but that nevertheless exists in fact. Perhaps like the meaning a viewer gives to a work of art, especially one like a soup can, or DaDa, art in the form of purposely deconstructed, indecipherable, meaningless objects or sounds or "text." Or the word "fuck" anonymously shouted in a crowd. Such "speech" is much different than the speech we historically associate with the First Amendment.

Traditionally, the speech guarantee applies to the known message of a speaker to an audience intended to inform or convince or influence, most often in a cognitive way. We might call such speech structural, or liberty based, as it grows out of the First Amendment's purpose of protecting the liberty of individuals to hold political and other beliefs and to express them purposefully to others in order to spawn an open and free marketplace of ideas. Only intentional human speech that is understood by an audience serves these constitutional purposes. Indeed, the structuralist nature of protected speech is the reason that art, obscenity, and related forms of largely emotional and aesthetic expression have found uncertain protection under the First Amendment.

So we must think of Dale's case as something like a pacifist driving a car with the license plate motto "Live Free or Die" (New Hampshire), which leads other drivers to believe that he believes in war. And think of the Scouts as an organization that stands for moral straightness, but whose ability to do so is frustrated by the emergence of a new message accepting homosexuality that is now attributed to *it*. Is the pacifist forced to speak a message with which he wishes not to be associated? Is the license plate speaking such a message, forcing it on him?[5] Is speech an artifact of communicated meaning, or is it instead a manifestation of communicative intention? Can a speaker and a message be dispensed with, leaving only an audience that constructs its own meaning out of one's failure to speak (as with the Scouts)? These questions go to the core of what is meant by freedom of speech.

The *Dale* case involves a conflict between artifact—the fact of communication—and intention. It involves the absence of a speaker or author. The message in *Dale* was constructed by bystanders and attributed to the Boy Scouts (absent Dale's discharge). An unwanted message "by" the Scouts was therefore actually communicated to an audience. But the Boy Scouts did not intend to speak any message whatever. Is the fact of a message alone sufficient to qualify an act as speech under the First Amendment, or must intention by an author or creator *also* accompany a message in order for it to amount to a First Amendment claim of the messenger?[6]

The Justices who would hear oral argument on this confusing and largely unprecedented First Amendment claim were a pretty deeply divided group in terms of the judicial role (constrained or creative) and ideology (conservatives who claimed to be bound tightly to the text and original meaning, versus liberals who saw the Constitution as a charter whose purposes could evolve over time). The former group was led by William Rehnquist, the chief justice. The latter, more liberal group was led by John Paul Stevens.

The lawyers arguing before the Court were George Davidson of New York, representing the Boy Scouts, and Evan Wolfson of New York City, representing James Dale. The lawyers had their job cut out for them, as the justices came armed with plenty of difficult questions.

At shortly after 10:00 A.M. on Wednesday, April 26, 2000, the chief justice called the case.

CHIEF JUSTICE REHNQUIST: We'll hear argument now in Number 99-699, *Boy Scouts of America and Monmouth Council v. James Dale.* Mr. Davidson.

MR. DAVIDSON: Mr. Chief Justice, and may it please the Court: This case is about the freedom of a voluntary association to choose its own leaders. The New Jersey supreme court has held that the State and not Boy Scouting may decide who will wear the Scout leader's uniform and act as a role model of Scouting's values for a group of 10 to 15 boys in a Scout troop.

Far from a business networking organization, Boy Scouting is so closely identified with traditional moral values that the phrase "He's a real Boy Scout" has entered the language.

QUESTION: Do we take this case as one in which Dale was terminated because of the reasonable likelihood that he would use his position to advocate for his cause?

The question goes to the exact definition of the issue in the case. Is the claim that Dale will advocate homosexuality and its legitimacy to the scouts, or instead is the claim that knowledge of Dale's sexual orientation by scouts would influence them in some way? Neither is the case. There was no evidence in the record that Dale had promoted or discussed sexual orientation with scouts, and no claim that Dale retaining his position would harm or influence the scouts. Instead, the claim is that Dale's official position would convey a message by the Boy Scouts as an organization about its views of homosexuality. In the questions that follow, we will see the Justices agonizing over the precise definition of the issue presented in the case and the harm claimed by the Boy Scouts of America.

MR. DAVIDSON: Your Honor, Mr. Dale had created a reputation for himself by the newspaper article which appeared, and the reputation would have carried into the troop meeting and affected his ability to be a role model to the youths in his troop. . . .

QUESTION: If a troop leader simply said to other officials, not to the newspapers, not in any public forum anywhere, "I am a homosexual," would he be excluded from his leadership position for that alone?

MR. DAVIDSON: That precise question hasn't come up. I believe that there would be the right to do that.

Davidson is doing a little evading of the question here. He doesn't want to say that the Scouts could not exclude a homosexual (scout or troop leader, presumably), but that's not the question here. Yet he seems a bit uncomfortable about saying that the issue in this case is strictly limited to the Scouts' "institutional" right to express their views free from the inferences people might draw from their failure to fire him when his sexual orientation becomes known—even though the Scouts' firing of Dale was simply an act, not intended as expression, and even though the New Jersey nondiscrimination law applied only to acts, not speech. It's tricky business for Davidson.

QUESTION: But you're defending an expressive policy, and that's one of the things that's confusing. Are you saying the policy is don't ask, don't tell, or is the policy, if you are gay you are not welcome in the Boy Scouts? Which is it?

MR. DAVIDSON: The policy is not to inquire. The policy is to exclude those who are open . . . being openly homosexual in [the sense that he] communicates the concept that this is okay. This is an all-right lifestyle to pursue.

Now we're getting down to brass tacks. The problem isn't that Dale is homosexual. The problem isn't that Dale is acting it; his actions are private. It's just that he is being open by communicating (not to the Scouts specifically, or even at all) about who he is.

QUESTION: All right. Now, clarify for me, because I—it is not clear to me yet. A heterosexual male adult who wants to be a Scout leader who openly espouses the view that homosexuality is not immoral, and that it is consistent with Scout law and oath, is that person qualified for membership as a troop leader?

MR. DAVIDSON: That person could take that position in Scouting Councils to urge that a change be made, but if that person were to take that position to the youth in the program and urge it on the youth in the program, that person would not be able to continue as a Scout leader.

QUESTION: How about if he just made speeches about this in the community as a whole? Did anything happen here, other than what's in the complaint, which I take it was that Mr. Dale, sometime in the past, was a member of the Gay Alliance at a university, gave some seminars, was interviewed then, and it was in the newspaper. Then he received a letter of termination.

MR. DAVIDSON: I have no information as to how that situation would be resolved. I would observe that it would be open to the Scouts to conclude that somebody who is himself presenting a personal example, as well as advocating, might be more unacceptable than somebody who was merely advocating.

QUESTION: All right. How are we supposed to know—and this is genuinely bothering me—how are we supposed to know whether the basic principle that the Scouts is operating on is thinking that this is very, very bad conduct, or is simply being quite concerned about public reaction? I mean, if it were very, very bad conduct, it's surprising you don't look into it, but if what you're concerned about is public reaction, it all makes quite a lot of sense.

That is, why don't the Scouts not only prohibit openly gay leaders, but also those who are not gay but support gay rights in public or in Scouts? For purposes of the First Amendment argument, after all, it is the public perception and message, not the fact of homosexuality itself. This is a hard question for Davidson.

QUESTION: I ask the question in terms of the expressive association claim. The problem is that we're not at the point where anyone is using the Boy Scouts, or proposing to use the Boy Scouts, for expression. Mr. Dale has not, in effect, asked to carry a banner. He's saying, I'm not going to carry a banner, I'm not going to get into it.

The point of the question has to do with intent to speak. Generally in a First Amendment case the person claiming a free-speech right has to intend to speak a message and convey it to an audience. Inadvertence is not enough, and mere intended conduct others might see as "expressive" of a view—say, racism by not hiring minorities—doesn't count at all. Why shouldn't the same be true of claims by a white-supremacist organization or association to speak collectively for its members?

MR. DAVIDSON: Justice Souter, he put a banner around his neck when he got himself into the newspaper and Scout leaders throughout Monmouth Council sent the article in to headquarters. He created a reputation. This is a place he goes once a week, a camping trip once a month, summer camp for a week. These are people that see him all the time. He can't take that banner off. He put it on himself and, indeed, he has continued to put it on himself in this week's *Time Magazine*, the Out 100, the *New York Times*—

QUESTION: But in effect–I understand what you're saying, but you're saying he has created a kind of public persona for himself and therefore simply for him to be in the Scouts in that position does carry a message.

MR. DAVIDSON: Well, it requires Boy Scouting to identify with that message that Mr. Dale has created. Mr. Chief Justice, I would like to reserve a bit of time for rebuttal.

Davidson finally got to the heart of the case, but only at the very end. Most of the argument was spent trying to clarify what the exact question presented in the case—a free speech case, not a nondiscrimination case—was. But perhaps this was best for Davidson, as greater attention to the free-speech/association claim would have delved more deeply into the center of the free-speech claim: Why should people's reaction to the Boy Scouts be seen as forced or garbled speech by the Scouts?

An example might reveal the peculiarity of the claim. In the law of libel a person whose reputation in the community is harmed by another's false but allegedly factual claim about him or her can sue for damages for the harm. But to recover damages the harmed person must overcome the libeler's (speaker's) claim that imposing liability and damages on the libeler would violate his or her free speech. The harmed person's right is to their reputation as protected in common law or statutory law; the libeler's protection is the First Amendment. In *Dale* the Scouts are turning the tables. If Dale is the speaker whose message harmed the reputation of the Scouts, he would be the libeler and have the protection of the First Amendment. But the Scouts are arguing that Dale's speech is subordinate or irrelevant to the case, except to the extent that it forced a false image on the Scouts, effectively libeling them. They don't claim a right to reputation and damages. The Scouts instead claim a right to free speech that protects them against liability to Dale, the speaker, through the New Jersey law. Why should this be the result even though the Scouts didn't intend to say anything?

These are the important questions raised by the *Dale* case and the act of speaking. The Court didn't get to them in the first half of the oral argument. And even if it could have, there is also the question of whether it should ever get to them. The NEA is probably a better judge of art and aesthetics—even decent art—than nine cognitively skillful lawyer-Justices without experience in such matters.

CHIEF JUSTICE REHNQUIST: Mr. Wolfson, we'll hear from you.

MR. WOLFSON: Mr. Chief Justice, and may it please the Court. The State of New Jersey has a neutral civil rights law of general applicability that is aimed at discriminatory practices, not expression. The law protects gay and non-gay people within New Jersey against discrimination based on their sexual orientation.

QUESTION: You seem to suppose a dichotomy between an entity that's a public accommodation and an entity that has expressive rights. Surely there can be both.

MR. WOLFSON: Oh, absolutely, Your Honor.

QUESTION: If that's so, then in your view a Catholic organization has to admit Jews, a Jewish organization has to admit Catholics. That's your view of the constitutional law?

MR. WOLFSON: The constitutional question that would be before the Court in that case, as in this case, is whether the organization has born its heavy burden of winning an excuse from compliance with the law based on its ability to show a specific expressive purpose that brings its members together that is being significantly burdened by the exercise—

Wolfson can't win the case by arguing that discrimination against gays, as such, is the issue, nor that discrimination against gays is higher or lower on some nonconstitutional pecking order than race and gender, or religion and national origin. He's got to argue a First Amendment case, and he has some very good arguments to make (which I mentioned earlier), but not these. Where is the speech? Why should it count for much, when the Scouts didn't even intend to say anything? If the speech claim, which the Court wants and intends to address, is weak, then Wolfson wins because the State can define a large range of persons and groups against whom to prohibit discrimination. If instead Wolfson effectively concedes that the speech claim is a real and important one—even by his failure to contest it—he will likely lose.

QUESTION: Well, suppose that it says this is basically a Jewish organization, or this is basically a Catholic organization. And it is. Suppose it is. Then what?

MR. WOLFSON: Well, that may very well be the kind of criterion that would have taken it out of being a public—

QUESTION: Fine. If that's so, if that's what we're supposed to do, then how are we supposed to determine, in your opinion, whether or not the relationship of the anti-gay to the Boy Scouts is or is not fundamental, or core, in the way that I've just described in respect to other organizations?

MR. WOLFSON: The Court, Justice Breyer, looks for that specific expressive purpose that brings the members together, not simply the views that some may happen to hold, and not simply a policy or a practice of discrimination.

QUESTION: Why doesn't that exist here? That's what I don't understand. I mean, is there any doubt that one of the purposes of the Boy Scouts, if not its primary purpose, is moral formation, the Scout's oath, and all that good stuff? Isn't that what you say—he's a Boy Scout, as you say.

MR. WOLFSON: Right. That's correct, Your Honor, and—

QUESTION: Okay. So moral formation is. You concede that. And they say, and I don't know why we have any power to question it if the leadership of the organization says so, that one of the elements of that moral formation is that they think that homosexuality is immoral. Now, how does that not make it an essential part of Scouting's purpose?

MR. WOLFSON: What New Jersey has prohibited, Justice Scalia, is identity-based discrimination in its membership practices. It has not limited what Boy Scouts may say. It has not limited its ability to express whatever message it wishes to express. It has not limited its ability to require that members—

Wolfson keeps focusing on identity-based discrimination. The Boy Scouts, however, is not challenging the law's prohibition on discrimination against gay people. It is instead arguing its First Amendment right to free expression—the ability to control its own message. Its claim is not a right to exclude scoutmasters if they are gay, but only if they are avowedly and openly gay in their scouting capacity. The Court (finally, we might add) takes Wolfson to this distinction.

QUESTION: You think it does not limit the ability of the Boy Scouts to convey its message to require the Boy Scouts to have as a Scout master someone who embodies a contradiction of its message, whether the person wears a sign or not? But if the person is publicly known to be a contradiction of its moral message, how can that not dilute the message?

MR. WOLFSON: Assuming, arguendo for your question, that they have established that is such a message and such a purpose that they wish to convey, Justice Scalia. Nevertheless, a human being such as Mr. Dale is not speech. A human being is certainly not speech as to a view, or as to a message, other than perhaps the message, I am who I am, I am here, and this Court has taken great—

This has the makings of a good argument. First, the Boy Scouts did not convey the anti-gay message Justice Scalia seems to be implying, because the message is not anti-gay, but instead the Scouts wish to disassociate themselves with the message that gay is moral. Second, Dale's identity is not speech; it just *is*. So how can that be transferred to the Boy Scouts as speech?

QUESTION: I don't know that our law requires that it be speech. I think our law simply prevents the State from diluting or imperiling the message that an organization wants to convey, whether the State does it by speech, or whether the State does it by dropping a bomb. It seems to me that's what's going on here.

MR. WOLFSON: Well, no. What's going on here, with respect, Justice Scalia, is that the BSA bears the obligation of showing that it needs a First Amendment shield to excuse it from this neutral law, content-neutral law.

QUESTION: Well, I think you assume in your answer to Justice Scalia that the Boy Scouts do have a moral message.

MR. WOLFSON: I accepted that for purposes of answering Justice Scalia's question. But what this Court should look to is the record as to what burden is placed on the organization's members' ability to deliver the *specific* expressive purpose for which they come together. That's what the right protects.

QUESTION: Well, are you saying, Mr. Wolfson, that it has to be a definite expressive purpose? I mean, supposing you have some of the kinds of organizations that Justice Breyer hypothesized: We're a Catholic organization and we just feel much more comfortable with Catholics, and we do Catholic work, or a Jewish organization. Now, they don't have any great message of substantive message. Can they be required under a public accommodations law that is construed as broadly as New Jersey's is, to take on non-Catholics, or non-Jews?

MR. WOLFSON: Well, with respect, Your Honor, I don't believe that that's how the public accommodations law would be interpreted with regard to those organizations, but accepting that arguendo, the question before the Court would be, is there a specific expressive purpose of those organizations that is impaired or infringed, warranting—

The answer is not directly responsive. Is the Boy Scouts' message any less a message than Catholicism or Judaism as referents for the specific beliefs they contain? Specifics are implied in both cases.

QUESTION: Let's get away for a moment, because my question was intended to direct you away from freedom of speech to freedom of association, which is also guaranteed by the First Amendment.

MR. WOLFSON: That's correct, Your Honor, as a right in furtherance of the expression of the members.

QUESTION: And in almost all of your answers it seems to me that you say once there is a public accommodation, that right of expression is somehow secondary, or somehow must be subordinated. You simply cannot find that proposition in our cases.

MR. WOLFSON: I totally agree, Justice Kennedy. I'm certainly not arguing that at all. What I'm saying is that this Court has held that the creation and implementation of public accommodations laws fulfilling those important interests is a legitimate and important exercise of a State's power, and what is at issue here, Justice Kennedy, then is, has this organization shown that for its First Amendment expressive purposes there is a burden on its ability to convey its messages warranting excusal from that law.

Of course, the First Amendment would trump the public accommodations law in such a setting, but this Court has made it very clear that it will not simply allow the mere statement "We don't want to comply with the civil rights law" to be the exception that defeats the civil rights law.

QUESTION: All right. Let's assume, then, that the Boy Scouts tomorrow morning take formal steps to amend all of their official statements of objective, and they say in the Boy Scout manual, the troop leader's manuals and so on, that it is essential to our objective of moral decency that homosexual conduct not be permitted, and that those who avowedly engage in it or believe, indeed, that it is appropriate, may not be members of the organization. Would your case, on your view, then be different?

MR. WOLFSON: That's correct, Your Honor, but if I understood the hypothetical you were giving, there were two elements in it. One was this establishment of a specific expressive purpose that has in fact not been shown here, with the additional point that the organization is actually requiring that it be conveyed to members and others.

QUESTION: Does the case, then, turn on the sufficiency of the Boy Scouts' statement of its position as essential to its message? Does it turn, then, on how well they have made their message known?

MR. WOLFSON: No, Justice Souter. Even were you to assume that they have the implicit moral they say they have, what they have failed to show is that their expressive messages, that their activities are burdened—

Why so? Implicit messages are still messages. What about divinity of Jesus? The infallibility of the Pope? Both can be said to be implied in a message of Christianity or Catholicism.

QUESTION: Yes, but doesn't it follow that if their message is clear, the burden upon the message, by putting an avowedly homosexual person in a leadership position, would be [clear]?

MR. WOLFSON: Well, that's correct up as far as it goes, but it doesn't mean it shows the significant burden that then gets to—

QUESTION: But it shows a more significant burden than you believe they are entitled to be given credit for now?

MR. WOLFSON: That's correct, but—

QUESTION: So if this is the basis on which you prevail, what you will have succeeded in doing is inducing the Boy Scouts of America to be more openly and avowedly opposed to homosexual conduct in all of its publications. Is that what this case is all about?

Whoa! This question smacks of unfairness, but it is a full court press to get Wolfson to the point of the case, too. Wolfson should probably just say yes, in the sense that the message should be a clear one in order for the state's regulation to rise to the level of a violation of the right of free speech of the Scouts. Instead, Wolfson descends into pure speculation of the Scouts' real motives—speculation that has no basis whatever in the record in the case.

MR. WOLFSON: Actually, Justice Scalia, there is most likely a reason why they have not—why they in fact concede in their own brief that they are not an antigay organization, and they do not require members and sponsors and Scout masters to inveigh against homosexuality, or to teach anything about sexual orientation, and the reason for that, Justice Scalia, is not so much that they're afraid of losing the gay people. It's that they are afraid of losing the non-gay people who, as Justice O'Connor's question pointed out, do not agree with this policy, whose charter is renewed year after year after year, despite their not sharing this moral view, or having disagreement over this, because that's not why they come into Scouting.

QUESTION: I think there's a distinction between being an antigay organization and having a policy of disapproving of homosexual conduct. You don't have to have as your raison d'être to oppose homosexuality in order to believe that it is part of your moral code that that conduct is inappropriate, and that's the position that the Boy Scouts have taken. You insist that they go further and make that a prominent part of their promotion.

MR. WOLFSON: It's their burden, Justice Scalia, to show that their specific expressive purposes, not simply views they hold implicitly, but the expressive purposes of conveying any such views, are significantly burdened, and then that those outweigh the State's interest in this neutral law. The State—

QUESTION: How do we do that? That is, I'm back to Justice Scalia's earlier question, and the Chief's. Maybe you've answered it. I'm not sure. I think we both agree that a basically Jewish or a basically Catholic organization, expression or not, maybe association, would be immune from New Jersey's law under the First Amendment. B'nai B'rith, Knights of Columbus, et cetera. I mean, you know–don't we agree about that?

This is a hard and good question. Wolfson's answer should be "Yes, we agree." But instead he dissembles. Why?

MR. WOLFSON: They certainly draw in many other strands, free exercise or other principles that would protect them as well.

QUESTION: You're saying that if a church were a public accommodation, that the church could then deny admission to the church, to non-Catholics, the Catholic Church?

MR. WOLFSON: Well, in the unlikely event that it were a public accommodation, which it would not be, then what we also have operating with religion, and perhaps this goes to your question, Justice Breyer, is that that's addressing people on the basis of views. It's addressing people on the basis of message and expression. It is not the identity-based discrimination.

QUESTION: My question was—maybe we don't agree on the assumption—that if there are some groups, say religiously oriented groups that could keep out people of the other religion—that on the other hand if you take these basic organizing principles and push them to the periphery, so that now they're only a peripheral principle, and you accept that, you could submerge all civil rights laws? You said that at one point. In other words, if you take what is a basic principle, and say the same law applies if it's just a secondary or tertiary or sort of peripheral principle, if we accept that as an excuse, there will be no civil rights laws left.

MR. WOLFSON: Certainly, if—

QUESTION: All right. Fine. [S]o I thought we were agreeing about those two things, and then I wanted to know what the Court is supposed to do to figure out when an association claims that a principle is very important, whether it is really central, or whether it is one of these things that you call peripheral, or tertiary, that it would submerge the civil rights laws. Are we supposed to—how are we supposed to find that out?

MR. WOLFSON: With respect, Justice Breyer, I don't know that it turns on centrality so much as it turns on specific expressive purpose. The Scouts do not require any Scout master or sponsoring entity or whatever to convey that to youth, and in that case it's an easy determination for this Court to see that there's no burden on this conveying of an expressive message—central, specific or otherwise—because they themselves do not convey it. They themselves don't do it, and therefore these—

QUESTION: Mr. Wolfson, there seems to be some conflict on that point, because I believe counsel for the Boy Scouts told us that one troop's charter was continued only when it agreed that it was going to adhere to this policy, and that it wasn't going to advocate gays are okay.

MR. WOLFSON: But Mr. Dale is not here to advocate that he be allowed to advocate that gays are okay within Scouting, nor does New Jersey tell the Boy Scouts what they can or can't say within Scouting, nor does it tell them that they can't limit what is said within Scouting. What it tells them is, identity-based discrimination, the equation of a human being with forced speech, or a speech, or an assumed message, is off the table.

Ah! Identity-based discrimination is unrelated to the free speech argument the State must make, but the speech argument needn't be made because Dale did not speak with the Scouts. This is a good point (too late, though) that needs to be driven home. The issue in the case is what is "speech" protected by the First Amendment. Dale did not want to profess his beliefs to the Scouts. The Scouts didn't want to speak on the question. So where is the "speech" for purposes of the First Amendment?

QUESTION: But of course, they're saying that it's not merely identity-based discrimination. They're saying it's advocacy-based, that by making the public statements that he has made, he in effect has put himself in a position of being identified, understood by people as an advocate, and therefore if he's in a leadership position in the Scouts, by that very fact he's going to carry sort of the aura of the advocacy with him. How do you respond to that?

MR. WOLFSON: Well, in this specific case, Your Honor, Mr. Dale was expelled for taking part in a seminar outside of Scouting, in which he made no connection to Scouting, in which he asserted a view that, as questions have indicated, had non-gay people asserted them, would have been perfectly fine.

QUESTION: Well, your opposing counsel I think gave us an example of non-gays who were taking that position who were challenged by the Scouts and backed down, so I don't know whether the differential treatment is as clear as I thought when I came in here.

This is a very good point. The heterosexual pro-gay man is equally not allowed to speak in public. So it's not about gays or homophobia by the Scouts but about keeping issues off the moral agenda of the Scouts' educational activities. We're back to the beginning of the oral argument. And if so, this case is about speech, or at least avoidance of speech about a belief, not about discrimination against gay versus non-gay, and it's therefore not about identity-based discrimination under New Jersey law.

The oral argument, unfortunately, ends with this critical point hanging. Wolfson must have been as intent upon avoiding the speech issues in the case as was Davidson.

CHIEF JUSTICE REHNQUIST: Thank you, Mr. Wolfson. The case is submitted.

▪ ▪ ▪

The oral argument in *Dale* was, frankly, disappointing. On both lawyers' parts it seemed an exercise in avoidance. For its part, the Court was trying mightily to pin the lawyers down, clarify the exact issue and the posture in which the case presented it, and then engage the lawyers in grappling with it. But it just didn't work out. So the Court had to do it on its own. With such fundamental questions as were presented in the *Dale* case—questions going to the construction of meaning and the act of speaking—doing it on one's own can be dangerous business.

The Court's opinion in the case was issued at the very end of the Court's term, a fate virtually guaranteed by the difficult First Amendment questions raised by the case. The decision was 5–4 in favor of the Boy Scouts, with Chief Justice Rehnquist and Justices O'Connor, Scalia, Kennedy, and Thomas in the majority, Justices Stevens, Souter, Ginsburg, and Breyer in dissent. The majority opinion represents a very broad and important—*and creative*—expansion in the reach of the First Amendment. The dissenters stuck to the hallowed and well-trodden ground of traditional free-speech law. So much for the conservatives being constrained in the exercise of judicial power and the liberals being creative.

Chief Justice REHNQUIST delivered the opinion of the Court:

To determine whether a group is protected by the First Amendment's expressive associational right, we must determine whether the group engages in "expressive association." The First Amendment's protection of expressive association is not reserved for advocacy groups. But to come within its ambit, a group must engage in some form of expression, whether it be public or private.

The Boy Scouts asserts that it "teach[es] that homosexual conduct is not morally straight," and that it does "not want to promote homosexual conduct as a legitimate form of behavior." We accept the Boy Scouts' assertion.

We must then determine whether Dale's presence as an assistant scoutmaster would significantly burden the Boy Scouts' desire to not "promote homosexual conduct as a legitimate form of behavior." As we give deference to an association's assertions regarding the nature of its expression, we must also give deference to an association's view of what would impair its expression. That is not to say that an expressive association can erect a shield against antidiscrimination laws simply by asserting that mere acceptance of a member from a particular group would impair its message. But here Dale, by his own admission, is one of a group of gay Scouts who have "become leaders in their community and are open and honest about their sexual orientation." Dale was the co-president of a gay and lesbian organization at college and remains a gay rights activist. Dale's presence in the Boy Scouts would, at the very least, *force the organization to send a message, both to the youth members and the world, that the Boy Scouts accepts homosexual conduct as a legitimate form of behavior*. (Emphasis added.)

Here, we have found that the Boy Scouts believes that homosexual conduct is inconsistent with the values it seeks to instill in its youth members; it will not "promote homosexual conduct as a legitimate form of behavior." [T]he presence of Dale as an assistant scoutmaster would . . . interfere with the Boy Scouts' choice not to propound a point of view contrary to its beliefs.

The judgment of the New Jersey Supreme Court is reversed, and the case is remanded for further proceedings not inconsistent with this opinion.

It is so ordered.

Justice STEVENS, with whom Justice SOUTER, Justice GINSBURG, and Justice BREYER join, dissenting:

The majority does not rest its conclusion on the claim that Dale will use his position as a bully pulpit. Rather, it contends that Dale's mere presence among the Boy Scouts will itself force the group to convey a message about homosexuality—even if Dale has no intention of doing so. The majority holds that "[t]he presence of an avowed homosexual and gay rights activist in an assistant scoutmaster's uniform sends a distinc[t] . . . message," and, accordingly, BSA is entitled to exclude that message. In particular, "Dale's presence in the Boy Scouts would, at the very least, force the organization to send a message, both to the youth members and the world, that the Boy Scouts accepts homosexual conduct as a legitimate form of behavior."

It is true, of course, that some acts are so imbued with symbolic meaning that they qualify as "speech" under the First Amendment. At the same time, however, "[w]e cannot accept the view that an apparently limitless variety of conduct can be labeled 'speech' whenever the person engaging in the conduct intends thereby to express an idea." Though participating in the Scouts could itself conceivably send a message on some level, it is not the kind of act that we have recognized as speech. Indeed, if merely joining a group did constitute symbolic speech; and such speech were attributable to the group being joined; and that group has the right to exclude that speech (and hence, the right to exclude that person from joining), then the right of free speech effectively becomes a limitless right to exclude for every organization, whether or not it engages in *any* expressive activities. That cannot be, and never has been, the law.

The only apparent explanation for the majority's holding, then, is that homosexuals are simply so different from the rest of society that their presence alone—unlike any other individual's—should be singled out for special First Amendment treatment. Under the majority's reasoning, an openly gay male is irreversibly affixed with the label "homosexual." That label, even though unseen, communicates a message that permits his exclusion wherever he goes. His openness is the sole and sufficient justification for his ostracism. Though unintended, reliance on such a justification is tantamount to a constitutionally prescribed symbol of inferiority. As counsel for BSA remarked, Dale "put a banner around his neck when he . . . got himself into the newspaper. . . . He created a reputation. . . . He can't take that banner off. He put it on himself and, indeed, he has continued to put it on himself."

It is not likely that BSA would be understood to send any message, either to Scouts or to the world, simply by admitting someone as a member. Over the years, BSA has generously welcomed over 87 million young Americans into its ranks. In 1992 over one million adults were active BSA members. The notion

> that an organization of that size and enormous prestige implicitly endorses the views that each of those adults may express in a non-Scouting context is simply mind boggling. Indeed, in this case there is no evidence that the young Scouts in Dale's troop, or members of their families, were even aware of his sexual orientation, either before or after his public statements at Rutgers University. It is equally farfetched to assert that Dale's open declaration of his homosexuality, reported in a local newspaper, will effectively force BSA to send a message to anyone simply because it allows Dale to be an Assistant Scoutmaster.
>
> As Justice Brandeis so wisely advised, "[We] must be ever on our guard, lest we erect our prejudices into legal principles."
>
> If we would guide by the light of reason, we must let our minds be bold. I respectfully dissent.

▪ ▪ ▪

The logic of the majority's reasoning in *Dale* was that (1) Dale himself expressed a message legitimizing homosexuality by public awareness of his sexual orientation and political activism on behalf of homosexuals, which took on symbolic meaning; (2) Dale's formal association as a scoutmaster with the Boy Scouts would cause the public to attribute Dale's message (legitimacy of homosexuality) to the Boy Scouts, becoming, in effect, the Boy Scout's selection and adoption of Dale's message as its own; (3) by having the unwanted and disagreeable message attributed to it, the Boy Scouts would be forced by any legal prohibition on Dale's exclusion to express a message with which they did not concur; and (4) therefore the public accommodation statute denied the Boy Scouts either its First Amendment right not to speak, or its right to speak its own message, or both. The majority's opinion, in short, is one of attribution on attribution; artifact built upon artifact—attribution to the Boy Scouts of a message constructed by an audience and attributed to Dale.

For us, the *Dale* opinion is important for what it may imply about unconventional forms of expression qualifying as free speech. The Dale case involves "speech" without a willing or even knowing author, and a text, or meaning, discovered metaphorically (at best) and assigned to an unwitting act or actor. This form of communication may be inherent in much artistic and aesthetic expression; is it inherent also in cognitive expression? Can we stretch free speech far enough to cover the fact of inadvertent message and meaning, and can we reasonably speak of the unwitting "author" as having liberty?

Free Speech and Constitutional Theory

The competing arguments about the meaning of speech in *Dale* boil down, in the end, to a sharp divide. On the one side are those who argue, much as the *Dale* majority did, that the First Amendment should protect the mere transmission of speech—communicative stimuli of human or corporate origin, whether words, acts, images, identities, or even institutional policies and programs that are of communicative significance to the actor or to those who perceive the act.[7] On the other side are those who argue, as Justice Stevens did in his dissent in *Dale*, that speech should consist only of purposeful communicative acts that reflect the speaker's freely formed communicative intention.[8] The first view, which focuses the First Amendment's protection on the stimulus of speech, itself, I will call the artifactual, or "just speech," position: First Amendment freedom attaches to the fact of speech alone. It is a position taken most recently in the *Citizens United* corporate-speech decision. The second view, which focuses the First Amendment's protection on expressive acts of individuals, I will call the liberty, or "speaker," view: First Amendment freedom attaches to the speaker and the act of speaking. Our focus will be on speech as an artifact of meaning.

The artifactual theory of speech extends the Constitution's protection to speech itself. As Justice Harlan put it in the seminal case of *Cohen v. California*, the First Amendment claim rests, in the end, on the "fact of communication." Only if a communicative artifact is *understood as expressive*, as conveying a message or meaning, is it protected speech under this theory. The artifact of speech is protected, as was the unwelcome message in *Dale*, irrespective of the knowledge or intention of the person or thing that produced it. Attaching protection to speech makes questions of origin, authorship, authority, and intention unimportant.

The artifactual theory nicely avoids the complex, even inscrutable, definitional intricacies of the alternative liberty view, which protects the human free-willed act of expression. If an instance of speech by a person turns out, upon examination, to be inadvertent, that fact makes no difference under the artifactual theory, for the presence of a communicative fact (and, more important, its meaning) is not dependent on knowledge or intention of a person or thing that originates the speech. Similarly, the fact that speech is originated by an artificial entity such as an organization or business corporation—or even an object—is a matter of constitutional indifference. The speech still receives First Amendment protection if it is understood as expressive by others. Indeed, under the artifactual theory, there is no reason to disqualify communicative stimuli produced by a machine, or by an inanimate object, or even by a different species. After all, a painting is expressive. It conveys meaning to the viewer even though it is inanimate, and this is especially true when the expressive meaning bears no relation to the original communicative design of its producer.

But if speech is grounded in the fact of communication—the fact of something being *understood* expressively—a host of complications are immediately confronted. What is an expressive understanding? Is it simply the fact that a person has interpreted a stimulus metaphorically—as saying something more than the thing itself: not letters only but words, not words but a new message; not a soup can but a symbol of culture; not a beggar's tin cup but a metaphor of despair; not a parade but a cultural ritual? Must the understanding be rational and reasoned, or can it be a feeling, a purely sensory experience, such as Yo-Yo Ma's playing Bach in the deep woods, or love at first sight? The stimulus of fear visited by the cross burning, the stimulus of lust fostered by obscenity (which the Supreme Court implicitly acknowledges to be "speech" in artifactual form by the Court's Herculean efforts to define it out of the Constitution on other grounds), or the stimulus of gay rights arising symbolically from Dale's very existence, suggest that both possibilities, and perhaps others, qualify for First Amendment status.

What about the problem of varying meanings that arise when different persons receiving a stimulus have different expressive understandings? Is the important point the fact of *an* understanding, indeed *any* understanding, or must the understanding be "reasonable"—shared by many, or a product traceable to skill or genre—as the Court has sometimes suggested? What if the meaning differs from that intended by the speaker? If the feminist performance artist Karen Finley intends to convey a qualifying message, such as the banality of sex, but those who witness the stimulus of the speaker understand instead a message of prurience and obscenity, should Finley be just out of luck? Conversely, if the speaker's intention carries no weight, should the speaker get the advantage of speech protection due to the fact of communication even though no communication was intended? This, of course, was what happened in *Dale*, where the Boy Scouts disclaimed any intention to speak the symbolic message attributed to them, yet were granted the status of a speaker—an involuntary one, to be sure, but a speaker nonetheless. If a racist slur is not intended to be communicative but is in fact so understood, is the racist protected by the First Amendment?

The artifactual theory implies that the answer to all of these questions will be affirmative, for the "speech moment" is not the production of a stimulus but its reception. The speaker is instrumental only to the First Amendment's practical enforcement. Indeed, the artifactual theory should not, to be consistent, place the First Amendment claim of "right" in the hands of the speaker at all—not to the council in *Hurley* or to Andy Warhol, who simply transmitted the Campbell's soup can on his canvas, or to the business corporation that cannot speak for itself (an artificial entity) but can produce "just speech." The speech claim belongs, instead, to the audience, which serves as the interpreter, the giver of meaning, and either the beneficiary of liberty lodged in the act of perception or the instrument of a larger social good that grows out of the collective perceptions of millions of persons and millions of meanings.

Some scholars contend that the speech right belongs to the audience. This is the view articulated by the "right to receive ideas" and the "marketplace of ideas" schools of First Amendment thought most recently made famous in the *Citizens United* case. The purpose of the First Amendment, it is said, is to encourage the dissemination of information and views and communicative stimuli to the audience, the viewers or receivers, or the public: to educate, presumably, and to stimulate. By so doing, exposure to ideas and information communicates new ideas and stimulates mental and emotional activity, thus enhancing the capacity of the individual as a free-willed and thinking human being. In short, the audience-centered view of free speech is based on protecting liberty, but not the liberty of the speaker. Instead it protects the liberty of the recipient of communicative stimuli. The point is a valid one, as we know that the brain's development is stimulated and expanded by mental activity of all sorts. A cacophony of speech is thus a useful and basic human enterprise: a free, open marketplace of ideas.

If the First Amendment seeks primarily to secure intellectual and aesthetic stimulation, then the fact of stimulation is central and meaning is incidental. The fact of stimulation, and indeed its manner and subject and object, are truly idiosyncratic. I see a Marlboro Man and want a cigarette; my friend sees a cultural icon. I see Dale and feel good about liberty and equality; the Boy Scouts see him and think "morally crooked." A general, or reasonable, meaning given by an audience need play no part in this scheme; indeed, even as with art, the fact that most people are not stimulated in the least may make no difference. The audience is important only as a universe of persons in whom stimulation might occur (and when it does, those who enjoy it receive constitutional protection in the form of protection of the object as an instrument for their stimulus). The audience, as a collective group, plays no definitional or instrumental role in whether there is a generally understood communication or what meaning it might reasonably be assigned. Indeed, this view so deconstructs communication that one is left to wonder why the Constitution used the word speech at all.

Let us, then, remain with the audience as a body that is at once the beneficiary and the locus of definition of speech. If the audience's liberty is dependent on persons or things producing the needed stimuli, but if the producer has no independent freedom to produce but is instead subordinate to the audience—if, that is, the speaker's First Amendment claim is only that of the audience, and the speaker's standing to raise the audience's speech claim is made dependent on the audience's (often unascertainable) expressive understanding—then the fullest realization of the audience's interest cannot be achieved. The problem, in other words, is which comes first: freedom to speak or freedom to hear; free expression by the artist, which audiences then may enjoy though not control; or freedom to receive artistic stimulation, which may thus, if not naturally forthcoming, be compelled or controlled? If speech or art are stimulation, and stimulation is idiosyncratic, how can we know when and how they will occur, with what effect, and to what public or private end? The answer may be that we do not and cannot know, so government cannot manage speech. It must be satisfied with a world of random stimuli.

An alternative justification for the audience-centered view rests on the cognitive premise that speech, itself, produces a more informed and educated citizenry better capable of engaging in self-government and better equipped to preserve freedom in a democratic society. It is these ends, not individual liberty, to which the First Amendment is principally directed. As the Court said in *Citizens United*, corporation speech is a "voice[ ] that best represent[s] the most significant segments of the economy"[9] The audience's elucidation is thus treated not as an end of the First Amendment but instead simply as a means for achieving other structural ends of democracy and a free civilization.

This view, too, can be described as a "right to receive" speech theory, but it is of a different ilk. The structural ends of self-government and freedom serve to define the scope and nature of protection accorded the free speech. They serve to justify virtually complete immunity for some speech because its content is deemed central to the business of self-government and freedom; but they also serve to disqualify other speech that does not serve, or even disserves, those ends, not because the other stuff is not speech, artifactually speaking, but because it is not useful speech when judged by the structural purposes of the First Amendment.[10] Directly political speech, even false political speech, is given nearly complete immunity from government regulation, but nonpolitical speech, including false nonpolitical speech, *and much art*, is given markedly less protection.

The arrival of commercial speech on the First Amendment scene also nicely illustrates the point. Commercial speech is protected, the Court says, because of the audience: it provides information needed by people when making individual choices in a free economic market. Previously, the Court deemed commercial information less important to the structural ends of the First Amendment, but it is hard to dispute its importance in the late twentieth century postindustrial, information age. The standard of value, in other words, can change, as can the breadth of the audience's right—need, really—to receive. But the audience's "right to receive" commercial speech depends on its truthfulness and accuracy. These dimensions are evaluated from the perspective of the receiver: commercial speech must be neither false nor misleading—ideas lodged firmly in the communicative understanding of the recipient.

A few serious problems attend this branch of the artifactualist view. First, when one must regulate speech for structural purposes—impose disclosure or equal time or decency requirements, setting preferences for certain types or subjects of speech—the artifactualists seem to have forgotten their own main premise: that speech is a communicative stimulus whose meaning is lodged in the audience whose understandings are far from uniform (and, it should be added, far from understood). Truth, accuracy, balance, fairness, decency, and equality as regulatory instruments are thus often likely to be incoherent, resting on assumptions that topple like a house of cards.

The second problem is that the democracy-serving view of speech and its meanings, driven to theoretical conception as an instrument of expression in the service of self-government and preservation of a free society, places the definition of structural purposes, the means by which they will be achieved, and their regulatory enforcement against offending speech, in the hands of the very government over which people are to have control and from which they are to be free. This is accomplished largely by justifying government action on the skeptical impulse that people are not free agents—at least not interpretive free agents able to discern for themselves—but are instead easily manipulated by artifacts of communication and thus must be protected against them. This is a fundamental premise of campaign finance and speech restrictions. It is also a premise of "decency and respect" requirements applied to art. Since people cannot discern, government should do the discerning for them, a position that, notably, leaves no room for an intervening liberty to speak or be free from unwanted speech, which the *Hurley* and *Dale* cases recognized. It is the government, after all, that now defines obscenity for all of us. Indeed, it is the Supreme Court.

At a more basic level, however, the deeply skeptical premise of nondiscernment—whether true or not—is flatly inconsistent with the premise that underlies the structural objectives of self-government and a free social and political order. If one tries to preserve freedom by denying its possibility, the remaining game will be only about who holds power. This, as Robert Post has so nicely argued, is precisely what this branch of artifactualist speech theory is all about.[11]

Art and aesthetic expression are easier to value as speech under the artifactualist view, which rests the First Amendment's protection on the *audience's* freedom to be stimulated, unconditioned by the servicing of other structural constitutional ends. This is because aesthetic perceptions, sensory stimuli, are arguably as conducive to the development of one's human potential and mental growth as are facts and logic and reason. The mind is not simply a computer driven by logic; it is a complex system of senses and structures. Who we are is a combination of all of our senses, all of our experience, all of our capacity for feeling and insight and reason and language.[12]

The artifactualist thus can claim a theory premised on an appeal to universal "truth": that protecting speech in the interest of the individual's growth and development (and incidentally, but incidentally only, the capacity for freedom and free-willed choice) is coherent in the abstract. But the artifactualist cannot explain why expressive stimuli are limited to those of human or corporate origin only, as opposed to the wind whistling through the pine trees, or why, if stimulation is the key, "speech" was made the constitutional prerequisite. If speech is a function of meaning, and if stimulation does not depend on an ascertained or standard meaning, then stimulation does not seem to have much to do with speech.

The *Dale* case, on reflection, seems a strange combination of artifact and liberty. The "speech" in *Dale*—the message or meaning—arose from Dale as a symbolic artifact of meaning, the meaning lodged not in Dale's intention but in the audience's construction, which was then assigned by the audience as an act of speech to the otherwise mute Boy Scouts. This is artifactual analysis. Yet having created the speech by artifact, the Supreme Court extinguished it in the name of liberty—the liberty of the Boy Scouts of America to be free from bearing Dale's message as its own speech. Some might describe this alliance of artifact and intention as unholy.

It is, at the very least, messy.

Too Much Free Speech?

In *Hurley* and *Dale* the Supreme Court walked right up to the edge of a chasm . . . and then leaped in. The chasm, of course, is the elimination of a required speaker who intends to express a message that the audience understands. After the two cases it is possible to eliminate a speaker, an identifiable message, and a coherent and understanding audience. This is a dramatic and radical leap. It is a leap that the Court reinforced in its later *Citizens United* opinion, where Justice Kennedy said that the First Amendment protects speech, not just, or even primarily, speakers, and in the hands of corporations it matters not whether the owners of the corporation agree with the message, or even intend one. Like a parade, or a mute symbol made expressively immanent by those who see or hear it.

It takes the strictest of textualists—the amendment talks of speech, not speakers—combined with the most creative of non-originalists—it's a marketplace metaphor that controls First Amendment interpretation—topped off by the most creative of communication theoreticians—speech is cultural dissemination—to arrive at the *Citizens United/Hurley/Dale* view of freedom of speech. Not separately, but all in one package. Can judicial interpretation countenance such schizophrenic creativity?

The answer is that it can, and it has on many occasions over the history of the Supreme Court and judicial review: one person, one vote; desegregation; gender equality; and on and on. Some such decisions, like perhaps the Dred Scott decision, have been tragic. Others, like the reapportionment cases, have been wildly successful and universally accepted. But such instances of interpretation, no matter how principled and analytically thorough, are not the meat and potatoes of *this* Supreme Court.

Ironically, in the *Hurley*, *Dale*, and *Citizens United* cases, it is the more interpretively liberal minority justices who are most cautious, and when they agree generally with the majority they are the ones to hew a more limited line and limit the scope of their interpretation. For Justice Kennedy "it's just speech, stupid," and that includes not just art but private associations and corporations and political speech. But not trees or polar bears, according to Justice Scalia. For the dissenters it's art and perhaps some historically sedimented cultural traditions and rituals, all with clear authors who fit the speaker-message-receiver paradigm. Corporations as speakers can qualify, but not all of them, and when they do qualify, their First Amendment protection may be more limited than that enjoyed by real liberty-bearing individuals.

So the problem is not, or not just, differences in interpretive methodology and the scope of judicial power. It is instead inconsistency at the most fundamental levels. Maybe the cases give us too much free speech. Maybe not. But they leave us guessing about the how and why, which are important questions in a democracy, especially when it comes to assertions of nondemocratic judicial power. We are left to our own personal preferences about the cases and issues, but the Court has effectively removed our capacity to act democratically on them should we disagree with the Court.

IV

Voting as Speaking, Expressive Association, and Privacy

Our final question, which we will explore through the recent *Doe* case and a gay rights referendum in Washington State, involves expansion of free speech to the largely mute act of voting in elections and to the protection of a person's affiliations and associations with others from public disclosure at the hands of the government. How should the freedom of speech be interpreted to protect such undeniably important acts as voting and joining with others—say, in a church or a charitable cause? More important, is it possible to read "freedom of speech" as protecting them without at the same time loosing all pretense of restraint on the Supreme Court's power to interpret the Constitution? In addressing these larger questions we will see the parts of the First Amendment that we first pulled apart—speaker, speech, purpose—stitched back together in the form of constitutional doctrine. Is the resulting web of free speech doctrine and theory coherent or symmetrical, or is it just a tangled mess?

And what does that say about the Supreme Court?

CHAPTER FIVE

The Secret Ballot

VOTING AS SPEECH

Doe v. Reed, 130 S. Ct. 2811 (2010)

On January 28, 2009, Senator Ed Murray led a group of Washington State senators in introducing Senate Bill 5688, a piece of legislation that would come to be known as the "Everything but Marriage Bill." The bill's statement of purpose declared: "It is the intent of the legislature that for all purposes under state law, state registered domestic partners shall be treated the same as married spouses. . . . The provisions of this act shall be liberally construed to achieve equal treatment, to the extent not in conflict with federal law, of state registered domestic partners and married spouses." Following a contentious legislative battle, the bill was enacted.

When Washington Governor Christine Gregoire signed S.B. 5688 into law on May 18, 2009, she portrayed it as the natural conclusion to several years worth of legislative progress. "From the first bill I signed in 2007 to today's bills," Gregoire explained, "we have proudly made immeasurable strides on behalf of LGBT individuals and families. [S.B. 5688] represents the culmination of incredible work to treat all Washingtonians equally."

In the weeks prior to Governor Gregoire's signing, as S.B. 5688 made its way through the state senate and house, opponents rallied in opposition. The most vocal critics of the bill were two political action committees: the Washington Values Alliance (WVA) and Protect Marriage Washington (PMW). Prior to S.B. 5688, the Washington Values Alliance had promoted several less-controversial conservative causes, including supporting legislation restricting minors' access to pornography and tightening scrutiny on minors seeking abortions. Protect Marriage Washington, conversely, was established exclusively to combat S.B. 5688. Its stated goal was to gather the signatures necessary to place a public referendum overturning S.B. 5688 on the November 2009 ballot.

The public referendum initiative, which became Referendum 71, was intended to give Washington voters the chance to uphold or reject S.B. 5688. If a petition on S.B. 5688 received enough signatures—about 120,000—S.B. 5688 would be suspended as law and its approval by referendum of all voters would be required for it to take legal effect. In pressing forward with the referendum, PMW and the WVA built upon the arguments posed in similar fights in Massachusetts and California, insisting that the passage of S.B. 5688 would dilute marriage and create a "genderless society" that would be thrust on children at an early age, primarily through school curricula focused on homosexual relationships.

The common thread between the WVA and PMW was a conservative political activist named Larry Stickney, who served as the campaign manager for Protect Marriage Washington and as the president of the Washington Values Alliance. Stickney's centrality in the two organizations is hard to overstate—he often operated as the sole spokesperson for the PMW and was the dominant board member of the WVA. As his organizations marshaled support for R-71, Stickney was also hosting the Values Action Radio Show, a weekly broadcast on the Liberty Broadcasting System.

With Stickney's organizations garnering media attention and attracting followers, gay-rights groups responded with their own campaigns supporting S.B. 5688 and opposing R-71. A group called Washington Families Standing Together (WFST) launched an effort to counteract PMW's campaign. WFST was founded primarily through the efforts of Anne Levinson, the former deputy mayor of Seattle and a prominent Seattle businesswoman. WFST distributed flyers and info sheets and held gatherings and events intended to persuade voters to vote to uphold S.B. 5688 by voting yes on R-71. WSFT was quickly joined by national organizations, most notably KnowThyNeighbor, which was founded in 2005 by Aaron Toleos and Tom Lang. KnowThyNeighbor grew out of the gay-rights debate in Massachusetts and then joined the ranks of similar fights in other states, including Florida, Oregon, and Arkansas.

The most aggressive opponents of Stickney's movement, however, were the members of a grassroots organization called WhoSigned. On June 1, WhoSigned formally requested the list of R-71 petition signatories from the secretary of state, maintaining that once it received the list, it would make the names searchable and flag the names that were unverifiable or erroneously included in order to allow Washington State voters to check to see whether their names had been incorrectly included and, if such was the case, report the errors to the appropriate body. Within a week, KnowThyNeighbor joined WhoSigned at a press conference to announce that they intended to publish a database of signers' names and make that database searchable.

The day after WhoSigned submitted its initial request, Washington Secretary of State Sam Reed announced that he would comply by releasing the names. The rapid response surprised some Washingtonians. Reed was, after all, a Republican, and much of the S.B. 5688 debate had splintered along party lines. Rather than couch the S.B. 5688 debate in terms of civil rights, Reed chose to frame the issue in a National Public Radio (NPR) interview as a stand for "open government, transparency in government and the people's right to know."[1]

PMW's opposition to S.B. 5688 and its efforts to place R-71 on the ballot were well organized and fast moving. Stickney's campaigning, however, made him the primary target for the ire of S.B. 5688 supporters. Critical emails to Stickney, ranging from philosophical to threatening, served as evidence for the initial *Doe v. Reed* complaint. A news article published by *The Stranger*, a Seattle-area weekly newspaper, detailed Stickney's divorce from his first wife fifteen years earlier, her accusations of domestic abuse, and allegations of tax evasion. Stickney reported feeling threatened and harassed by S.B. 5688 supporter emails and message-board posts. He also reported receiving menacing late-night phone calls and seeing individuals photographing his house and property during the summer of 2009. Stickney claimed the response "seemed like a blood sport for the other side. Any form of communication that could reach our home [did], including e-mail, telephone [calls], letters—we were the recipients of obscenities and threats and Internet harassment. I'm talking about an attitude of total war here."[2]

Blog posts and emails provided in the initial lawsuit supported Stickney's claims of implied threats, if not explicit ones. One poster raged, "[Gays] have been persecuted by religion enough . . . why must we also allow government to support and encourage the hate . . . that repeatedly slices our throats, bashes our head open, or shoots bullets into our heart or brain. Is it wrong to stab the person who is gay-bashing you? Would it be 'fighting hate with hate' or would it just be self-defense?"

In the posted comments following the online version of *The Stranger's* inflammatory article, Stickney's son Matt refuted the accusations and maintained that his father "has and always will be a caring and loving dad." Posters quickly shot back. One comment expressed a "hope [that these accusations] have given you a taste, however small, for the hardship and agony your father is placing upon our lives, our community and our livelihood." Some were even more spiteful: "Matt, your dad is a thrice married piece of shit. It runs in families so expect to have at least two marriages yourself, live with it." Others were plainly menacing: "Hey Matt Stickney . . . You are a hypocritical PIG, and have NO BUSINESS WHATSOFUCKINGEVER in blocking anyone's path—straight or gay—in the pursuit of marriage! Do us fellow Washingtonians a favor: get rip roaring drunk and replace the . . . guy passed out on the tracks!"

The opponents of S.B. 5688 claimed that such threats and harassment were more widespread, and that all signatories of the R-71 petition were targeted. The fear of intimidation seems to have been based on a KnowThyNeighbor press release dated June 8, 2009, which did suggest that their planned online publication of the names was partially intended to initiate "uncomfortable" conversations about the bill. The tone of the press release, however, was less than menacing. "Conversations are triggered between people that already have a personal connection like friends, relatives, and neighbors," said Toleos, KnowThyNeighbor's co-director. "These conversations can be uncomfortable for both parties, but they are desperately needed to break down stereotypes and to help both sides realize how much they actually have in common."

S.B. 5866 was initially scheduled to go into effect on July 26, 2009. One day before the deadline, however, PMW submitted its completed petition, with nearly 140,000 signatures, to Sam Reed's office. A flurry of legal activity followed. In short order, all major supporters of S.B. 5688 filed suit to prevent Secretary of State Reed from certifying the measure. WFST and the Washington Coalition for Open Government (WCOG) joined KnowThyNeighbor, which had already requested the petition names, by filing a public records request for all R-71 petitions, with the stated purpose of reviewing the petition for errors.

PMW responded immediately, seeking an injunction in federal district court to keep the secretary of state's office from complying with the public records requests. The injunction landed in Judge Benjamin Settle's court. Settle was sympathetic to PMW's intimidation concerns and granted a temporary order preventing name disclosure.

On September 1, the signatures were finally verified and the final count established: 121,757 Washingtonians had signed the petition, enough to suspend S.B. 5866 and require a referendum on the law. Two days later, Judge Settle heard arguments from each side in his district court.

Despite Larry Stickney's prominent role in promoting the Referendum 71 petition, he was not the primary plaintiff in the case before Judge Settle. Stickney's public statements and previous campaigning had long since eliminated his anonymity, and since the plaintiffs' argument focused on the protection of anonymity in political speech, it was appropriate that the plaintiff position be reserved for two anonymous signers of Referendum 71, Doe #1 and Doe #2. The Does were residents of Stevens County and Cowlitz County, respectively. Stevens County is in northeast Washington and Cowlitz in southwest Washington. Both are rural counties far from the more populated counties surrounding Seattle in the Northwest.

The Doe plaintiffs were represented by James Bopp, a prominent conservative attorney in Terra Haute, Indiana. Bopp was also affiliated with the James Madison Center for Free Speech, serving as the organization's general counsel since 1997, as well as general counsel for the National Right to Life Committee, special counsel to Focus on the Family, vice chairman of the Republican National Committee, and advisor to Republican presidential candidate Mitt Romney.

The defendants, in turn, were represented by Washington State Attorney General Robert McKenna. McKenna was elected attorney general in 2004, one of the few Republican candidates to perform well in that round of elections. In response to claims that organizations such as WhoSigned and KnowYourNeighbor sought referendum names in order to encourage petition opponents to engage in "uncomfortable conversations," McKenna told NPR that he "[didn't] think that encouraging uncomfortable conversations amounts to the kind of harassment or potential intimidation that would warrant keeping these petitions out of public view. In fact, in a democracy, there are supposed to be conversations which are occurring about difficult or contentious political issues," even if those conversations are "uncomfortable."

In the next six weeks, the status of the hotly debated petition names changed three times. When arguments concluded on September 10, Judge Settle issued a preliminary injunction, preventing the release of the R-71 names. With the November election fast approaching, the state acted quickly, announcing that it would file an appeal in the Ninth Circuit Court of Appeals. The Ninth Circuit took issue with Judge Settle's analysis of protected political speech, reversed the district court ruling and issued a stay of the preliminary injunction on October 15, allowing for the release of the names. As quickly as that permission arrived, it was revoked: the decision was immediately appealed to Supreme Court Justice Anthony Kennedy, who on October 20—just two weeks before the Washington general election—reinstated the district court injunction pending resolution in the Supreme Court.

Before the Supreme Court heard and decided *Doe*, Washington voters went to the polls to determine the fate of S.B. 5688. Despite the failure of the bill's many supporters to force the disclosure of the petition names, S.B. 5688 was approved, garnering more than 53 percent of the vote, and became law. But the lawsuit over public disclosure of petition signers' votes continued.

▪ ▪ ▪

The original Constitution of the United States didn't mention a right to vote as we think of it today. Voting and elections were left broadly within the control of the states, and might—indeed often did—consist of selection of representatives and senators by the state legislature, not by the people at a voting booth. It was left to the amendments to shore up the voting question, and even there, where the right to equal vote and the election of senators was provided for, the states retained much of the power to design and regulate, even define the meaning of, elections and voting. Notably, this included how and when and where voting was conducted, and whether it took place in public or private. There was then, and remains today, no constitutional right to a secret ballot—much less a ballot. As we will see, the now nearly universal right to a secret ballot, or vote, in elections was introduced by the states, and not until the late nineteenth century. Before then voting was generally a public affair in which everyone could see or watch how an individual voted—even the candidates being chosen. It may have looked much like the famous Iowa caucuses today. This was a brave world in which people were not shy about their political preferences. Or a local community affair with refreshments and conversation.

It is against this background of constitutional silence and essentially complete state authority that the *Doe v. Reed* case arose. It involved a claim of privacy or secrecy in voting by the people who signed the referendum petition in Washington, where referendum petitions are public records and the names and addresses of petition signers are available to everyone online. As we will see, the *Doe* case transcends petition signatures. It potentially applies to voting in elections, voting on bond issues, voting in government meetings, to campaign contributions and expenditures by individuals and groups—and to the Iowa caucuses, perhaps. It turns on one critical question: Is the act of casting a vote an exercise of free speech for purposes of the First Amendment? Is the vote's public anonymity constitutionally required? Or can our votes be made public records available to all—and for all purposes the mind of man can conceive—and to all parts of government?

These and other questions deeply split the Court—not into two blocks, but into seven little pieces. The *Doe v. Reed* case came on for oral argument before the Supreme Court of the United States at 10:11 A.M. on Wednesday, April 28, 2010.

CHIEF JUSTICE ROBERTS: We will hear argument this morning in Case 09-559, John Doe v. Reed, Washington Secretary of State. Mr. Bopp.

MR. BOPP: Thank you, Mr. Chief Justice, and may it please the Court: No person should suffer harassment for participating in our political system, and the First Amendment protects citizens from intimidation resulting from compelled disclosure of their identity and beliefs and their private associations.

JUSTICE SCALIA: What about requiring disclosure of campaign contributions? Why doesn't that fall within your principle that no person should be exposed to criticism for his political beliefs?

MR. BOPP: It could, potentially. This Court in Buckley subjected those requirements to the appropriate constitutional First Amendment analysis, found that there were sufficiently important governmental interests, some of which are not present when we are talking about a referendum or initiative, and then also created an exception from even a generally valid statute where there is a reasonable probability of harassment of that particular individual or group.

So the First Amendment analysis regarding the privacy of association, the privacy of identity and beliefs, the potential of intimidation, are all elements of the analysis that were employed by the Court in Buckley.

That is something of an overstatement of *Buckley v. Valeo*, the 1976 case challenging the 1974 political campaign reform act. In its opinion the Supreme Court set the constitutional framework for later reform legislation and Supreme Court decisions. Among other things, the *Buckley* opinion held that campaign contributions are speech by someone else, not by the contributor. Thus, it seems, contributions are not protected by the First Amendment. Bopp, however, implies that a decision in this case might change that reasoning. And with good reason, for it could be hard to distinguish making a contribution and signing a petition in terms of the acts' expressiveness.

The *Buckley* Court also approved campaign contribution *and* expenditure *public disclosure* requirements, with the narrow intimidation exception noted by Bopp. The scope of the exception and the standards of proof of likely intimidation were not specified in *Buckley*, nor was it clear that such exceptions were constitutionally required or, if they were, when or why.

Technically, at least, the *Doe* case raises a different question. Signing a petition is not an expenditure, nor is it a contribution. Instead, the question is whether a petition signature is speech and whether public disclosure of a petition signature violates that speech right. What, exactly, the speech right is, whether and when it is implicated by disclosure, and how an exception for intimidation relates to it, will be central to the *Doe* case.

> JUSTICE SOTOMAYOR: I'm trying to separate out the harassment aspects of this case from the working proposition that there is some sort of freedom of association privacy. Your theory, putting harassment aside, would invalidate all of the State laws that require disclosure of voter registration lists, correct? All of those States like New York that permit public review of voter registration lists and party affiliations, et cetera, that's unconstitutional?

This is a very good question. If the First Amendment protects one's freedom of expressive association—the privacy of one's expressive affiliations—or, even more, one's freedom of belief, including the right to hold one's beliefs in private, then it would not be sensible to limit the freedom only to instances of intimidation. Privacy of beliefs and expressive association would instead imply a broad right to anonymity.

But Bopp has proposed a much more limited "freedom," the freedom from physical harm and intimidation resulting from public disclosure of one's beliefs and associations. Is this a tactical choice? The broader freedom would require anonymity in a broad range of voting contexts and, just as important, could undermine the existing campaign-disclosure requirements. But has he achieved a tactically more modest and practical claim at the expense of the very First Amendment freedom he relies upon?

> MR. BOPP: No. [Voter registration lists] would certainly be subject to First Amendment analysis. But in the instance of voter registration, there are other governmental interests that are not present in petition signings for referendums.
>
> JUSTICE SOTOMAYOR: New York is a State that also permits or requires that petitions for candidate listing on the ballot be public as well. New York relies in part, as this State does, on the public reviewing those petitions. Would that be invalid as well for a candidate's running?
>
> MR. BOPP: Well, we believe it would be subject to First Amendment analysis. But again, there are different governmental interests when

you have candidates involved. This Court recognized in Buckley that there were disclosure interests that related specifically, and actually only, to candidates. For instance, people who contribute to a candidate, that information, to the voter, can signal the interest that the candidate, once he or she takes office, will be responsive to. When we have an initiative, we know what the law is that is being voted upon. It's not a matter of electing a representative.

The right to speak independently, or through a corporation or a group with common views, had been addressed by the Court just a few months earlier, in the *Citizens United* case, discussed in chapter 1. There the Court held that independent corporate or group political speech could not be restricted in the interest of preventing corruption or illegal influence. As the Court put it, "We now conclude that independent expenditures, including those made by corporations, do not give rise to corruption or the appearance of corruption." The interest, as Bopp notes, that disclosure "can signal the interest that the candidate, once he or she takes office, will be responsive to," seems even more ephemeral. Of course the *Citizens United* case involved direct regulation of speech, not simply public disclosure of people's votes or petition signatures. But the distinction may be a hard one to defend, especially in light of the *McIntyre* case, which protected a First Amendment right to speak anonymously . . . and will come up soon in the oral argument.

JUSTICE SOTOMAYOR: You don't think that—putting aside this kind of referendum, just a hypothetical referendum having to do with a certain tax scheme—you don't think the voters would be interested in knowing what kinds of people in what occupations are interested in that particular tax benefit or not?

MR. BOPP: Well, a few might be, but we think this is marginal information. First, they are adopting a law. And so we know what the law is. And while it might be marginal information for a few people, once the measure qualifies for the ballot, the petition signature and distribution is only for a very limited governmental interest. And that limited governmental interest is to preserve State money, to not conduct an election on the matter unless there is sufficient public support.

CHIEF JUSTICE ROBERTS: Now, counsel, the response you have given to a couple of the questions has been that the First Amendment analysis would apply. But given that you have a facial challenge, is that enough? Don't you have to indicate that the First Amendment analysis would prevail in either all of the other cases, most of the other cases, a significant portion? This is a facial challenge. And if the challenge is going to fail in some of those other cases, I think your facial challenge fails as well.[3]

MR. BOPP: Well, we are only challenging the application of the Public Records Act to petitions and referendum petitions. We're not challenging it as it would be applied to petitions to put people on the ballot.

CHIEF JUSTICE ROBERTS: So we have to decide in assessing your claim that no matter what the referendum issue was, that there's a significant intrusion on First Amendment rights?

MR. BOPP: Yes.

CHIEF JUSTICE ROBERTS: So that if, for example, the referendum involves a bond issue as to which people may have particular views, but they are not going to get excited about it, we still have to say that that is protected under the First Amendment?

MR. BOPP: Well, actually, with modern technology, it only takes a few dedicated supporters [with] a computer who are willing to put this information on the internet, MapQuest it, as they did with respect to the contributors of Proposition 8 [a similar ballot initiative in California] which then encouraged people to harass them, which resulted in hundreds of—

CHIEF JUSTICE ROBERTS: Well, my point is, though, you are not likely to get that with respect to, you know, a debt issue, raising the debt ceiling from 0.8 percent to 0.9 percent. You are not going to get a crowd outside your house because you signed that petition.

MR. BOPP: Well, it may not manifest itself in any particular initiative. We agree with that, but we think the potential is there. And there is usually a group of supporters of any measure that, you know, are passionate about that particular issue.

Bopp's argument here is that in all referenda—and, he suggests when pressed, all votes, campaign contributions, and the like—the First Amendment applies, though it is not always violated by public disclosure of the signatories. This is, frankly, confusing in terms of the facial challenge. Bopp appears to be arguing that a conclusion that the First Amendment applies to all referenda signatures is a facial one—free speech applies to every referendum—but the relief required by such a decision would be largely theoretical if, as he also argues, likely intimidation and so forth will exist only in a narrow band of cases, like this one. Bopp is effectively asking the Court to decide a wholly abstract question of constitutional law—is voting (or referendum signing, or contributing) an act of free speech? The Court almost never entertains such abstract questions when the result will be to give no relief to the challenger.

If Bopp's argument were that the signatures on a petition were acts of free speech and that they can never (or only rarely) be disclosed because they reveal a signatory's political associations and beliefs, a facial challenge would be appropriate. But Bopp's tactical strategy to narrow his claim in the Court to likely intimidation has effectively given up that ground for a facial challenge. This is the source, it seems, of the justices' confusion.

Bopp, it turns out, is trying to forge his way through a bramble bush. But might he also be undermining his very underlying free speech claim in the process? And what, exactly, is that free speech claim? Is it a right to anonymous speech or a right to privacy of expressive associations?

> JUSTICE SCALIA: Mr. Bopp, do you have any case in which we have held that the First Amendment applies to activity that consists of the process of legislation, of legislating or of adopting legislation? The person who requests a referendum is taking . . . part in that. And in light of the fact that for the first century of our existence, even voting was public—you either did it raising your hand or by voice, or later, you had a ballot that was very visibly red or blue so that people knew which party you were voting for—the fact is that running a democracy takes a certain amount of civic courage. And the First Amendment does not protect you from criticism or even nasty phone calls when you exercise your political rights to legislate, or to take part in the legislative process. You are asking us to enter into a whole new field where we have never gone before.

Justice Scalia's view, as we will see, is that the act of voting, or signing a referendum petition, is not an act of free speech protected by the First Amendment. It is instead an act of governing in a democratic nation, and nothing in the Constitution says that it is otherwise. In this Justice Scalia has history on his side. Is a petition signature that has legal effect, just like a vote does, sufficiently different that, despite the similarity, the history doesn't apply?

> JUSTICE SOTOMAYOR: Counsel, if we create this constitutional right of association in the manner that you are describing it, why is it limited to the voting area?
>
> Would we be inviting review if a group of citizens get together and send a letter to an agency that says: Please pass X regulation, or

rescind Y regulation? Would the agency be prohibited from making that letter public?

MR. BOPP: Well, potentially. And it would be required to be subject to a First Amendment analysis. It's this Court that created, in the NAACP case, the right of private [expressive?] association.

JUSTICE SOTOMAYOR: So you're suggesting that when the petitioner or a person engages in political discourse with the government, and they choose to do it, because the government is not compelling them to write to it, it is not compelling them to sign the referendum. It's just—

MR. BOPP: And they are not compelling Ms. McIntyre to distribute her brochure, either. But this Court held that—

The *McIntyre* case comes into the fray. As it should. There the Court held that Margaret McIntyre (*McIntyre v. Ohio Elections Commission*) had a right to express her views anonymously in a leaflet opposing a school bond issue, which she distributed at public meetings on the bond issue. The Court waxed eloquent on the anonymous authors of the Federalist Papers, among others. If voting is an act of protected speech—at least voting through signing a referendum petition that, if successful, would suspend the challenged law protecting domestic partners, and especially gay partners—it's hard to see why the broad right to speak anonymously guaranteed in *McIntyre* would not apply.

JUSTICE SOTOMAYOR: But Ms. McIntyre wasn't asking the government to engage its process in her favor. She was asking for political reform, but she wasn't asking to engage the government process on her behalf.

MR. BOPP: Well, the government, you know, has a lot of options. For instance, they don't have to conduct elections for the election of judge. But if they opt to do that and provide that procedure, well, then, the First Amendment applies to the political speech.

The distinctions being drawn here, including Justice Sotomayor's, are getting too detailed and complex—even picky. This is happening because the argument has lost all grounding in a general principle of expressive privacy and association, or anonymous speech. Without an underlying theory of free speech, all distinctions can be made without a need to explain and justify them. Maybe McIntyre was a widow. Would that make a difference?

JUSTICE SCALIA: You are objecting to the public being able to check whether the agency is indeed finding out whether this is a genuine petition or not, correct?

MR. BOPP: They have procedures to check and verify these signatures that do not involve full disclosure.

JUSTICE SCALIA: The people of Washington evidently think that this is not too much of an imposition upon people's courage, to stand up and sign something and be willing to stand behind it. Now, if you don't like that, I can see doing it another way. But the people of Washington have chosen to do it this way.

JUSTICE STEVENS: Isn't there another possible public interest? Would it be a legitimate public interest to say, I would like to know who signed the petition, because I would like to try to persuade them that their views should be modified? Is there public interest in encouraging debate on the underlying issue?

MR. BOPP: Well, it's possible, but we think it's a very marginal interest. The Ninth Circuit recently ruled that if you give a small contribution to an initiative, nobody cares. So why should it be publicly disclosed when it's so marginal?

A better argument would be that disclosure itself conflicts directly with a right of anonymity in one's expressive political associations. But Bopp misses the chance to make it. He's still stuck on the threat-of-harm theory. Justice Scalia forces his hand.

JUSTICE SCALIA: What about just wanting to know their names so you can criticize them? Is that such a bad thing in a democracy?

(Laughter.)

MR. BOPP: Well, what is bad is not the criticism, it's the government requiring you to disclose your identity and belief.

JUSTICE SCALIA: You know, you can't run a democracy this way, with everybody being afraid of having his political positions known.

MR. BOPP: I'm sorry, Justice Scalia, but the campaign manager of this initiative had his family sleep in his living room because of the threats.

JUSTICE SCALIA: Well, that's bad. The threats should be moved against vigorously, but just because there can be criminal activity doesn't mean that you have to eliminate a procedure that is otherwise perfectly reasonable.

MR. BOPP: But all we are asking for is a First Amendment analysis of the compelled disclosure of the identity of these people and whether or not these interests are sufficient.

CHIEF JUSTICE ROBERTS: Thank you, Mr. Bopp.

Mr. Bopp's argument is, frankly, tactical artifice. So, it seems, is the justices' understanding of the issues. Not once was the principle of expressive association explored in any depth. Nor was the principle of freedom to speak anonymously. This is the justices' fault, not Bopp's, who likely wants to stay away from general principles of free speech. The justices seemed genuinely perplexed by the case, and they are spread all over the map in their view of what should be relevant to judging the First Amendment claim. The reason, I suspect, is that the stakes in the case are so high, and the broader implications of a decision—public disclosure of voting in elections, caucuses, and public disclosure of campaign contributions and expenditures, to name a few—are very unsettling.

Chief Justice Roberts next calls Washington Attorney General Rob McKenna to the podium.

> GENERAL MCKENNA: Mr. Chief Justice, and may it please the Court: In Washington the petitions do not become public records after the verification process, but in fact are made available as public records before the verification process even begins. This is because the Secretary of State's first step after receiving submitted petitions is to take them to his archiving section and to have them digitized. As soon as they are digitized, they are available on disks for anyone who requests them. Then the verification process begins.
>
> JUSTICE SOTOMAYOR: So is there a time for the public to look through the disks before the people who are sent into the room are sent into the room [to do the verification]?
>
> GENERAL MCKENNA: Yes, that's correct.
>
> CHIEF JUSTICE ROBERTS: Counsel, if the State had a law that you could disclose voters and for whom they voted, would that implicate First Amendment interests?
>
> GENERAL MCKENNA: Yes, Mr. Chief Justice, we do believe that First Amendment interests would be implicated by revealing how people voted, and we don't see a legitimate State interest in knowing how people voted.

Now the excitement begins. What about disclosure—to the state and the public—of one's vote in an election? The state takes the position that the First Amendment requires that one's vote be anonymous, but not one's signature on a referendum petition which if successful will immediately suspend the challenged law until a statewide vote is taken. This is a hard distinction to justify: a vote is speech, but a signature isn't. Why doesn't McKenna argue that neither is speech? This is Scalia's view. Does he think that he would lose the case if he did?

Like Bopp's argument, McKenna's argument will be very difficult to make, given the implications of the case, and like Bopp, McKenna will try to escape hard questions by descending to the details and detritus of the case. Frustration will result. Justice Scalia bores in.

> JUSTICE SCALIA: So the country was acting unconstitutionally for a whole century before we adopted the Australian secret ballot? Do you really think that?
>
> GENERAL McKENNA: No, Justice Scalia, I didn't say that I thought that the secret ballot was constitutionally required. I was asked by the Chief Justice whether some First Amendment interests would be implicated. They probably would be.
>
> CHIEF JUSTICE ROBERTS: What would the First Amendment interests be?
>
> GENERAL McKENNA: It might be implicated by a potential chill from voting, if you know your vote is going to be revealed.
>
> CHIEF JUSTICE ROBERTS: Do you think having your name revealed on a petition of this sort might have a chilling effect on whether you sign it?
>
> GENERAL McKENNA: Mr. Chief Justice, some chill may result, just as some chill may result from having your campaign contributions disclosed, or the fact that you have registered to vote and provided your name, address, your voting history is being disclosed. So some chill will result, but we do not think that it is significant enough.

But if there is little if any chilling effect here, why is the chill different for votes in a general election, whether for a candidate, a bond issue, or whatever? Notwithstanding Justice Scalia's valiant attempt to raise the tenor of the argument to constitutional levels, we won't find out the answer, and the rest of the justices won't ask for it.

> CHIEF JUSTICE ROBERTS: You don't think revealing that you are a voter has the same chilling effect as revealing how you voted, do you?
>
> GENERAL McKENNA: No, I do not. I think how you voted would have a much greater chilling effect than the fact that you are registered to vote. And of course, this Court has not ruled on whether the secret ballot is a constitutional right. If it is, then is town hall voting in New England unconstitutional? Is the caucus system in

Iowa for presidential candidates unconstitutional? The Court in this case does not have—

CHIEF JUSTICE ROBERTS: I thought you told me that the First Amendment interests were implicated with respect to the secret ballot, that you couldn't require people to reveal how they voted.

GENERAL McKENNA: We don't—we don't know if this Court would rule that the vote could never be revealed. We know that in some places, votes are done in public. We know that before the late 1800s, there was no secret ballot. We just—we don't know what the constitutional ruling would be. But we—we do know that in this case, it's not necessary for the Court to reach that—that determination, because in this case—

McKenna is on very dangerous ground here. He doesn't want to concede the case by saying that there is a First Amendment claim in all of these situations. The only difference is the balance of interests: referendum; election voting; caucuses; letters to a government official or agency; faculty tenure decisions; and on and on. He tries to escape by saying that the central and larger questions need not be decided. The Court should limit its decision to referendum petition signatures in Washington only.

But how can that limit be justified? The differences between the Washington referendum and all the other situations, if there are any, are relevant only to the extent that a general constitutional principle justifies them. And the duty of the Supreme Court is to decide cases based on reasoning that transcends the specific facts, and to issue an opinion that explains its decision in terms of the proper interpretation of the Constitution. The executive and legislative branches decide issues and cases without worrying too much about inconsistency. The judicial branch must be different, bound to reason based on the Constitution's text, history, and values only. If it weren't bound by this discipline, it would become nothing more than a nonelected partisan political body.

JUSTICE ALITO: Well, I would like to know how far you want to go. You say in your brief that the availability of the referendum signature petitions allows Washington voters to engage in a discussion of referred measures with persons whose acts secured the election and suspension of State law. So would it be consistent with the First Amendment to require anybody who signs a petition to put down not just the person's name and address, but also telephone number, so that they could be engaged in a conversation about what they had done?

GENERAL MCKENNA: It would depend on the strength of the State interest in having the telephone number. The State does not have an interest in the telephone number on the petition form, because the State only needs to know from the petition form the name and the address in order to verify—

Oops. McKenna gets caught in his own justification for the public disclosure. The State doesn't need telephone numbers for citizen verification, which seems odd but wasn't Justice Alito's question. What about *disclosing* the telephone number as a means of fostering discussion by members of the public with the petition signer? McKenna ducks that one, as if it's not really a justification for the law. Justice Alito calls him on it . . . and then we descend into desiderata.

JUSTICE ALITO: I thought that you were saying that one of the interests that's served by this is to allow Washington citizens to discuss this matter with those who signed the petition. So putting down the telephone number would assist them in doing that.

GENERAL MCKENNA: Yes, it probably would make it easier for people to contact.

JUSTICE ALITO: So you would endorse that?

GENERAL MCKENNA: That would be a policy determination for the legislature to make, Justice Alito.

Precisely, Justice Scalia would say! The state's argument consists of nothing more than legislative policy, not Constitutional principle and law. McKenna hasn't yet even talked about the First Amendment principle of associational privacy. So Justice Alito strikes again.

JUSTICE ALITO: No, I'm not asking the policy question. I'm asking whether the First Amendment would permit that.

GENERAL MCKENNA: I believe it could permit that, yes, Justice Alito.

This isn't an answer. It's simply a declaration. Justice Alito drops the subject, probably because he already knows the answer—in other words, that there isn't one.

JUSTICE ALITO: Now, one of your Co-Respondents says that supplying this information provides insight on whether support comes predominantly from members of particular political or religious organizations. Would it be consistent with the First Amendment to require anybody who signs a petition to list the person's religion?

GENERAL MCKENNA: No, I do not believe it would, Justice Alito.

Again, just a declaration. Justice Breyer tries to get to the core of the issue from a different direction.

> JUSTICE BREYER: Suppose that in 1957 in Little Rock, a group of Little Rock citizens had wanted to put on the ballot a petition to require the school board to reopen Central High School, which had been closed because there was a sentiment in the community that they didn't want integration. And it was pointed out that if they signed this petition, there was a very good chance that their businesses would be bombed, that they would certainly be boycotted, that their children might be harassed. Now, is there no First Amendment right in protecting those people? And if there is, how does it differ from your case?

> GENERAL MCKENNA: Justice Breyer, that is count two. That is count two of the Petitioners' complaint. This Court ruled as recently as *Citizens United* that such situations should be evaluated on a case-by-case basis to evaluate the reasonable probability of threats, harassments, and reprisals. But that—

McKenna is trying to seek shelter from the question by deflecting it to the applied challenge, which hasn't been adjudicated yet. In any event the First Amendment question will arise in either setting. His deflection works, though, but the tactic proves very tricky for McKenna.

> CHIEF JUSTICE ROBERTS: Counsel, your answer to Justice Breyer was that they can bring an as-applied challenge. Now, that as-applied challenge would be small comfort unless the names were protected pending the resolution of that challenge, correct? Do you think a stay should be granted in this case to allow the Petitioners to pursue an as-applied challenge?

> GENERAL MCKENNA: Yes, of course.

> CHIEF JUSTICE ROBERTS: Do you think that the disclosure of the names, pending the resolution of their as-applied challenge, would subject them to incidents of violence and intimidation?

> GENERAL MCKENNA: There is no evidence of that in the record.

> CHIEF JUSTICE ROBERTS: There is no evidence of episodes of violence or intimidation?

> GENERAL MCKENNA: Involving the Referendum 71 signers? No. The evidence in the record is about people who are out circulating petitions, people who are out, you know, campaigning for the petitions,

> the campaign manager for the measure. But none of the evidence in the record speaks to petition signers, and none of the evidence in the record speaks to petition signers for other, similar measures which were cited by the Petitioners.

Come on! Of course there wouldn't be evidence involving the Referendum 71 signers, as their names haven't yet been publicly disclosed. But there seems to be some evidence of fear and intimidation on the part of the circulators and the campaign manager. Does that count?

> JUSTICE ALITO: Well, let's say somebody is thinking of circulating a petition on a sensitive subject and fears that people may be dissuaded from signing because they fear retaliation. At what point could they bring this as-applied challenge? Could they do it before they even begin to circulate the petition, arguing that if people are not assured ahead of time their name and address is not going to be revealed to the public on the internet, they are not going to sign this?
>
> GENERAL MCKENNA: Justice Alito, it would be possible procedurally for them to bring the motion for an injunction even before collecting the signatures, if they had sufficient evidence.

Ah! There's the rub. Mckenna says that harassment of petition circulators and the campaign manager are not enough to justify a decision not to publish the names of the signers. Moreover, there is no record of violence in three states—*in the record*. Was that in fact the case? If this reflects the standard of proof that must be met by the petition sponsors, proving future harassment, intimidation, and the like will be pretty difficult to do.

Justice Alito then asks a tricky question—not about likely intimidation, but about the chill on supporters signing petitions because their vote and name will be public, whatever the reason for their reluctance. That is surely a harm if the underlying First Amendment right is anonymity or privacy of expressive associations. McKenna simply ignores the question, however, saying nothing more than that seeking an injunction against public disclosure in advance is *procedurally* possible. But how about the interest in avoiding chill rather than escaping intimidation? Alito keeps pushing.

> JUSTICE ALITO: And how would they prove that there is a sufficient threat of harassment in that particular case, before the petition is even signed?
>
> GENERAL MCKENNA: I believe that the sponsors of the measure would bring to the court evidence, if they have any, of—because

the controversial nature of that particular measure, that is based on what's happened to some of the people who are planning to put the measure on the ballot.

JUSTICE SCALIA: But you have rejected that here. You said there is no evidence here that any of the petition signers were subjected to any harassment.

GENERAL McKENNA: Right.

JUSTICE SCALIA: Of course there isn't, because the names haven't gotten out yet. How could you possibly demonstrate before the names get out that petition signers are going to be subjected to harassment? Or otherwise, don't insist upon evidence that these very petition signers will be harassed.

GENERAL McKENNA: I imagine, Justice Scalia, that these individuals moving for that preliminary injunction would do what the Petitioners have done in this case. They would cite to an example from another State involving a comparable—

JUSTICE SCALIA: And you think that would be an acceptable type of evidence?

GENERAL McKENNA: They can bring it into the court. I'm not saying the court would accept it, because I don't know—

JUSTICE SCALIA: Well, if you don't think it's acceptable, then you are not making an argument.

McKenna is getting close to a precipice here. Justice Scalia is not at all happy. Justice Alito is in the wings.

JUSTICE ALITO: Well, the hypothetical is that before this petition is circulated, the supporters came into court and they said, look what is happening in California with Proposition 8. Don't disclose—enter an order prohibiting the public disclosure of the names and addresses here. Would that be sufficient?

GENERAL McKENNA: Justice Alito, I think that the evidence would have to be very strong. It would have to rise above criticism. I think it would have to rise to the level of threat and violence.

Whoa! They would have to prove a threat and violence, a very, very high standard? McKenna says nothing that even acknowledges, much less discusses, any harm from chilling prospective signers from participating in the referendum for fear that their identity and vote will be publicly disclosed, a ground on which the petition group could probably present real and solid evidence through testimony. The as-applied challenge seems to be diminishing to essentially nothing for signatories of petitions—or, for that matter, for general election voters whose votes are made a public record and disclosed. McKenna is trying to escape dealing with the hypotheticals posed by the justices as well as the substance of the First Amendment interest, by pawning the questions off to an as-applied process which, it now appears, is much sound and fury signifying nothing.

JUSTICE ALITO: Can I ask you this question? It seems to me the strongest State interest here is detecting fraud. And you mentioned that the records are digitized. And maybe you can correct my impression of this, but it seems to me that if the records are digitized, there are very simple ways of detecting fraud that would not require the disclosure of the list to the public.

If somebody wants to see whether his or her name has been fraudulently put on the list, wouldn't it be very simple to set up a website where the person could put in a little bit of identifying information and see whether that person's name is on the list? And if the purpose is to see whether a particular person lives at a particular address, couldn't you just cross-reference by means of a computer program the information on the referendum with the voting lists?

GENERAL McKENNA: Justice Alito, you are right. They do use computers because in the verification process, the Secretary of State staff, with the observers looking over their shoulder, will look at the petition and look up that voter in an electronic voter registration database. This is exactly why the information is so useful to the public as well. They have access to electronic online voter registration history as well, and they can also check.

JUSTICE ALITO: Well, what's the answer to my question? Couldn't you—couldn't this be done simply? If I want to see whether somebody has fraudulently signed my name, I could very quickly go to a website—it wouldn't be expensive to set up—and put in your voter ID number and your name, and see whether somebody signed your name to the petition?

GENERAL McKENNA: Yes, Justice Alito, that could be done.

So. . . . ? Does that mean that public disclosure is not needed? McKenna is close to giving up his case, or at least having to defend it on the highly questionable public-information and civic-engagement interest.

JUSTICE ALITO: So what is your interest?

GENERAL McKENNA: In addition to the fraud interest, there is a valid information interest in knowing who is it exactly who is calling for this election and suspending—

JUSTICE ALITO: Well, but how far does that go? When I asked whether you could know the religion of the people who signed? No, you can't do that. How much more demographic information does the State of Washington have an interest in making publicly available about the people who support this election? Let's say it's a referendum about immigration. Does the State of Washington have an interest in providing information to somebody who says, I want to know how many people with Hispanic names signed this, or how many people with Asian names signed this? Is that what you want to facilitate?

GENERAL McKENNA: I don't see what the valid State interest would be of knowing the ethnicity of the person—I mean, of course, anyone could look at petition ballot forms, I suppose, divine something about the ethnicity based on the last name, but the State's interest doesn't go—go to that. That we don't—we don't believe we need to know that. We believe we need to know [only what is] is requested—required on the—on the petition form.

JUSTICE ALITO: Then I don't understand what information you think you are providing to the public. Outside of the fraud area, if I see that John Jones from Seattle signed this petition, that tells me absolutely nothing.

Good question. The issue isn't the need for information for the state itself, but by the public for civic engagement and so on.

GENERAL McKENNA: Well, Justice Alito, it might—if you know John Jones, that might tell you something. Number two, we know that intermediaries and especially the press and sometimes social science researchers and others will—will look at the names, and they will be able to tell, for example, that a large number of employees at one company [voted in support of] a measure; maybe it's a measure that would cut a tax break for a particular industry. Or perhaps members of a union, large numbers have signed—

CHIEF JUSTICE ROBERTS: How can they—how can they find that out with just the name and address, that a large number of people from a company signed it?

GENERAL McKENNA: Well, a voter who—who works at that same company or does business with that same company might know that, gosh, I know these employees and they've—they have all signed this petition. The press may be able to do research to find this out. Intermediaries do play an important role.

This exchange is really too painful to reproduce in full. But it speaks volumes. The First Amendment does apply, McKenna says, but it means next to nothing. Inhibition or chilling of speech, a longstanding First Amendment harm, isn't even mentioned. McKenna is grasping at straws—and not good ones, at that. Perhaps he must do so since he has to defend a law that really isn't a law, but an administrative interpretation, which comes from a public records act, not a well-thought-out law governing elections and referenda. The truth is that nobody thought about these problems.

JUSTICE ALITO: You know, if somebody called your office and said, "I'd like the home address of all the attorneys who work in the attorneys general office because we want to go to their homes and have uncomfortable conversations with them"—

(Laughter.)

—which is what has been alleged here, would you release that information?

GENERAL McKENNA: We would not, Justice Alito. We could not release it because they can come to the office and have uncomfortable conversations with them—

(Laughter.)

GENERAL McKENNA: —which I can personally attest happens with some regularity.

(Laughter.)

CHIEF JUSTICE ROBERTS: Thank you, General McKenna.

Oh my! How about their home addresses? They aren't available, probably in order to protect their privacy, or because of the risk of threats? These are about the same interests as petition signers have. Mckenna escapes because the time is up. But he's done an absolutely unrevealing job of defending the Washington Public Records Act and its interpretation regarding petition signatories. It turns out that the law is an ugly, messy business; rough lines must be drawn, discretion exercised; the justifications for the distinctions made are weak and frankly political. Don't First Amendment issues require more than that of a legislature or an administration when their actions affect speech freedom?

Bopp contributed little in his remaining two minutes, and after that the argument was ended and the case was submitted for decision by the Court. It had been an unsatisfying and frustrating oral argument. One could come away from it without having the slightest idea what the First Amendment had to do with the case. Scalia's view was the exception to that rule. For him the First Amendment had nothing to do with it.

The main question one might ask after hearing the oral argument was: "How in the devil will the Supreme Court come to a decision in the case?" The answer turned out to be: "They won't." That's because the Justices came not to one or two views of the case, but instead arrived at no fewer than seven different views. The only common denominators were the result—send the case back to the district court for trial on the as-applied challenge—and, remarkably, a conclusion that the act of petition signing is an act of free speech! Eight justices agreed that the case should be sent back to the district court for adjudication of the as-applied challenge with the First Amendment vaguely in play. Justice Thomas dissented and would have invalidated the law on its face. But pretty well all of the eight disagreed about the reason for doing so. The opinion would be a mess, a lawyer's nightmare (or dream, as the case may be). Pity goes to the district court judge who must try the as applied challenge without any clear guidance on the legal and evidentiary standards that should be applied.

We won't prolong our discussion of the seven different opinions that were issued. Instead, we'll take just enough of each to get a taste of the different approaches to the case and the different views of the First Amendment's application to public disclosure of petition signatures, votes, and a broader range of questions. Thereafter we will turn to a discussion of the important free speech issues raised by the case and the implications of those issues for voting and campaign contributions and expenditures—this time from a *constitutional* perspective.

Chief Justice Roberts wrote the opinion for the Court. There was only one dissenting opinion, but there were many concurring opinions, some of which didn't fully join the Chief Justice's opinion. The Chief managed to get a majority of the Justices to join his opinion, but in order to do so he was forced to write a fairly opaque opinion, leaving room for future flexibility and leaving many of the largest issues undecided. The decision in the *Doe* case was announced late in the term, on June 24, 2010.

CHIEF JUSTICE ROBERTS delivered the opinion of the Court:

The compelled disclosure of signatory information on referendum petitions is subject to review under the First Amendment. An individual expresses a view on a political matter when he signs a petition under Washington's referendum procedure. In most cases, the individual's signature will express the view that the law subject to the petition should be overturned. Even if the signer is agnostic as to the merits of the underlying law, his signature still expresses the political view that the question should be considered "by the whole electorate." In either case, the expression of a political view implicates a First Amendment right. The State, having "cho[sen] to tap the energy and the legitimizing power of the democratic process, . . . must accord the participants in that process the First Amendment rights that attach to their roles."

Petition signing remains expressive even when it has legal effect in the electoral process. But that is not to say that the electoral context is irrelevant to the nature of our First Amendment review. We allow States significant flexibility in implementing their own voting systems. To the extent a regulation concerns the legal effect of a particular activity in that process, the government will be afforded substantial latitude to enforce that regulation. Also pertinent to our analysis is the fact that the PRA is not a prohibition on speech, but instead a disclosure requirement. "[D]isclosure requirements may burden the ability to speak, but they . . . do not prevent anyone from speaking."

We have a series of precedents considering First Amendment challenges to disclosure requirements in the electoral context. These precedents have reviewed such challenges under what has been termed "exacting scrutiny." . . . That standard "requires a 'substantial relation' between the disclosure requirement and a 'sufficiently important' governmental interest." To withstand this scrutiny, "the strength of the governmental interest must reflect the seriousness of the actual burden on First Amendment rights."

. . . Respondents assert two interests to justify the burdens of compelled disclosure under the PRA on First Amendment rights: (1) preserving the integrity of the electoral process by combating fraud, detecting invalid signatures, and fostering government transparency and accountability; and (2) providing information to the electorate about who supports the petition. Because we determine that the State's interest in preserving the integrity of the electoral process suffices to defeat the argument that the PRA is unconstitutional with respect to referendum petitions in general, we need not, and do not, address the State's "informational" interest.

The secretary's verification and canvassing will not catch all invalid signatures: The job is large and difficult (the secretary ordinarily checks "only 3 to

5% of signatures"), and the secretary can make mistakes, too. Public disclosure can help cure the inadequacies of the verification and canvassing process.

Disclosure also helps prevent certain types of petition fraud otherwise difficult to detect, such as outright forgery and "bait and switch" fraud, in which an individual signs the petition based on a misrepresentation of the underlying issue. The signer is in the best position to detect these types of fraud, and public disclosure can bring the issue to the signer's attention.

Public disclosure also promotes transparency and accountability in the electoral process to an extent other measures cannot. In light of the foregoing, we reject plaintiffs' argument and conclude that public disclosure of referendum petitions in general is substantially related to the important interest of preserving the integrity of the electoral process.

Plaintiffs' more significant objection is that "the strength of the governmental interest" does not "reflect the seriousness of the actual burden on First Amendment rights."

. . . Plaintiffs explain that once on the Internet, the petition signers' names and addresses "can be combined with publicly available phone numbers and maps," in what will effectively become a blueprint for harassment and intimidation. To support their claim that they will be subject to reprisals, plaintiffs cite examples from the history of a similar proposition in California, and from the experience of one of the petition sponsors in this case.

In related contexts, we have explained that those resisting disclosure can prevail under the First Amendment if they can show "a reasonable probability that the compelled disclosure [of personal information] will subject them to threats, harassment, or reprisals from either Government officials or private parties." The question before us, however, is not whether PRA disclosure violates the First Amendment with respect to those who signed the R—71 petition, or other particularly controversial petitions. The question instead is whether such disclosure in general violates the First Amendment rights of those who sign referendum petitions.

The problem for plaintiffs is that their argument rests almost entirely on the specific harm they say would attend disclosure of the information on the R—71 petition, or on similarly controversial ones. But typical referendum petitions "concern tax policy, revenue, budget, or other state law issues."

We conclude that disclosure under the PRA would not violate the First Amendment with respect to referendum petitions in general and therefore affirm the judgment of the Court of Appeals.

It is so ordered.

The chief justice begins by limiting the Court's decision to petition signatures and addresses on referenda. This is a prudent and likely necessary limitation, of a piece with Supreme Court practice and almost surely required for the chief to get a Court (a majority of the Justices joining the opinion). But it leaves many larger questions open: Is there a principled constitutional ground upon which such a limitation could be rested in the future; is the basic premise that acts of political intention—a petition signature, raised hand, a button hit on a ballot, a circle blackened—are acts to which the First Amendment applies? Are direct restrictions on signing or perhaps voting, such as registration requirements or disqualification of ex-felons, to be treated differently than disclosure requirements, which inhibit but do not prevent speech? The answers to these and other related questions will ultimately determine the scope of the *Doe* opinion.

The Chief then states the constitutional test to be applied in the *Doe* case. It requires the state to show a "sufficiently important" interest in disclosure when balanced against the "seriousness of the actual burden" placed on the signer's free speech, and a "substantial relation" between the disclosure requirement and "a 'sufficiently important' governmental interest." If one reads this test carefully, the inescapable conclusion is that it is not very "exacting scrutiny," a conclusion that the remainder of the opinion bears out.

The Chief then turns to the state's interest in disclosure. By most any standard the case he makes is pretty weak. The Secretary of State only checks 3 percent to 5 percent of the signatures, he says, and the actual signer, armed with an electronic database of everyone who signed the petition, is in the best position to uncover fraud or mistake. Without any information about the reliability of the secretary's audit or the incidence of fraud or mistake in the referendum petition process, or any investigation into alternative or additional audit steps that don't require public disclosure, the opinion represents little more than the Court's taking the state's word for it. Hardly "exacting scrutiny." Throwing in a dab of openness and transparency doesn't really add anything.

The chief then turns to the harm from disclosure. He first minimizes the degree and extent of the harm, with justification. Intimidation and threats and the like, it seems (happily), are quite rare, and laws already exist to punish such acts. If the state's valid interest in disclosure were simply providing public information, the low incidence of harm would surely not, under most constitutional standards, invalidate a disclosure requirement. But that's not the interest the Court's opinion rests upon. If instead we balance the state's weak case for preserving integrity by discovering fraud and mistake against the challengers' narrow and weak interest in preventing intimidation and threats, it's far from clear which side comes out ahead in the balance.

The larger point, however, is that Bopp had settled on the risk of intimidation and threats as his whole justification for challenging the disclosure requirement. And apart from a bloviation or two about disclosure inhibiting petition signers for reasons other than risk of intimidation and threats, he always stuck to his narrow definition of harm, even saying that general inhibition or chill by signers would be the result of risk of intimidation or threats, not the risk of violating the signer's right to privacy of political belief or right to anonymity of speech.

The chief justice held Bopp to his argument, not even addressing other forms of expressive harm from disclosure. By doing so (whether justifiably or not), the outcome was inevitable: notwithstanding a vastly overreaching justification for the state's policy, the claimed harm of intimidation and threats was even weaker, or at least as weak, and it could be taken care of by allowing the petition sponsors to seek judicial protection from public disclosure in advance of launching a petition campaign. The chief, in an act of prudence, or by this sleight of hand, tied the case up in a pretty bow and sustained the disclosure law.

Even accepting the chief's exceedingly narrow approach to the case, perhaps the most noteworthy thing about the opinion is that it said virtually nothing about when, whether, and how an injunction in advance of disclosure was to take place. What would the standard in such an action be? What kinds of proof would be relevant? Would the question be incidents of intimidation or threats already experienced in the particular referendum effort; the incidents of such harms in other efforts in Washington or in other states; the intuitive possibility of such harm; the actual harboring of such fears, baseless or not, in the minds of prospective signers who would not participate in the face of public disclosure of their signature and address?

More basically, it said virtually nothing about the basis of the Court's decision. Was it freedom from harm by others based on the signer's speech? Or the right to privacy of expressive association, with public disclosure of one's beliefs being the harm? Was it a right to anonymous speech? This is an important—indeed critical—question that the chief leaves untouched. Doing so is hard to justify if the Constitution does apply in the case. The Court's duty is to make decisions based on open reasons. That is what distinguishes the Supreme Court from the other branches of government and gives lower courts (including the poor district court judge who will have to pick up the case and try it again) guidance for future cases. The likely reason for the chief's evasion of the question is that he couldn't get a Court—in other words, five votes—for the opinion if he were any clearer—or even clear at all. The only thing he said clearly is that signing a petition is an act of free speech.

So Chief Justice Roberts left these questions as an open text to be filled in later. But the filling in would be one of the principal sources of concern expressed by the concurring justices, as we will see. The concurrences began with Justice Breyer.

> Justice BREYER, concurring:
>
> In circumstances where, as here, "a law significantly implicates competing constitutionally protected interests in complex ways," the Court balances interests. "And in practice that has meant asking whether the statute burdens any one such interest in a manner out of proportion to the statute's salutary effects upon the others." . . . For the reasons stated in those opinions (as well as many of the reasons discussed by Justice Sotomayor), I would uphold the statute challenged in this case. With this understanding, I join the opinion of the Court and Justice Stevens' opinion.

That's it. Pretty opaque, it seems. Justice Breyer joins the opinion but states the applicable constitutional test in different and overtly open-ended terms, and requires great deference to the state. None of this "exacting scrutiny" stuff, unless by that phrase he means that the Court is going to have to get into the nitty-gritty details against a background of deference to the state. Why did he "join" the chief justice's opinion? Because, it appears, that seems to be exactly the test actually applied by Chief Justice Roberts, notwithstanding the more muscular language the chief employed. And while it has no affect on the Court's opinion, Justice Breyer does qualify his "joining" with that understanding.

Why is his preferred approach so open and deferential? We don't know for sure, though we do know from experience that Justice Breyer is smitten with balancing. By joining the Court's opinion Justice Breyer states his agreement that the signing of a petition is an act of speech protected by the First Amendment. He also appears to agree on the very limited scope of the decision, leaving the larger First Amendment questions to simmer a while and venturing no opinion on the process and standards to be employed by the (poor!) district court on remand. But on the how, why, and when questions he is silent, except for his joining also the concurrence of Justice Stevens, to which we will turn in due course. But first comes Justice Alito.

> Justice ALITO, concurring:
>
> The possibility of prevailing in an as-applied challenge provides adequate protection for First Amendment rights only if (1) speakers can obtain the exemption sufficiently far in advance to avoid chilling protected speech and

(2) the showing necessary to obtain the exemption is not overly burdensome. With respect to the first requirement, the as-applied exemption becomes practically worthless if speakers cannot obtain the exemption quickly and well in advance of speaking. . . . The only way a circulator can provide such assurance, however, is if the circulator has sought and obtained an as-applied exemption from the disclosure requirement well before circulating the petition. Additionally, speakers must be able to obtain an as-applied exemption without clearing a high evidentiary hurdle.

In light of those principles, the plaintiffs in this case have a strong argument that the PRA violates the First Amendment as applied to the Referendum 71 petition. . . . Indeed, if the evidence relating to Proposition 8 is not sufficient to obtain an as-applied exemption in this case, one may wonder whether that vehicle provides any meaningful protection for the First Amendment rights of persons who circulate and sign referendum and initiative petitions.

The state maintains that publicly disclosing the names and addresses of referendum signatories provides the voting public with "insight into whether support for holding a vote comes predominantly from particular interest groups, political or religious organizations, or other group[s] of citizens," and thus allows voters to draw inferences about whether they should support or oppose the referendum.

The implications of accepting such an argument are breathtaking. Were we to accept respondents' asserted informational interest, the State would be free to require petition signers to disclose all kinds of demographic information, including the signer's race, religion, political affiliation, sexual orientation, ethnic background, and interest-group memberships. Requiring such disclosures, however, runs headfirst into a half century of our case law, which firmly establishes that individuals have a right to privacy of belief and association. Indeed, the State's informational interest paints such a chilling picture of the role of government in our lives that at oral argument the Washington attorney general balked when confronted with the logical implications of accepting such an argument, conceding that the State could not require petition signers to disclose their religion or ethnicity.

Respondents also maintain that the State has an interest in preserving the integrity of the referendum process and that public disclosure furthers that interest by helping the State detect fraudulent and mistaken signatures. But I harbor serious doubts as to whether public disclosure of signatory information serves that interest in a way that always "reflect[s] the seriousness of the actual burden on First Amendment rights."

Washington could easily and cheaply employ alternative mechanisms for protecting against fraud and mistake that would be far more protective of

> circulators' and signers' First Amendment rights. For example, with a digitized list, it should be relatively easy for the secretary to check for duplicate signatures on a referendum petition. And given that the secretary maintains a "centralized, uniform, interactive computerized statewide voter registration list that contains the name and registration information of every registered voter in the state," the secretary could use a computer program to cross-check the names and addresses on the petition with the names and addresses on the voter registration roles, thus ensuring the accuracy and legitimacy of each signature.
>
> Additionally, using the digitized version of the referendum petition, the State could set up a simple system for Washington citizens to check whether their names have been fraudulently signed to a petition.
>
> As-applied challenges to disclosure requirements play a critical role in protecting First Amendment freedoms. To give speech the breathing room it needs to flourish, prompt judicial remedies must be available well before the relevant speech occurs and the burden of proof must be low. In this case plaintiffs have a strong case that they are entitled to as-applied relief, and they will be able to pursue such relief before the District Court.

Justice Alito joins the Court's opinion and then proceeds to fill in many of the answers to questions left open by the Chief Justice. First, the State's "informational" interest is not, in Alito's opinion, worth the paper it is written on; indeed, it is potentially harmful because it opens the specter of excessive government intrusion into people's lives. Whether this is a constitutional problem or not, he doesn't say. But it is logical to assume, given his reference to a "right to privacy of belief and association," that the informational and civic engagement purpose is itself flatly inconsistent with the First Amendment right. Second, while the fraud and mistake interest of the State are legitimate, the State has so many alternative (and often technologically superior) ways to shore up its auditing in a more effective way than through public disclosure, that even the fraud interest may fail any serious scrutiny by a court. Finally, the First Amendment requires an easily available, pre-petition method of limiting or prohibiting public disclosure of signers, and the threshold of supporting evidence and burden of proof should be very low for the petitioners. Indeed, he suggests that on the record of the case at present, the referendum petition group should win.

Whether one agrees with Justice Alito or not, it is refreshing to see some clear answers and arguments. But it must be said that on the foundational questions of why and when the First Amendment protection should apply—referenda only; caucuses; election votes; campaign contributions and expenditures;

missives to government agencies; faculty tenure decisions, and so forth—Alito joins the crowd and is silent. But at least we have a flavor of his constitutional principle with which to consider the broader applications of the case.

> Justice SOTOMAYOR, with whom Justice STEVENS and Justice GINSBURG join, concurring:
>
> Regulations of this nature . . . stand "a step removed from the communicative aspect of petitioning," and the ability of States to impose them can scarcely be doubted. It is by no means necessary for a State to prove that such "reasonable, nondiscriminatory restrictions" are narrowly tailored to its interests.
>
> On the other side of the ledger, I view the burden of public disclosure on speech and associational rights as minimal in this context. As this Court has observed with respect to campaign-finance regulations, "disclosure requirements . . . 'do not prevent anyone from speaking.'"
>
> Likewise, because the expressive interests implicated by the act of petition signing are always modest, I find it difficult to see how any incremental disincentive to sign a petition would tip the constitutional balance. . . . Accordingly, courts presented with an as-applied challenge to a regulation authorizing the disclosure of referendum petitions should be deeply skeptical of any assertion that the Constitution, which embraces political transparency, compels States to conceal the identity of persons who seek to participate in lawmaking through a state-created referendum process. With this understanding, I join the opinion of the Court.

Well, that's clear . . . maybe. There is some kind of First Amendment interest, but it doesn't count for much. Indeed, it counts for so little that one wonders why she even mentioned it. Justice Sotomayor seems to say disclosure regulations, whatever their purposes (public information included), are not really regulations of speech at all, but instead are one step removed from any form of speech and are directed to entirely speech-unrelated interests (like requirements that you give your driver's license to an officer when you are stopped). She also says, as if to bolster the point, that the burden of public disclosure on speech is minimal at best, and in any event disclosure requirements do not "prevent" anyone from speaking. Prevent is a key word in that statement. Therefore, courts should be "deeply skeptical of any assertion that the Constitution, which embraces political transparency, compels States to conceal the identity of persons who seek to participate in lawmaking through a state-created referendum process."

With this understanding Justice Sotomayor *joins the opinion of the Court*! What can this mean, when there is virtually nothing left in the Court's opinion with which she agrees? The Court's opinion doesn't say much anyway. Justice Sotomayor has, perhaps, left enough unspoken ambiguity at the far edges of her otherwise pretty definitive statements, but for all practical purposes that might have been done simply to leave a smidgeon of purchase on the Chief's opinion in order to *say* that she joined the Court's opinion and thus to dispose of a horrid mess of a case and a ghastly set of constitutional issues that the Court will *never* want to see again.

Perhaps the district court judge on remand is not to be pitied. She or he will have a completely free hand—subject, of course, to the nettlesome Ninth Circuit Court of Appeals which seems to delight in forcing the Supreme Court to step into controversial cases it doesn't want to decide . . . like this one.

> Justice STEVENS, with whom Justice BREYER joins, concurring in part and concurring in the judgment:
>
> Any burden on speech that petitioners posit is speculative as well as indirect. For an as-applied challenge to a law such as the PRA to succeed, there would have to be a significant threat of harassment directed at those who sign the petition that cannot be mitigated by law enforcement measures. Accordingly, I concur with the opinion of the Court to the extent that it is not inconsistent with my own, and I concur in the judgment.

The first thing to say about this is that the counting of votes has become awfully complicated. Justice Breyer has joined the Court's opinion, but only on *his* understanding of its meaning, yet has also joined Justice Stevens's opinion, which concurs specially *and* in the result only. How can Justice Breyer do that? And then Justice Stevens joins Justice Sotomayor's concurring opinion, in which Justice Sotomayor joins the Court's opinion. Of course Justice Sotomayor joins the Court's opinion "with this understanding," whatever that means. And then Justice Breyer expresses agreement with "many of the reasons discussed by Justice Sotomayor," and joins *both* the chief justice's opinion for the Court *and* Justice Stevens's opinion, which does not *really* join the Court's opinion. All of this presents a mathematical and logical puzzle that defies understanding. It is surely a strange way to run a Supreme Court and an even stranger way to enforce the rule of law.

The only other thing to say is that Justice Stevens says next to nothing, and implicit in doing that is a general agreement with what the chief justice said in his opinion for the Court, which is precious little. Stevens just wants to make clear his view that the standard of proof on remand must be close to impossibly high, a question that the Court's opinion left entirely open. So why in the world did Justice Stevens refuse to join fully the Court's opinion?

Finally, we find our way to the two most constitutionally reasoned and very clear opinions, one reaching the same result as the Court but for very different reasons, by Justice Scalia; and one reaching the opposite result on the ground that the Court's First Amendment reasoning was too weak and the government should never be able to require public disclosure of petition signatures or, for that matter, votes at elections.

> Justice SCALIA, concurring in the judgment.
>
> Plaintiffs point to no precedent from this Court holding that legislating is protected by the First Amendment. Nor do they identify historical evidence demonstrating that "the freedom of speech" the First Amendment codified encompassed a right to legislate without public disclosure. This should come as no surprise; the exercise of lawmaking power in the United States has traditionally been public.
>
> Moreover, even when the people asked Congress for legislative changes by exercising their constitutional right "to petition the Government for a redress of grievances," they did so publicly. The petition was read aloud in Congress. The petitioner's name (when large groups were not involved), his request, and what action Congress had taken on the petition were consistently recorded in the House and Senate Journals. Even when the people exercised legislative power directly, they did so not anonymously, but openly in town hall meetings. Petitioning the government and participating in the traditional town meeting were precursors of the modern initiative and referendum.
>
> Legislating was not the only governmental act that was public in America. Voting was public until 1888 when the States began to adopt the Australian secret ballot. We have acknowledged the existence of a First Amendment interest in voting, but we have never said that it includes the right to vote anonymously. The history of voting in the United States completely undermines that claim.
>
> Initially, the Colonies mostly continued the English traditions of voting by a show of hands or by voice—viva voce voting. One scholar described the viva voce system as follows:
>
>> "'The election judges, who were magistrates, sat upon a bench with their clerks before them. Where practicable, it was customary for the candidates to be present in person, and to occupy a seat at the side of the judges. As the voter appeared, his name was called out in a loud voice. The judges inquired, "John Jones (or Smith), for whom do you vote?"—for governor, or whatever was the office to be filled. He replied by proclaiming the name of his favorite. Then the clerks enrolled the vote, and the judges announced

it as enrolled. The representative of the candidate for whom he voted arose, bowed, and thanked him aloud; and his partisans often applauded.'"

Although there was variation, the election official would ordinarily compile a poll with the name and residence of each voter, and the name of the candidate for whom he voted. To prevent fraud, the Colonies in Rhode Island, New York, and New Jersey adopted the English rule that "copies of the poll must be delivered on demand to persons who were willing to pay a reasonable charge for the labor of writing them." Some colonies allowed candidates to demand a copy of the poll, and required the legislature to examine the poll in a contested election. Thus, as in this case, the government not only publicly collected identifying information about who voted and for which candidate, it also disclosed that information to the public.

Of course the practice of viva voce voting was gradually replaced with the paper ballot, which was thought to reduce fraud and undue influence. There is no indication that the shift resulted from a sudden realization that public voting infringed voters' freedom of speech, and the manner in which it occurred suggests the contrary. States adopted the paper ballot at different times, and some States changed methods multiple times. New York's 1777 Constitution, for example, explicitly provided for the State to switch between methods. Kentucky's 1792 Constitution required paper ballots, but its 1799 Constitution required viva voce voting. The different voting methods simply reflected different views about how democracy should function. One scholar described Virginia's and Kentucky's steadfast use of viva voce voting through the Civil War as follows: "[I]n the appeal to unflinching manliness at the polls these two states insisted still that every voter should show at the hustings the courage of his personal conviction."

The new paper ballots did not make voting anonymous. Initially, many States did not regulate the form of the paper ballot. Taking advantage of this, political parties began printing ballots with their candidates' names on them. They used brightly colored paper and other distinctive markings so that the ballots could be recognized from a distance, making the votes public. Abuse of these unofficial paper ballots was rampant. The polling place had become an "open auction place" where votes could be freely bought or coerced. Employers threatened employees. Party workers kept voters from the other party away from the ballot box. Ballot peddlers paid voters and then watched them place the ballot in the box. Thus, although some state courts said that voting by ballot was meant to be more secret than the public act of viva voce voting; and although some state constitutional requirements of ballot voting were held to guarantee ballot secrecy, thus prohibiting the numbering of ballots for voter identification purposes, in general, voting by ballot was by no means

> secret. Most important of all for present purposes, I am aware of no assertion of ballot secrecy that relied on federal or state constitutional guarantees of freedom of speech.
>
> It was precisely discontent over the nonsecret nature of ballot voting, and the abuses that produced, which led to the States' adoption of the Australian secret ballot. New York and Massachusetts began that movement in 1888, and almost 90 percent of the States had followed suit by 1896. But I am aware of no contention that the Australian system was required by the First Amendment (or the state counterparts). That would have been utterly implausible, since the inhabitants of the Colonies, the States, and the United States had found public voting entirely compatible with "the freedom of speech" for several centuries.
>
> The long history of public legislating and voting contradicts plaintiffs' claim that disclosure of petition signatures having legislative effect violates the First Amendment. Just as the century-old practice of States' prohibiting anonymous electioneering was sufficient for me to reject the First Amendment claim to anonymity in *McIntyre*, the many-centuries-old practices of public legislating and voting are sufficient for me to reject plaintiffs' claim.
>
> Plaintiffs raise concerns that the disclosure of petition signatures may lead to threats and intimidation. There are laws against threats and intimidation; and harsh criticism, short of unlawful action, is a price our people have traditionally been willing to pay for self-governance. Requiring people to stand up in public for their political acts fosters civic courage, without which democracy is doomed. For my part, I do not look forward to a society which, thanks to the Supreme Court, campaigns anonymously (*McIntyre*) and even exercises the direct democracy of initiative and referendum hidden from public scrutiny and protected from the accountability of criticism. This does not resemble the Home of the Brave.

Now that's a clear opinion, right or wrong. Referendum petitions in Washington have immediate legal effect on the law. They are lawmaking, and like legislative votes in Congress public knowledge is a requirement. While Washington is not bound by the rule governing Congress, the widespread practice of openness in legislative voting belies any constitutional argument that petition signatures must be protected from disclosure. And with petitions to Congress under the petition clause of the First Amendment, disclosure or availability of a petitioner (or a petitioning group or organization) was the rule. There is no basis for concluding that the First Amendment has any application to these acts.

Justice Scalia then turns to voting in elections. There, he says, the record is even clearer. For more than a century voting was a public act, sometimes quaint, sometimes messy, but nevertheless done without any shade of concern about the First Amendment. The current near-universal use of the secret ballot was a matter of legislative judgment, not judicial requirement under the First Amendment. And, it might be added, open voting by show of hands still exists in local government settings—including the Iowa caucuses.

So there is no basis for a constitutional claim to secret ballots or secret voting. Voting is an expressive act, to be sure, but it is also a distinct act of governance that always has been, and always should be, constitutionally distinct from freedom of speech. And by the way, the *McIntyre* Court's conferral of a *broad* First Amendment right to speak anonymously in political settings, while distinct from the act of voting, was likewise unsupported by historical practice. "Requiring people to stand up in public for their political acts fosters civic courage." America is the Home of the Brave.

If a state decides to make people's votes public, so be it. Get a life! End of case. End of any problems with voting rules, end of any questions about the scope of the *Doe* opinion's application.

Justice Scalia was alone in his view. And perhaps he was right, too. Justice Thomas was likewise alone in his quite opposite view, and perhaps right also.

> Justice THOMAS, dissenting:
>
> Just as "[c]onfidence in the integrity of our electoral processes is essential to the functioning of our participatory democracy," so too is citizen participation in those processes, which necessarily entails political speech and association under the First Amendment. In my view, compelled disclosure of signed referendum and initiative petitions under the Washington Public Records Act (PRA) severely burdens those rights and chills citizen participation in the referendum process. Given those burdens, I would hold that Washington's decision to subject all referendum petitions to public disclosure is unconstitutional because there will always be a less restrictive means by which Washington can vindicate its stated interest in preserving the integrity of its referendum process. I respectfully dissent.
>
> This Court has long recognized the "vital relationship between" political association "and privacy in one's associations," and held that "[t]he Constitution protects against the compelled disclosure of political associations and beliefs." This constitutional protection "yield[s] only to a subordinating interest of the State that is compelling, and then only if there is a substantial relation between the information sought and an overriding and compelling state interest." Thus, unlike the Court, I read our precedents to require application of strict scrutiny to laws that compel disclosure of protected First Amendment association. Under that standard, a disclosure requirement passes

constitutional muster only if it is narrowly tailored—i.e., the least restrictive means—to serve a compelling state interest. Washington's application of the PRA to a referendum petition does not survive strict scrutiny.

We should not abandon those principles merely because Washington and its amici can point to a mere eight instances of initiative-related fraud among the 809 initiative measures placed on state ballots in this country between 1988 and 2008. If anything, these meager figures reinforce the conclusion that the risks of fraud or corruption in the initiative and referendum process are remote and thereby undermine Washington's claim that those two interests should be considered compelling for purposes of strict scrutiny.

There is no apparent reason why Washington must broadly disclose referendum signers' names and addresses in this manner to vindicate the interest that it invokes here. Washington—which is in possession of that information because of referendum regulations that petitioners do not challenge—could put the names and addresses of referendum signers into a similar electronic database that state employees could search without subjecting the name and address of each signer to wholesale public disclosure. The secretary could electronically cross-reference the referendum database against the "statewide voter registration list" contained in Washington's "statewide voter registration database," to ensure that each referendum signer meets Washington's residency and voter registration requirements. Doing so presumably would drastically reduce or eliminate possible errors or mistakes that Washington argues the secretary might make since it would allow the secretary to verify virtually all of the signatures instead of the mere "3 to 5%" he "ordinarily checks."

An electronic referendum database would also enable the secretary to determine whether multiple entries correspond to a single registered voter, thereby detecting whether a voter had signed the petition more than once. In addition, the database would protect victims of "forgery" or "'bait and switch' fraud." In Washington, "a unique identifier is assigned to each legally registered voter in the state." Washington could create a Web site, linked to the electronic referendum database, where a voter concerned that his name had been fraudulently signed could conduct a search using his unique identifier to ensure that his name was absent from the database—without requiring disclosure of the names and addresses of all the voluntary, legitimate signers.

Washington admits that creating this sort of electronic referendum database "could be done." Implementing such a system would not place a heavy burden on Washington; "the Secretary of State's staff" already uses an "electronic voter registration database" in its "verification process."

In *McIntyre v. Ohio Elections Comm'n*, the Court held that an Ohio law prohibiting anonymous political pamphleting violated the First Amendment.

One of the interests Ohio had invoked to justify that law was identical to Washington's here: the "interest in providing the electorate with relevant information." The Court called that interest "plainly insufficient to support the constitutionality of [Ohio's] disclosure requirement." "The simple interest in providing voters with additional relevant information does not justify a state requirement that a writer make statements or disclosures she would otherwise omit." "Don't underestimate the common man," we advised.

The historical evidence shows that the referendum and initiative process first gained popularity as a means of "provid[ing] an occasional safety valve for interests that failed to get a fair hearing in the legislatures." Unsurprisingly, such interests tended to be controversial by nature. Early examples include "the single tax, prohibition, women's suffrage, prolabor legislation, and the graduated income tax." And proponents of initiative measures tended to include politically marginalized groups such as the "Farmer's Alliance" in rural states; "[t]housands of labor federations, notably the miners"; and "the Women's Suffrage Association," which "saw the initiative and referendum as a possible new means to overcome" repeated failed attempts in state legislatures to secure for women the right to vote.

The difficulty in predicting which referendum measures will prove controversial—combined with Washington's default position that signed referendum petitions will be disclosed on-demand, thereby allowing anyone to place this information on the Internet for broad dissemination—raises the significant probability that today's decision will "inhibit the exercise of legitimate First Amendment activity" with respect to referendum and initiative petitions.

This chill in protected First Amendment activity harms others besides the dissuaded signer. We have already expressed deep skepticism about restrictions that "mak[e] it less likely that" a referendum "will garner the number of signatures necessary to place the matter on the ballot, thus limiting [the] ability to make the matter the focus of statewide discussion." Such restrictions "inevitabl[y] . . . reduc[e] the total quantum of speech on a public issue." The very public that the PRA is supposed to serve is thus harmed by the way Washington implements that statute here.

The question before us is whether all signers of all referendum petitions must resort to "substantial litigation over an extended time" to prevent Washington from trenching on their protected First Amendment rights by subjecting their referendum-petition signatures to on-demand public disclosure. In my view, they need not.

Justice Thomas's opinion is two-dimensional. In its first dimension, the First Amendment right to privacy in one's expressive beliefs and associations applies fully to the Washington disclosure law. That right guarantees that people can keep their political and associational beliefs private as an end in itself. This is what the *McIntyre* anonymous speech case said and meant. The scope of the right's application is universal, applying not only to referenda and signatures but also to votes in elections, caucuses, political or public leafleting, and so on. The state cannot condition the right to anonymity on only the risk of physical or psychic fear like intimidation and threats, because those harms are not directly related to the harm implicit in the First Amendment right, which is loss of an individual's right to keep beliefs and expressive associations private. McIntyre did not have to justify her anonymity on the leaflet by proving some threat to her safety. Indeed, her anonymity was little more than a mistake, as she intended to provide identifying information but it was inadvertently left off some of the fliers. Like McIntyre, the petition signers should not have to justify their anonymity either. This is because the denial of anonymity or privacy is itself sufficient harm to violate the First Amendment, which guarantees it.

The second dimension of Justice Thomas's opinion is that, *assuming* the state can justify its abridgement of the right of anonymity and privacy of expressive associations and beliefs, Washington's fraud-and-mistake justification doesn't even come close to the mark. There is little evidence that universal disclosure helps to ferret out fraud or mistake, and there is ample reason to believe that if Washington does, indeed, need help, it can obtain it by using additional or alternative technological means to uncover it without public disclosure. The constitutional requirement that the state's means (public disclosure) be narrowly tailored to its ends (fraud, etc.) and least restrictive of the competing First Amendment right to anonymity—in other words, the strict scrutiny test ordinarily applied to restrictions on speech rights—makes the invalidation of Washington's disclosure law inevitable.

Justice Thomas then says that even if risk of intimidation or threats of harm were needed to override the disclosure requirement, as Bopp argued without serious objection by the state, the obstacles to proof of the standards of risk required would render the exception a nullity, when in fact such apprehensions by signers in the internet age will always be present. And the resulting inhibition of voting or signing casts a costly chill over the democratic process.

Finally, on the question of whether the names of voters or petition signers or the authors of leaflets are necessary information upon which the judgment of others may be made—the public-information justification Washington offered—Justice Thomas said the purpose is facially invalid. As to the need for people to know and judge based on authorship, he said, quoting the *McIntyre* opinion, "Don't underestimate the common man."

For Justice Thomas, laws requiring disclosure of identity of the voter and his or her vote in the political setting are virtually all unconstitutional. For Justice Scalia they are virtually all constitutional. Justice Thomas was the only Justice who tried to give substantive definition to the First Amendment right of expressive association. Justice Scalia didn't even try, as he read the Constitution as imposing no free-speech-based restriction on open or secret voting. Theirs are the most (perhaps the only) open and honest, principled, and clear constitutional opinions in the case.

The rest are mush.

Reflections on the *Doe* Opinion

So what can be said more generally about the *Doe* case? The first and most important thing is that the Supreme Court has opened the door to application of the First Amendment in the voting setting, a prospect that Justice Scalia predicts will end in a prolonged course of constitutional decision making by the Court, without the guidance of underlying principle and with a complex and messy conclusion that can only be described, not justified.

Second, the justices' dramatic divisions on the practical and fundamental levels are likely to persist. It is possible, however, that when the Court takes on the next case (as it now must given its indecision in *Doe*), the justices will try to extricate themselves by limiting *Doe's* First Amendment holding only to referenda petition signatures and no more—or even more narrowly to referenda petition signatures under laws that suspend an existing law immediately if the referendum is successful. Clean up the mess, limit the damage, and get on to other matters. But the fact that Chief Justice Roberts couldn't cobble together enough votes to do that in *Doe* doesn't bode well for such an exit, expedient and unprincipled as it would likely be.

Third, there are surely divisions among the justices on the precise meaning of the right to expressive association and on the scope of its application. We didn't see the divisions in *Doe* because, frankly (and surprisingly), everyone chose to be silent, except of course Justices Scalia (overrule *McIntyre*) and Thomas (privacy in beliefs and associations) who had nothing to lose. But unless the Court forgoes principle and effects an escape, those constitutional divisions will, and must, emerge. Is the secret ballot in elections now a constitutional requirement? Can voting in elections (federal and state or one or the other) be constitutionally explained as a special case to which First Amendment rights don't apply?

Fourth, might the Court try in the future to rest its decision on the proposition, mentioned in more than a few of the opinions, that disclosure of identity and political belief is different from a regulation of speech, for it never limits speech directly? On this question there may be an answer, for no matter how rhetorically attractive the proposition may be, the Court from the formative years of its modern First Amendment jurisprudence has treated disclosures, alone, as classic instances of the restriction and inhibition of speech freedom under the First Amendment. A lot of cases and doctrine, in other words, would have to be overruled or undermined to install disclosure as a benign phenomenon. Only Justice Scalia (Home of the Brave) would find that prospect thinkable.

Fifth, if disclosure is considered a First Amendment problem, what are the implications of that conclusion on the very generous use of government-required disclosure in the campaign-finance-and-reform setting? What if we take the First Amendment right of anonymity or the First Amendment right of expressive association seriously in the campaign-finance setting? It is likely that "disclosure" will take more than one strong hit. Can categorical campaign finance and contribution disclosure laws be justified? Can corporations, now full First Amendment speakers under the *Citizens United* decision, claim anonymity in their expressive associations? That case is already on its way to the Supreme Court. Will all of these questions become constitutional questions under the First Amendment?

The *Doe* decision breeds confusion. Perhaps that's a price that must be paid for getting five justices to join an opinion. Yet one might wonder, in retrospect, whether Justice Scalia's escape from the First Amendment's grasp would have been preferable. As he said to Bopp in oral argument, "You are asking us to enter into a whole new field where we have never gone before."

Voting as Free Speech in *Doe*

It is worth stepping back at this point to consider two questions. The first is the fundamental question left open: What is the substance and constitutional basis of the First Amendment right and the status of voting in relation to it? The second question is equally important and equally untouched in the opinions: what are the practical consequences that would flow from a substantial First Amendment right to expressive association grounded in privacy, or a right to anonymity in one's own speech independent of expressive privacy—for voting, caucuses, town meetings, faculty hiring and tenure decisions, public disclosure requirements in election laws, and so forth?

The first question is the precise meaning of the First Amendment right invoked in *Doe*. The oral argument and the opinions in the *Doe* case contain three possible meanings of the speech right that is implicit in the act of signing a referendum petition: (1) freedom from intimidation and harm related to expressive acts like signing petitions and voting; (2) signing as a form of expression and therefore classic free speech; and (3) freedom of expressive association (for example, through membership in expressive groups whose ideas the person shares, such as a church, the NRA, or the ACLU) and a correlative right to privacy about one's association with the group.

Freedom from Harm

The first right, on which Bopp primarily based his oral argument, and which McKenna implicitly accepted, can be dispensed with quickly. The right has no theoretical foundation in freedom of speech or association but instead rests on private reactions to a person's speech or conduct that involves no government action at all, and could be as easily framed as private interference with the right to vote, to play music, or even to rake one's yard. To the extent such a right is connected to private retaliation for one's speech, the lack of government involvement in it (other than failing to prevent it, which is a problem with all crime) makes its denomination as a constitutional right against state action (to which the First Amendment is limited, as are virtually all of the constitutional rights contained in the Bill of Rights) awkward, to say the least. Finally, to the extent that the freedom from harm is claimed to be an aspect of one of the other two forms of free speech rights discussed below, the harm interest can't justify a heavy presumption in favor of disclosure, as it is but one harm that may flow from denial of the free speech right, and not the most important one. Instead, if the free speech right is freedom from state disclosure of expressive association, which protects the person's privacy or anonymity, the principle harm will be the invasion of privacy of one's beliefs and associations. If the right is a straightforward right to speak, the harm will be denial of one's right to speak anonymously. If the speaker in these senses is inhibited in speaking, that itself is a serious harm. If the speaker is threatened or harmed physically by others, just as if the person is denied credit, for example, that may be a harm but it is secondary in nature and extrinsic to the core values protected by the free speech right itself. Such extrinsic harms cannot be characterized as the right itself, which Bopp and

McKenna tried to do. Indeed, it is this very misunderstanding that led to the apparent incoherence of the oral argument.

Voting as a Speech Act

So the forms of the free speech right in *Doe* are, at base, two. The first is the right to speak and the correlative right to speak anonymously, which the state's public disclosure of the names and addresses of signatories directly violated, and thus could only be justified under strict scrutiny. The principal harm is from denial of anonymity (a right that may apply to signatures, though we don't know from the Court's opinion whether it should or does), and the consequences that flow directly from disclosure, like future inhibition of people's right to associate, or inhibition of potential signatories' or voters' willingness to participate in the referendum or election process, thus subverting the process itself. A general disclosure requirement could not satisfy strict scrutiny in the face of such a harm—at least in the absence of giving people an opportunity to keep their signature publicly anonymous.

The right to speak anonymously is of recent vintage, though it has long-standing historical roots extending, for example, to the Federalist Papers, essays written anonymously that debated the provisions of the Constitution and their meaning and value during the process of ratification by the states. As a First Amendment anonymous speech right, however, it wasn't fully recognized, explained, and enforced until the *McIntyre* decision in 1995, and even then its precise contours were not defined.

But the right to anonymous speech, applied to signatures on petitions or votes in an election, presents serious problems. Textually, the right is hard to square with the act of voting (including signing petitions) because voting and the circumstances surrounding it are broadly lodged in state government by the Constitution. It would be peculiar to see the First Amendment as cutting such a deep swath out of that state authority without recognizing it in the parts of the Constitution that expressly vest the power in the states. And as Justice Scalia well says, the history of voting in the United States has been marked by the use of public voting mechanisms, many of which, by the way, are still in use today. A strong right of anonymity in voting or signing petitions would condemn the past and upset the current situations in which open voting is still used (town meetings, caucuses, and so forth).

The only way to escape these problems in the *Doe* case—other than just declaring the right and to hell with the consequences—would be to distinguish referendum petition signing from everything else, like voting, caucusing, faculty tenure decisions, communications with government, and their like. But it is hard to see how such a distinction could be explained and justified by constitutional reasoning (like distinguishing the expressive nature of referendum signing from voting in public; or the greater constitutional importance of referenda as opposed to voting, neither of which seem to make constitutional sense). Maybe someone can draw a persuasive distinction, but for the moment I'm coming up empty handed.

Voting as an Act of Expressive Association

The upshot of this is that the right to speak anonymously is a possible, but highly problematic, form for the right at stake in the *Doe* case. If I am right about that, then the remaining definition of the First Amendment right in the *Doe* case is the right freely to associate in expressive groups or with like-minded persons and its correlative protection of individual privacy in such associations.

The right to privacy in expressive associations presents many of the same textual difficulties as did the right to anonymity in speech. Yet the right is more limited and thus may be more easily seen as existing within the values underlying the First Amendment, even though it lay dormant for these many years. From the beginning the First Amendment was intended to protect individuals speaking through groups, like the Sons of Liberty and others Justice Scalia discussed in his concurring opinion in the *Citizens United* case, covered in chapter 1. The ability to form and speak through such groups was well established at the time of the Bill of Rights, and the need for such organized expression of a message was obvious, given the limited technologies and attendant difficulties of communication in a rural and frontier country. Tocqueville remarked on Americans' "skill of association" that served a vital role in the American democracy. Indeed, he said that "if [men living in democratic countries] failed to acquire the practice of association in their day-to-day lives, civilization itself would be in danger." Protection of such associations was therefore important, and the First Amendment can be easily read to include such protection.

The difficulty with such a reading as applied in the referendum and voting contexts, however, is the long history of public petitioning and voting, which flies in the face of an expansive expressive association right, as that in *Doe*. Even here, though, we can see the general practice in nineteenth century petitioning before Congress (the right of petition was then very central to checking and seeking assistance from government), where, it appears, the names of *members* of petitioning groups were not usually provided, and though I am no expert on the history of petitioning, it seems likely that such names were not required by Congress.

But how could this be squared with the public voting practices of the time? The answer might lie in the meaning of "associations." Voting was public, but public voting did not entail any disclosure of expressive or ideological groups with which the voter associated. To be sure, a vote for a federalist candidate, or today a Democrat, revealed political beliefs, but party preferences, without more, need not be considered expressive associations, and the voter need not, in today's terms, reveal a membership in the Federalist Society or the NRA or the Democratic Central Committee. Moreover, being a Republican, say, didn't and doesn't reveal very much about one's beliefs and preferences on the range of political views.

This reading can be squared with the public voting practices and with open voting in all kinds of situations. It implies a fairly narrow definition of "associations" to which the First Amendment extends: not just the revealing of preferences or even of personal thoughts and beliefs; not associations in the word's most general sense, but instead affiliations through membership or the like in publicly active expressive groups of like-minded individuals. These are the very kinds of affiliations that the Supreme Court has protected in prior cases (the NAACP and not the Jaycees), and this narrower view is at one with the liberty-based purposes of the amendment and the practices at the time of ratification. A strict textualist—just speech and nothing else—would have difficulties, but in the evocative and open-ended setting of the Bill of Rights guarantees there aren't many strict textualists because the language of the Constitution is too (purposefully or inescapably) ambiguous. What is freedom, or liberty, or equality, to give just a few examples in addition to "speech"? For those who seek original intent of the framers and general pubic understandings at the time of ratification, like Justice Scalia, the narrow meaning of expressive association may not be a stretch. This is not to say that contrary views aren't possible, for they are, but at least the Court's extra-textual interpretation of the First Amendment isn't simply a reading of personal political or philosophical preferences into the Constitution.

Yet one big problem remains, and it is seen in the *Doe* case. There the state's public disclosure of signatories and addresses required no disclosure of affiliation with expressive, ideological groups like, hypothetically, a "preserve the sanctity of marriage" club, or the "gay marriage is a sin" group. The state simply required disclosure of a "vote." So how does the disclosure violate the narrower right of expressive associational privacy that requires more than a vote? There may be an answer, but I frankly admit that it isn't all that clear or even persuasive. The answer could be that, in referendum campaigns and more specifically in deeply ideological and hard fought, controversial referendum campaigns, the disclosure of a signature on a petition favoring one side of the controversy is the equivalent of a disclosure of expressive group affiliation. Literally speaking, of course, it is not that, but perhaps indulging a contrary assumption is an important means of preserving those associations for those who have them, especially in light of the fact that others, knowing of the signature, may attribute such associations to the signatory whether they exist or not.

As a matter of policy this is a reasonable explanation, or at least a less radical one than a right of anonymous speech or an expansive view of association. But as the first Justice Marshall reminded us (in the course of an interpretive stretch of his own in *McCulloch v. Maryland*), it is a *constitution* that we are interpreting. Good policy is not enough. Thus, while it is possible to interpret the First Amendment right to include public distribution of the *Doe* signatures and addresses, and indeed while the need to protect their anonymity may be more pressing in today's internet culture than in the late eighteenth century, the justices making such an interpretation of the freedom of speech clause can't hide in the text or history. They must instead engage in some measure of principled creativity to bring the Constitution up to date—or, more benignly, to square its purposes with the evolved values and culture in which they must be applied today. But if the unelected branch is to justify its final power to so interpret and apply the Constitution, it simply must accompany its decision with open, frank, and full constitutional reasoning that reveals the basis for its extrapolitical, independent claim to power in an otherwise democratic, representative nation.

Consequences of the *Doe* Decision

A final question that needs to be addressed involves the practical consequences of the *Doe* decision and its First Amendment principle. I have posited a narrow constitutional approach that could avoid many of the consequences, and certainly the consequences for voting in elections, the regulations surrounding which would remain with the states and their democratic political processes. The more general reading of the case, which I have suggested would not easily be squared with the text and history of the First Amendment, would of course have broad consequences in voting contexts where open voting remains the rule, and in broader government settings where secret voting would have to become the rule and communications with government could be secret as well. Those consequences are clear enough for our purposes.

But the fate of disavowal (I'm not speaking for candidate X, and so on) and disclosure (X gave $y to candidate Z, or spent $y on a political ad or spot) requirements are more uncertain. A narrow view of expressive associations—an exemption, perhaps, for disclosure of members in ideological groups; and otherwise a disclosure only of name, authorship, and amount and type of contribution or expenditure—might avoid most problems. Such qualified rules for disclosure could avoid the very large problem looming on the horizon, which is disclosure of corporate political expenditures, including endorsements. With the exception of our illustrative group of expressive organizations in corporate form—the NAACP, NRA, ACLU, and the like—*business* corporations don't easily fit the traditional definition of ideological expressive organizations. To be sure, most of them are committed to capitalism, but only in the sense that we are all committed to our own set of "isms," like consumerism, and that's not enough to transform the shareholder-investor of Microsoft from one interested in "profitism," whatever the surrounding political and ideological climate, to an affiliation with an organization whose ideological beliefs and expressive actions are but a product of the beliefs of like-minded speakers expressing, through the corporation, individual "speech" protected by the First Amendment. A broader view of expressive association, however, would make mincemeat of disclosure laws.

So we can say, by way of conclusion on the *Doe* case, that the oral argument was disappointing, the opinions were unsatisfying and (with but a few exceptions) unacceptable, the free speech principle was unelucidated but inescapably broad, and the Court's conclusion so ambiguous that we were forced to feel great sympathy for the district court judge who would inherit the case on remand. But the Court's studied ambiguity makes it just possible, though not certain at present, that in the wake of the decision the First Amendment freedom of speech has, perhaps inadvertently, been left as an undiminished, principled, and coherent whole—in other words, that free speech doesn't have much to do, really, with voting.

Or maybe not. . . .

Voting and Free Speech

This leaves us with the central question with which we began: can the First Amendment to the Constitution be interpreted to include voting as an act of free speech? And assuming that the Court has so concluded despite the interpretive problems, why should we worry, since more First Amendment protection—more free speech—is better than less?

The first thing to be said is that it is hard to conclude that voting is a special, one-of-a-kind act of free speech *because* of its importance in the Constitution. The Constitution, it will be recalled, hardly mentions voting by citizens in elections. The protections for voting later introduced in the Constitution after the Civil War confer no freestanding right to vote but rather protect against the unequal distribution of voting among citizens based on race or gender or other unjustifiable grounds. While the Supreme Court dubs the right to vote as a fundamental right, this means only that if the vote is given in a particular setting, it must be given equally to all. I can't claim, for example, that the appointment rather than election of major state or federal officers denies me any freestanding right to vote, as long as no one is permitted to vote.

In light of this, it is hard to imagine how the First Amendment could protect what the Constitution otherwise does not. That is, it is hard to make the argument that voting itself, as a special and unique case, is protected as an act of speech because of its—*and only its*—seminal role in the constitutional order.

The second point is, then, that voting, like petition signing, must qualify as an act of speech because the act is but one of many other such acts that are expressive and thus qualify for First Amendment speech protection: like burning a flag, or camping in protest on the National Mall in Washington, D.C. But such acts aren't necessarily "expressive" in a way that triggers free-speech protection. If I burn a flag to start my charcoal fire, having no paper at hand, the act of burning is not one of free speech—at least unless it is attended with other expressive statements or gestures and carries a message to others. The same is true of camping on the National Mall.

If voting is to be considered expressive because of the message it communicates to others, *it is the message that counts*. And what is the message of the act of casting a secret ballot? Other than the message that "I am voting now," there isn't any message expressed, and "I am voting now" isn't really any different from the message to anyone watching that "I am starting my charcoal fire with a flag." Voting, it seems, is a uniquely noncommunicative act. One might reach the same conclusion with signing one's name on a referendum petition, though the act of signing might make a political preference on the referendum likely, and thus expressed. But to whom? To the person seeking the petition, to any watchers, to the state officials who receive and verify the petitions? Maybe, but it's a thin reed, as the signer would likely disclaim any intention to voice their preferences and beliefs to these people through the act of signing.

In *Doe*, of course, the problem was the state's disclosure of the signatories to the public. But the Court's opinion explaining the signature as an act of speech focused on the signing, not the disclosure. And this is as it should be. By disclosing the signatories to the public, the State of Washington might convert a nonexpressive act of signing into an expressive one, but that's the state's doing, not the signer's. The interest in expressive association might well be triggered by the state's disclosure, protecting the signers (or voters) from the consequences of the state's act, but this would not be tied in any way to whether the act of signing or voting, when done, was expressive for purposes of the First Amendment.

Ironically, it could be said without great difficulty that the act of voting (or signing) was clearly an act of expression in the old days when voting was not secret, and when people had to raise their hands in public or come forward to vote for a candidate with their fellow citizens present and the slate of candidates watching. But as Justice Scalia reminds us, the act of public voting was then considered an act of public duty and courage *because it was expressive*, and allowing exceptions for those too timid to vote in public in the name of freedom of speech would have been flatly inconsistent with the act of voting itself. Indeed, this history is not only inconsistent with the view that voting is free speech, but it is also inconsistent with the view that affiliations disclosed through a vote would conflict with the privacy of one's expressive associations.

There are many mute acts in which we engage that could, by the Court's apparent reasoning in *Doe*, be considered expressive and thus protected by the free-speech guarantee. Kicking my dog. Spitting on the sidewalk. Signing my name on an application for a driver's license. Walking out of a room. Some might be intended as expressive. Some might not, but may still be seen by others as expressive. But despite intention and perception, these acts alone are not considered speech acts protected by the First Amendment. If I pass a beggar on the sidewalk asking for a dime, I may interpret his acts as a metaphor for the uncaring society in which we live, but that doesn't make his act of holding out the cup an exercise of free speech any more than if he means the metaphor but no one sees it. Is signing a credit card slip expressive—say of consent to or agreement with the free enterprise system, or capitalism?

Chief Justice Roberts declares in his opinion that "[a]n individual expresses a view on a political matter when he signs a petition under Washington's referendum procedure. In most cases, the individual's signature will express the view that the law subject to the petition should be overturned. Even if the signer is agnostic as to the merits of the underlying law, his signature still expresses the political view that the question should be considered "'by the whole electorate.' In either case, the expression of a political view implicated a First Amendment right." That's it. That's his full explanation for why the act of signing is expressing a view for purposes of the First Amendment. It's not a matter of the signer's intention (for he or she probably has none). It's not that the act of signing communicates a message to the public. It just is.

Surely the chief justice means more than he said. Perhaps he couldn't say it for fear of losing votes for the opinion. So we only know the conclusion, not the reason. If in fact there is nothing more to it, then the First Amendment risks gobbling up, Pac-Man like, the whole of human conduct and all things uttered by anyone, any time, any place. Kicking my dog, for example. Or, more to the point, the act of making a campaign contribution to a candidate, which the Court said many years ago isn't an act of free speech, it's just an act of giving money to someone else who decides on what to say and who does all the speaking for political campaign purposes. How can signing the check for a campaign contribution be distinguished from signing a referendum petition? It can't. And voting, an act of expressing a preference on a ballot though no one will ever see it, can't either. Voting is every bit as expressive as signing a petition, and it's less ambiguous about the choice made.

Signing a petition or casting a ballot are difficult to square with the First Amendment speech guarantee. To find them adequately expressive and thus a gloss on the Constitution's silence requires an interpretive act of considerable creativity. Textualism, original intent, purpose, and original understanding just won't do the job. For an open-ended interpreter of the text who is not bound by its plain meaning and history, the conclusion that signing and voting are protected by the First Amendment as expressive acts might be justified by the historical and cultural shift toward the secret ballot and the values that change reflects. Or it may be based on today's technology, which allows immediate and universal and permanent distribution of the signer's or voter's act, and so must be protected in a new way to prevent technology from undermining the very democratic process the nation has chosen under the Constitution. But there is none of this kind of explanation in the Chief Justice's opinion for the Court; Justice Thomas is alone in expressing such concern.

Too Much Free Speech?

Finally, we should ask, even in the absence of a clear constitutional reason or principle, whether we should care about the Court's decision in *Doe* and its logical application to voting (by secret ballot, by caucus, by town meeting). The result of the *Doe* opinion is an expansion of freedom achieved through an expansion of the meaning of "speech" under the First Amendment. More speech is better than less speech, right?

Not necessarily. In the setting of the *Doe* case, two undesirable results might flow from the expansion of the First Amendment's reach. The first is that the enlargement of "speech" cannot be limited to signing or voting. Depending on the reasoning that supports the expansion (which we do not know), much other activity might also fall within the grasp of "speech" newly defined, and some of it might be downright unacceptable or might place limits on desirable government regulation that serves important democratic aims. If, to give one example, campaign contributions or expenditures on behalf of candidates (electioneering, in the *Citizens United* case) are acts of free speech, requirements that such acts be disclosed publicly and that such independent expenditures identify those who support a message (corporation or not) would at best be crippled. Ultimately, the old saw that "disclosure" doesn't affect speech won't hold.

Another example might be committing *acts* (like voting?) of racial harassment or intimidation, which under general law today are considered conduct that can be restricted independently of and unaffected by the expressive meaning of the act. The reason is practical: much conduct, such as murder, intimidation, and fraud, would be much harder to regulate and punish if the First Amendment became a hurdle in every case. In the absence of speech the government has broad and largely unrestricted authority to regulate conduct (like spitting in public or smoking). After *Citizens United* it is difficult to make the argument that money (used to buy time for speech) is not itself speech, but conduct entitled, at best, to a lesser order of protection under the First Amendment. The claim that money is separate from resulting speech was rejected, though perhaps a bit too casually, in *Buckley*, the first major campaign-finance decision by the Court. But with the Court seeming to treat the act of signing or voting as speech in *Doe*, the likelihood of the Court revisiting the "money is speech" conclusion is slim, as it would be hard to square with the *Doe* case.

The second problem that may result from an expansion of speech is the watering-down of the protection afforded speech. With a potentially vast category of speech added to the First Amendment, practicality if nothing else will tend to weaken the historically very tight limits on government restriction of speech. Notably, we see this very thing happening in the *Doe* case, where the state's justification for public disclosure of signers' names was the prevention of fraud and mistake. The Court purported to apply "strict scrutiny" under the First Amendment to the disclosure law—requiring a compelling state interest with the speech restriction narrowly tailored to that interest and no more restrictive on speech than absolutely necessary. But as we have noticed previously, the test actually applied in *Doe* under the name of strict scrutiny can only be described as loose and deferential scrutiny. The state's fraud interest was compelling in theory but weak in fact, as the incidence of fraud in other referendum petitions was extremely low and hardly justified the blunt-edged instrument of public disclosure. The alternative state interest in public information and civic engagement was, most likely, facially invalid under the First Amendment, and in any event it was so laughable that the Court didn't even discuss it. Finally, as Justice Thomas so effectively pointed out in his dissent, the disclosure of signatories was unlikely to be of help in uncovering fraud, and many other steps short of disclosure were available to the state and probably much more effective against fraud. Yet the state had not used any of them. This hardly fits the narrow tailoring and least restrictive wings of the strict scrutiny rule. It wouldn't even satisfy a test of reasonableness, seriously applied.

It appears, instead, that Chief Justice Roberts watered down the elements of strict scrutiny in order to accommodate the problems that a tough constitutional test would have produced. Notably, the same thing appears to have been done in *Citizens United*, where the Court extended full First Amendment rights to all corporations and then, in what can only be described as brazen dicta, concluded that the disclosure requirements applicable to all electioneering communications were perfectly constitutional, under the theory that disclosure does not prevent or restrict speech in any constitutionally relevant way. Tell that to Margaret McIntyre or to the members of the NAACP in mid-twentieth-century Alabama or to the people who feared intimidation or harm or loss of privacy if their petition signature was disclosed in Washington.

It can't be said that free speech is a free good, the more the better. Sometimes this may be true. Other times it won't be true. It depends, and therefore it is incumbent on all of us to ask and answer the question.

In this, too, the Court failed us.

■ ■ ■

Meanwhile, back in Washington the *Doe* case continued. Disclosure of the signatories was enjoined until a trial on the "as applied" issue—whether in fact there was a reasonable apprehension of harm to signators warranting nondisclosure of the names under the First Amendment.

Trial was set for September 2011.

For all practical purposes the Does won.

V

Is There Such a Thing as Too Much Free Speech?

The question we have been examining in this book is limited but fundamental: how should the Supreme Court's recent definitional expansions of the meaning and scope of "speech" protected by the First Amendment be judged? In the cases we have reviewed, the constitutional term "speech" has been expanded to include speech by corporations, speech by government, voting and petitioning, and speech "out of thin air." These decisions are not just extensions of the freedom enjoyed by speech. They are extensions—indeed very substantial ones—of the definitional range of the free speech guarantee itself.

Over the long history of the First Amendment "freedom of speech" has been variously understood by the Court to mean very little—initially a prohibition on prior restraints on speech only—and to mean a great deal—speech includes conduct that is expressive, for example, because it has an actor/speaker who intends to communicate a message understood by an audience. The sparse and open-ended words of the Constitution, "Congress shall make no law . . . abridging the freedom of speech," provide few guideposts for the Supreme Court.

The freedom of speech guarantee is textually and historically ambiguous. This is partly because of its terseness and partly because of the paucity of helpful historical material with which to divine its intended meaning or, even, its fundamental purpose(s). More basically, though, the open-endedness of the speech guarantee is a necessity, for its meaning, scope, and application must change with the changing social, economic, political, technological, and cultural landscape. The free-speech guarantee is, perhaps uniquely among the constitutional guarantees, a social guarantee that must always change faces as it reflects changing social conditions. It was born in a largely oral and infant-print environment. There were few printing presses, and they were dependent on laborious hand setting and printing. There were few printed images, much less photography and video. No radio. No television. The culture was rural and communication over large distances was difficult, not instantaneous and cheap, as today. And so on.

The speech guarantee therefore *must* change over time, just as the meaning of communication and the instruments it relies upon will change. And with the constitutional guarantee of freedom of speech the Supreme Court will be the creative instrument of change. The creativity the Court brings to the question, however, must be bounded by the text and the purposes of freedom of speech, as well as the methods by which a *judicial* exercise of power must be limited.

As a country and a culture we have an abiding faith in the power of speech and a concern for its proper role in the scheme of things. But our personal and political preferences cannot be the measure of whether in a particular instance speech freedom has gone too far. The question of the meaning of "speech," after all, is a *constitutional* one, and, for better or worse, it has been almost exclusively lodged in the hands of the justices of the Supreme Court. So we must look to the Constitution's meaning and to the power wielded by the Supreme Court to answer the "too much" question.

Have the methods of interpretation and creative law making been true to the Court's assigned function in the Constitution? Have the Court's treatments of the text, its history and meaning, been correct? Have the purposes assigned to the terse "freedom of speech" been adequate and appropriate? Have the Court's decisions been true to the "judicial" quality of its constitutional power? Have the consequences of its decisions, unintended and intended, been acceptable and appropriately limited? Is the Court acting as a court, abstaining from power where and when it cannot use it well?

As Alexander Bickel, perhaps the greatest constitutional scholar of the past century, said:

> [T]he Court should not tell itself or the world that it draws decisions from a text that is incapable of yielding them. That obscures the actual process of decision, for the country, and for the judges themselves, if they fall in with the illusion. And it is a menace, to the Court and to the country. . . . [The illusion] gives them a great sense of freedom, it induces a happy activism without afterthought and sometimes even without forethought; in short, it lightens the load of personal and institutional responsibility. But behind the screen of the illusion, thus embraced, will operate—and operate less deliberately than they should—the judge's own convictions. These convictions will be decisive, even after the illusion has engulfed him; it is to these that he will have fitted his reading of "the literal meaning of the text." . . . And so judges fear for the survival of passionately held presuppositions of their own and wish to preserve them for the ages in the deathless body of the Constitution. But the Constitution is merely words—deathless words, but words. And the future will not be ruled; it can only possibly be persuaded.[1]

A partial response to Bickel's fear of unbridled judicial power was provided by Herbert Wechsler of Harvard:

> "The main constituent of the judicial process is that it must be genuinely principled, resting with respect to every step that is involved in reaching judgment on analysis and reasons quite transcending the immediate result that is achieved . . . [;] on grounds of adequate neutrality and generality, tested not only by the instant application but by others that the principles imply."[2]

Our concluding assessment of the Court's work will, then, reflect the obligations owed to us, as citizens, by the Supreme Court as it carries out its constitutional duty. It is, after all, a *constitution* that the Court is *interpreting*. The main criteria we will look to in our inquiry will be:

1. The methodology of decision, including the consistency with which the justices apply approaches to ascertaining constitutional meaning (such as textualism, original intent, and interpretivism), and the Court's commitment to open, analytical, principled reason;
2. The judicial power and capacity to decide the case;
3. The need and justification for constitutional intervention by the Court;
4. The consequences of a decision.

Judicial Methodology

The methodology employed by the Supreme Court is at once the most important and the most elusive criterion by which the Court's performance must be measured. We have special expectations about the exercise of judicial power, as distinguished from executive or legislative power. This is in large part because its constitutional name—judicial power—connotes a distinct scope of power and a distinct form of its exercise. Courts decide cases; they do not legislate or administer. They act, generally, after the fact, rendering judgment in hindsight on the actions—laws, treaties, wars, law enforcement actions—of others. They are not elected and they are protected from the political process by life tenure. Courts must, therefore, operate by reason based in the law and traditions of a society, and the reasoning must be open, complete, intellectually honest, and it must rest on principled grounds that transcend the narrow ambit of a case—grounds that reflect more broadly applicable law and practice and serve as a basis for future conduct by those similarly situated. This is what lawyers mean when they talk about precedent and the need to conform decisions to the past or, if not, to openly explain the grounds that justify departing from it.

In matters of speech freedom and its meaning and range, the Supreme Court plays a peculiarly sensitive constitutional role. Decisions about the meaning of "abridge," "freedom," and "speech" are ultimately the Court's responsibility. And given the sparseness of text and the lack of definitive historical meaning, the Court's role is more than ordinarily creative: it must *make or create law* and the means of its enforcement. So the Court's reasoning, while constitutional, is likely also to be philosophical: what is free speech's function in our form of democratic government; what is its relation to liberty of the individual in our organized society; what role does speech play in political discourse and elections; and so on. Armed with knowledge of the structure of the Constitution and our form of government and our social order and culture, and then helped only by one spare text, "Congress shall make no law . . . abridging the freedom of speech," the Court must work its way through a subtle and complex analysis as it reaches a result in a case—say, whether burning a draft card is protected "speech"—and it must base its decision on reasoning that will have wider meaning for the law of free speech throughout time in America.

It is this obligation of creative interpretation and law-making that best explains the Court's political independence; its habits of decision; and frankly the requirement that the Justices be highly intelligent, very wise, and well educated—nonrepresentative and nondemocratic, in short. And, perhaps most important, the Court is powerless. It has no purse strings and no army. The Court depends only on respect for its decisions and confidence in its methodology to effect obedience to its law.

One final note about interpretive methodologies is in order. In general, the alternative methodologies, or approaches, to constitutional interpretation are textualism, originalism, and interpretivism. Textualism looks almost exclusively to the constitutional text—freedom of speech—and no more; if there is no answer to a case and issue forthcoming there, the Court must refrain from decision and leave the matter to the other branches or the states. Originalism looks, in varying ways and degrees, beyond the text to what otherwise uncertain textual language was intended by the framers to mean or how it was understood by the contemporaneous public. Absent a clear answer from the text and the historical intent materials, the Court must refrain from decision and leave the matter to the other branches and the states. Finally, interpretivism looks to the text and its intended meaning, but finding no answer, or an unacceptable answer in terms of current conditions (like speech by video and not just words and text), proceeds further based on later history, changing social values, changing circumstances, and the like, basing a decision on the purposes of the guarantee brought up to date through constitutive, or fundamental, tides of change.

Each of these interpretive methodologies is principled and, indeed, valid. But to judge a Supreme Court decision by the interpretive methodology used would be, in essence, to judge it by our personal and ideological preferences. We can always agree or disagree with the Court—indeed we should do so—but to address a question like "Is there too much free speech?" we must stick to matters of constitutional and judicial legitimacy, not personal preferences among otherwise justifiable choices.

We can, however, make judgments about a few aspects of interpretive methodology. First, we can ask whether the claimed methodology can be squared with the reasoning and interpretation in a case. Textualism that is truly based on current social values and circumstances just won't work, and should be loudly criticized. We can also judge a Justice's consistency in avowed methodology. If Justice Thomas claims, as he does, to be a textualist, we should be very critical of a decision he makes based on interpretivism. Justice Scalia, for example, has described himself as a "faint-hearted originalist," an admission, perhaps, that he can and will entertain an interpretivist methodology where appropriate. But we will want to know what his criteria for "appropriate" are, lest he simply decide based on his personal "Can't Helps," as Holmes described them.

So what can we say about the Court's methodology in the cases we have discussed? Quite a lot, as it turns out.

In *Citizens United* the Court, speaking through Justice Kennedy, declared that business corporations have the same First Amendment protection for their political speech as individuals do. Given the text and history of the First Amendment and the free-speech guarantee, the interpretation that corporations are fully protected "free speakers" simply must fall into the interpretivist camp—and even there it seems to be a stretch based on current public values and legal practices. There is virtually no evidence that corporations, as they existed at the time of the founding, were seen as protected speakers. To read the text—freedom of speech—as *literally* not excluding corporations in light of the clear contemporaneous history (and indeed the virtual absence at the time of private business corporations with legal identities separate from their owners') would require the staunchest and most wooden of textualists, and even Justice Thomas didn't go that far in his concurrence.

If you are with me so far, then you will understand why the *Citizens United* decision reflects a large degree of fallibility, or worse. The five Justices who made up the majority are all self-confessed conservatives when it comes to interpretive methodology. They are avowed originalists with the possible exception of the author, Justice Kennedy, who cannot be said to be consistent on his interpretivist methodology, but is instead selective on largely unarticulated grounds. And it is Kennedy who is both textualist and creative at the same time. In *Citizens United* he says that the First Amendment literally protects "speech" and corporations can emit speech (textualist); corporate speech is essential to protecting the functioning of the marketplace of ideas because it is the primary source of information about the economy in today's political system (distinctly interpretivist). One might say Kennedy has both bases covered, but the point of a methodology is that you can't pick and choose or combine them. Meanwhile, Thomas is a textualist; Roberts and Alito are originalists (judge the balls and strikes, but don't make the rules); and Scalia is at least a "faint-hearted" originalist whose concurring opinion is originalist in virtually all respects . . . except his conclusion.

The dissenting justices shouldn't be excused from inconsistency either, though in this case we know only about the opinion of Justice Stevens, whom the other justices joined fully and without separate opinions. This is, in common parlance, the liberal group, which means, methodologically, a group heavily inclined toward interpretivism and creativity in the job of construing the constitution. Yet there is a heavy dose of textualism and originalism in the Stevens opinion. But criticism of this is harder with the dissenting group, for two reasons. First, while interpretivists will go beyond text and intention when interpreting "speech," for example, they all agree that the text and original intent are always the starting point of interpretation, and often the decisive point. And Stevens does go beyond textualism and originalism to the current economic and social values of the society, which interpretivists will, of course, do. In effect, the interpretivists get the best of the interpretive deal; they needn't reject the text or original intent (except for the "isms" attached to them) when they do their job, but they can chose any or even more than one of them. This is why, of course, they are less restrained in their view of the judicial power than the textualists or originalists, who limit themselves in the very interest of restraining the exercise of judicial power.

More can be said about *Citizens United* on this front. The (methodological) conservatives in the majority appear to have wiped out any independent constitutional significance for freedom of the press, the textualist and originalist support for which is perhaps the strongest of any provision in the First Amendment. And they did so by citing as authority only the dissenting views expressed by a few justices in some earlier cases. No explanation, no principled legal reasoning to speak of, nothing really. This is the worst of all methodological judicial worlds: ignore the text and history; ignore full and open reasoning; ignore prior opinions of the Court; rely only on dissenting opinions. Such a methodology is hard to justify as an exercise of judicial power as we have described it earlier.

Finally, the opinion in *Citizens United* announced, at its end, that the decision about business corporation free speech would have no impact on the campaign finance act's avowal and disclosure requirements, all of which would be constitutional when enforced against claims of corporate free speech. There are again many methodological problems with this portion of the decision. First, apart from making a statement of the obvious—that disclosure requirements don't prohibit speech—the Court gave no reasons for its holding. Yet in a long line of free speech decisions the Supreme Court has held the opposite—that while disclosure requirements don't prohibit speech, as such, they can inhibit free speech and thus require careful First Amendment scrutiny. Second, the Court's stated conclusion is squarely inconsistent with a recent decision announcing a First Amendment right to anonymous political and campaign speech. Perhaps that case—the *McIntyre* case—was wrong or should be limited, but the Court would have none of any explanation, much less constitutional reasoning or even serious mention of the text or history of the First Amendment. Justice Scalia wrote a scathing and fully reasoned dissent in the *McIntyre* case, but again, dissents are no substitute for authority or open reasoning and explanation in constitutional terms. This all leaves a lingering suspicion—surely wrong because it would be so seriously inappropriate—that the unnecessary absolutist rulings on freedom of the press and disclosure restrictions were demanded by Justice Scalia in order to get his agreement with the Kennedy opinion. Such things lend strength to critics of the opinion and, over time, compromise the essential public trust upon which the Court relies.

We can turn next to the *Doe v. Reed* case, involving the First Amendment's protection for signatures on referendum petitions and more broadly for the act of voting in elections. The opinion was written by Chief Justice Roberts and was characteristically spare. The decision to expand the reach of the First Amendment to the act of signing petitions and, by necessary inference, voting was spare also. The spareness, unfortunately, was analytical, with the reasoning reduced essentially to the conclusion that because signing and voting were expressive acts they were protected by the First Amendment speech guarantee. But not very much protected, it seems. And not very expressive, it turns out.

For a decision that expands the reach of the First Amendment in unprecedented ways, the absence of open reasoning and thorough analysis borders on the shocking. And the likelihood that the chief justice simply couldn't say any more because to do so would mean that there could be no "Court" (five votes joining) opinion is hardly a justification for a lack of reasoning on virtually all aspects of the opinion: the extension of free speech; the test to be applied under the First Amendment; the precise basis (speech or expressive association) for the decision. As I described the decision earlier, the justices actually broke into seven little pieces, each writing their own different views separately. Sometimes such an opinion may be required, but why here? The inability to supply clear reasoning, especially in the face of Justice Scalia's remarkable dissent rejecting voting as free speech in light of the text, intention, and history of voting under the Constitution, is, if anything, a compelling reason for the Court *not to decide* the case.

Deciding the case as the Court did violates most of the methodological premises of judicial power and, thus, most of the constitutional justifications for a Court, rather than another branch, resolving the question. The opinion is neither openly and thoroughly reasoned or even clear in its holding and thus partakes of legislative power and mere judicial preference.

What, then, of the *Summum* case? There the Court was dealing with a recent but fairly well established doctrine of "government speech." The decision was not closely divided in its result. There were, however, significant differences of view expressed in the separate opinions. But the constitutional reasoning and analysis were well and openly expressed by both the majority and concurring opinions. The principled grounds for decision were openly voiced and the implications of the constitutional interpretation were acknowledged. At the most basic level the methodological demands imposed on the Court were well satisfied.

There are, however, some grounds for concern. First, the precise constitutional grounds for the government speech doctrine remain surprisingly ambiguous. Does the government's immunity from First Amendment challenge take the form of a "right" under the speech guarantee, or is the immunity more in the nature of a practically necessary but nonconstitutional rule of deference that limits the individual's First Amendment rights? This is not a small question. If the doctrine is based on a "right" to speech immunity for the government, the doctrine will take a much stronger and less flexible form and would be the first time the First Amendment was read to protect government as a speaker. Many would say that this result would be oxymoronic, as the First Amendment speech guarantee has always taken the form of a right *against government* and on behalf of the individual.

The Court seems, in other words, to be hiding the ball. But as long as the question is genuinely one of constitutional interpretation that calls for judicial power in the main, the remaining vagueness of the doctrine may be for the best. It leaves the political branches room for entering the fray and playing a role in limiting the scope of protected government expression, and it leaves the Court free to welcome that executive and legislative involvement on some aspects of a potentially broad power. The judicial branch has been required to act in order to protect the individual free speech rights as well as the expressive government action in specific cases. But that does not mean that the scope of the doctrine must be exclusively judicial business.

Finally, how should we judge the *Hurley* and *Dale* cases on the methodological scale? The two cases are distinct, to be sure, but they have in common an expansion of First Amendment speech that threatens to realign the traditional and linear speech paradigm: a speaker with a cognitive message getting through to an audience. *Hurley* displaces such a traditional speaker—GLIB with its pro-gay message—with a message formed only in the minds of the spectators of a parade, a cultural celebration without a single or even a main cognitive meaning. *Dale*, by contrast, eliminates the need for a speaker in favor of a message neither Dale nor the Scouts intended or even wanted to express. The message, instead, was a function of meaning imagined (and unwanted) by the Scouts—Gays are good scouts too—whose source is the equally imagined attribution by "hearers" of pro-gay sentiments attached out of thin air to the silence of the Scouts.

I have suggested elsewhere[3] that these cases represent the deconstruction of the speech paradigm and the constitutional self-government and exchange-of-ideas purposes behind it, and its replacement with a constitutional protection for mere artifacts of meaning, whatever their source or audience. Speech out of thin air, in short. I have also suggested that while this idea of speech is truly radical, it may serve a valuable service in the very limited setting of nonrepresentational art, or pure aesthetic "expression." But to apply this methodology of loosed meaning in the cognitive speech setting would be to open up a new and uncontainable form of speech indifferent to any author or, for that matter, any intended meaning. Yet in some respects this is the very idea the Court loosed in *Citizens United* with respect to that most cognitive of speech settings, political speech. It was done by the Court's justification for business corporation speech because, and only because, it is "speech" and is therefore protected by the First Amendment without regard to—and perhaps without—any speaker. The only limit, Justice Scalia says in his concurring opinion, is that the rationale doesn't extend to trees or polar bears (whatever that means).

It is this common denominator of the cases—that the First Amendment protects the *fact* alone (or mere artifact) of speech that looses meaning—that we must examine in order to determine if the Court's dramatic expansion of the meaning of speech protected by the First Amendment is warranted as an act of judicial power—if, in short, it is "too much free speech."

In the purely aesthetic and artistic setting—nonrepresentational art like Pollock's *Mural*, or music, for example—the *Hurley* decision is perfectly justified as a creative but soundly reasoned instance of constitutional interpretation of the meaning of the term "speech." Justice Souter, who wrote the opinion, wrote a remarkable and fully reasoned justification for viewing aesthetic and artistic expression as speech that should be protected under the First Amendment. While there is little evidence that art was to be protected by the guarantee at the time of ratification—and indeed what art there was at that time could hardly be described as nonrepresentational in the sense of a Pollock painting—the text of the speech guarantee is done no injustice by the inclusion of such expression, and the history of changes in art and the evolving importance of artistic speech in America over two centuries justify Souter's interpretivist conclusion. The conclusion is not, of course, free from doubt; indeed my colleague Mark Tushnet of Harvard has expressed sound reservations about it.[4] Moreover, Souter's application of the genre of aesthetic and artistic speech is perfectly apt for most parades whose "meanings," like the meaning of Pollock's paintings, emerge free of an author or specific message from out of the thin air of the audience's interpretation. But the interpretation of speech should be restricted only to certain forms of aesthetic and artistic speech.

Application of the "out of thin air" speech analysis to the meaning and scope of cognitive speech is an altogether different thing. Yet that is precisely what the Court did in the *Dale* case as well as some aspects of the *Hurley* opinion. The linear speaker-message-audience model of protected free speech reflects precisely the form of communication that serves the ends of truth seeking, political liberty building, and the exchange of ideas in the service of democratic self-government. To loose the moorings of speaker (liberty), message (information and ideas), and audience (discourse) requisites from speech would be to loose speech meaning from any possibility of limitation and any form of constitutional purpose. This does not mean, of course, that emotion and aesthetics play no part in cognitive speech, but the part they play (apart from art) is in service of the *cognitive message* and *its* force or clarity. As Justice Harlan said in the famous "fuck the draft" case, the emotive force of the word *fuck* is valuable under the First Amendment as a means of reinforcing or amplifying or dramatizing the cognitive "speech" message, which was "I really dislike the draft." In contrast, emotion itself, let loose, is not speech; otherwise my act of kicking my dog out of frustration would have to be counted as speech. While I can, to be sure, engage in First Amendment speaking through conduct alone—like burning the flag or my draft card—the acts are only speech if I intend them to express a message that will be understood cognitively by an audience. Lighting my charcoal fire with a flag or a draft card simply won't do.

On the "cognitive message out of thin air" issue, there is precious little to justify the Court's interpretation of the First Amendment speech guarantee from a methodological point of view. While the bare word "speech" in the First Amendment might not foreclose such "out of thin air" meanings as First Amendment speech, there is little but the shallowest form of literal interpretation to support it. There is simply no evidence of an original intent to read the speech guarantee that way. More damningly, there is no evidence (outside of art or music or the like) of historical and cultural changes that could lead to any other than the traditional meaning of cognitive speech. Such an extension of speech freedom would not be simply creative interpretivism, it would be making meaning up from scratch. In *Dale* the speech protected under the First Amendment was people's assumptions about the meaning of the Boy Scouts' failure to fire Dale in light of Dale's earlier statements in another context. There is literally no speech here by the Boy Scouts. There isn't any forced speech either, as the "meaning" was a product of audience construction and nothing else. *Hurley* suffers the same problem. The problem is that the case allows the "fact" of the parade organizers' speech, and any specific message conveyed by the "speech," to be constructed almost entirely from assumed audience interpretation of the message of the parade based on the organizers' publicly unknown act of noninclusion of GLIB. If as a student I miss a class, does that make others students' belief that I don't like the professor my speech?

So we can say that the new and significantly altered meaning of speech in the *Hurley* case can be justified as an exercise of interpretivism by the Supreme Court, but only with respect to aesthetic and artistic speech. Methodologically, the opinion and the decision, so limited, are quite sound. The use of the *Hurley* speech definition in the setting of cognitive speech, however, as in *Dale*, is hard to defend methodologically, and thus the decision in the *Dale* case must be placed in serious doubt. It is an exercise of judicial power, to be sure, but not by any methodology that justifies judicial—unelected—governmental power. It simply cannot be connected to the text or purposes of the First Amendment by any of the principled limits on judicial interpretation—textualism, originalism, or interpretivism—and the Court fails to express openly the reasoning behind its interpretation.

Judicial Capacity to Decide

We start this discussion of judicial *capacity* with a simple yet very important observation: the Supreme Court is almost *never* required to decide a case. It always has a choice. This is reflected in the statutes that govern its jurisdiction. With very few and narrow exceptions, the Court decides which cases to consider from among the thousands that are appealed to the Court. These days the Court only decides to decide, and thus grants review, in perhaps one hundred cases each year. And it needn't give any reasons for refusing to grant review to a case. The Court has full and unreviewable discretion in the matter.

More basically, the Court is only empowered to decide what the Court itself calls justiciable cases—cases susceptible to judicial resolution. As a general proposition the Court deems nonjusticiable any cases in which the legal and constitutional issues are beyond the capacity of courts to decide. Why? Perhaps because the facts, on which courts rely, are unascertainable (say, ongoing foreign affairs matters) or are incapable of reliable assessment by a court; or because the decision on an issue is committed to the political branches (say, review of impeachment). Perhaps most relevant to our discussion is another category of issue that the Court has held is beyond the capacity of judges: Can the issue raised in a case be reduced to reasoned and principled dimensions for a decision by judges; are the consequences of any decision on an issue too broad or uncertain to be resolved by a judgment between the parties with precedential effect in the future; are the consequences of decision so great that deference should be accorded the political branches which alone possess the power to enforce any decision? These are considerations that must be judged in every case the Court decides, and to one degree or another they are factors that the Court takes into account in all the cases presented to it for discretionary review.

Each of the cases we have discussed involve issues that are *capable* of reasoned and principled interpretation of the First Amendment free-speech guarantee. In this sense of capacity to decide a free-speech issue, most cases fit the judicial model for principled interpretation with precedential weight, as the speech guarantee is a limit on government power whose enforcement depends almost exclusively on the judicial branch.

The capacity concern in our cases thus boils down to a relatively narrow one of whether the consequences of an interpretation are so complex or large or unforeseeable that heavy deference to the enforcement and policy powers of the executive and legislative branches is warranted, at least for the moment, thus circumscribing the scope or timing of the Court's own interpretive power. This is a potential problem in three of the cases we have discussed: *Citizens United*; *Summum*; and *Dale* (assuming that *Hurley* is narrowly limited to aesthetic and artistic expression).

The *Citizens United* decision that corporate political speech is fully protected, just like individual free speech, has potentially vast consequences. First, in an increasingly corporatized society, the decision threatens to unleash a voice in the political marketplace that has the power and resources to dominate that marketplace and diminish the self-government purpose of individual speech. This is a problem with the absoluteness of the Court's interpretation that speech itself is protected without regard to its source. Government is structured on the premise that voters ultimately control, and voters are *only* individuals whose active involvement and expression in the marketplace is foundational. The effect of the Court's interpretation is to treat corporations, when speaking, as fully equal participants in the self-governing system and not as entities whose main legal existence for the past 150 years has been as a creation of the state as a highly regulated form of organization. The *Citizens United* interpretation that corporations must be treated equally alongside individuals in the speech realm threatens to undermine much of the regulatory framework for corporations (governance laws, securities laws, and fair-trade laws, for example).

Perhaps more basically, the corporate-equality-with-individual speech premise will certainly preempt a wide range of methods of controlling elections and lobbying in the United States, methods that the political branches, reflecting popular will, must consider in shaping political rules and reforms bearing on the voting rights of individuals. The Court will have to rely in the future on the political branches to shape political compromises and to enforce the Court's power alongside those branches in seeking solutions. In an area in which the relevant decisions are necessarily political (expedient, compromising) and not principled, it is unwise for the judicial branch to act in broad and absolute ways, as opposed to more realistic and respectful smaller steps.

The *Summum* case is similarly troubling for analogous reasons. Government speech is an act undertaken by the political branches—legislative, executive, and administrative (in other words, mixed). The decision to use speech as an exercise of government power and policy resides in the first instance in those branches, and can equally be restrained or justified by those branches. The Supreme Court should be careful not to preempt the field, for in doing so it will be left with the inherently nonjudicial tasks of shaping law on the specifics of how and when government can make such choices—tasks that the Court would itself disclaim the capacity to do. The Court should thus be very apprehensive about creating a doctrine that grants government a First Amendment *right* to do as it chooses. The only right-holding party to government speech disputes should be the individual (and corporate?) speakers. The broader the Court's government speech doctrine, the greater will be the conflict between government and individual rights holders. In sum, the government speech doctrine, suitably limited in rights terms, is a matter over which the Court's capacity to decide is undeniable . . . as long as the Court proceeds cautiously and nonexpansively—in other words, prudentially. Many people, including me, see the *Summum* opinion as dangerously crossing the line of prudence.

Finally we turn to the *Dale* case, in which the Court unleashes a wholly new and radically reconstructed (or deconstructed) principle of free speech. It holds that the mere existence of expressive meaning (the artifact of speech), without the need for a speaker or an intended cognitive message, constitutes protected "speech" under the First Amendment. The implications of this idea, which I hope the Court simply did not see or think through, are almost limitless. It is more than doubtful that the Court has the ability to foresee where its decision may lead, much less to shape its interpretive principle to anticipate the future and avoid the possible undesirable consequences. No "trees or polar bears or trees" doesn't make much of a limit. For this reason, if no other, the decision should be overruled as an unwise expedient, and perhaps replaced by a different and more directly applicable protection for private expressive associations, not just their imagined speech.

It is interesting that the capacity problem in the three cases just mentioned is not a lack of capacity to decide the interpretive issue but instead a lack of judicial capacity in light of the specific decision/interpretation made by the Court. In a peculiar way the lack of capacity resides in, or is reflected only by, one of many possible interpretations. But this is not uncommon in lack-of-capacity cases, which regularly call on the Court in advance of a decision to anticipate the decision and the results it will produce. If the result would create nonjusticiability, then the Court needs to step back from making any decision and either dismiss the case altogether or limit or revise its decision to avoid the capacity problems.

The conclusion that judicial-capacity problems arise in these cases, and were ignored, is thus a conclusion that the Court failed to think seriously about its own power when interpreting the meaning of speech. The problems need not and should not have arisen; they did so, perhaps, because of an unseemly haste to settle firmly certain issues the justices deemed too important to leave to future Courts.

If that's the case, the Court failed us miserably.

The Need for Judicial Intervention

The Supreme Court does not so much decide cases as it addresses important questions of law, including constitutional law. The Court is a lawmaking body, not a place for the correction of mere error in courts below. In practice the Court's criteria for cases turn on necessity: Are the lower courts in conflict about the legal question, thus causing damaging inconsistencies across the nation; is the legal issue one of fundamental importance in its field of law, and is that issue presented clearly in the case being considered for review; are there other factors that practically require prompt review and decision, such as an issue affecting foreign affairs, or an issue important to upcoming elections?

Do the cases we have considered here meet the high threshold for decision? Most of them do: *Summum* and the law governing government monuments and parks; *Hurley* and the protection for artistic forms of expression; and certainly *Citizens United*, which involved the constitutionality of the key restriction placed on independent expenditures by corporations and unions for ads in the final days of an upcoming federal election.

One might question the degree of necessity in two of the cases, however. The first of these is the *Doe* case, in which the Washington public records law would require disclosure of referendum petition signatures. The Court below had permitted the release of the names of signatories, though some further proceedings on the question of harm could be held in the district court. The case, then, might have come to the Court again at a later time. But even if that were not possible or likely, the harm to the parties was not great, many states had or were considering similar policies, and cases would surely be considered in other federal circuits, thus allowing the Court to learn from the variations in statutes among states and the variation in opinions among the federal courts.

Virtually the same thing could be said about the *Dale* case. The issue of state nondiscrimination laws that conflicted with private expressive associations was important, but it had been (nondefinitively) addressed in two previous cases. Moreover, a little further thought about the case might have disclosed that the expressive-association claim was not well presented and an alternative (and unprecedented) free-speech theory would be needed to decide the case in favor of the Scouts. Finally, there was a lot of litigation throughout the country on expressive-association claims, so opportunities to decide the expressive-association issue, assisted by a fuller sense of its scope and the different ways Courts have dealt with it, were available. All of this would, at least, have counseled the Court to dismiss the case as improvidently granted once it became clear that the expressive-association issue was not well presented in the case.

In the end it is hard to conclude that the Court's decisions in any of the cases to grant review and address the constitutional issues were improper or failed to satisfy the general criterion applied to all cases by the Court, but in the *Doe* and *Dale* cases the decisions may have been unwise and imprudent.

The Consequences of a Decision

By consequences of a decision I mean the decision's impact, whether the consequences were anticipated and whether their scope exceeds the capacity of the judicial branch to manage. This factor does not yield perfect yes or no answers, but rather a judgment about the balance between the imperative to decide and the likelihood that the decision will be effectively carried out.

Citizens United is the decision that has most prominently featured concerns about its consequences, in two forms. The first is the predicted consequences of corporate-speech power on the outcome of political elections. Such objections rest largely on distaste for the decision on the merits and thus are not of great concern to the larger questions of judicial power and legitimacy that we are discussing.

Some of the corporate-speech-power objections, however, go to the distinct question of whether the decision will effect a fundamental change in the political election marketplace, with corporate speech suffocating individual voter speech and ballot choice. Were this consequence to be at all certain, *Citizens United* could be roundly condemned as an exercise of judicial power. The difficulty with the argument, however, is that there is really no evidence of corporate domination—yet, some would say—and even less evidence that the corporate views will significantly affect voter choice in an election. In this respect there is some substance to Justice Kennedy's statement in the Court's opinion that voters are fully capable of reaching their own judgments, and that the First Amendment rests on that fundamental premise.

A second concern about consequences of the decision is quite different. It is that the breadth and absoluteness of the corporate speech holding will have the effect of displacing the political branches from a significant portion of political campaign reform in the future. The judgment of legislators themselves will be critical to how effective reform can be structured. But that structuring cannot easily take place without the ability to regulate one of the primary actors in the campaign and larger political system—unions, corporations, and related interest groups. Many people believe, for example, that the entire campaign system is deeply flawed and that a reexamination of the process from bottom up, including the problem of lobbying, must take place because the system operates as an open auction process for political favoritism and access and influence (short of bribery or corruption). It seems clear that a fully protected population of corporate speakers will make such fundamental reforms virtually impossible.

The ultimate question on consequences, therefore, is whether regulation of campaigns (and lobbying, perhaps) is necessary and whether such regulations must come first from the political branches. The answer to each of these questions seems obviously "yes." If the breadth of *Citizens United* (not the issue in the case, which was pretty narrow) is as great as Justice Kennedy made it seem, the Court will have preempted action by the political branches unnecessarily with the consequence that the Supreme Court will have become the main locus of election reform and regulation. Indeed, this result is suggested in the final parts of the *Citizens United* opinion, where the Court states, in overly broad dicta, that disclosure regulations for individuals and corporations alike are constitutional. Has the Court basically limited the scope of election (and lobbying) reform to the single instrument of disclosure? Can the Court justify a decision of such fundamental importance being made exclusively by the unelected branch of government?

Related concerns can be expressed about the *Doe* case and its decision—tepid to be sure—that the act of voting is an act of free speech. Only time will tell what the practical consequences of this ambiguous but broad First Amendment holding will be. It certainly has implications for the states' constitutional freedom to establish election and voting systems. Such choices as whether open caucuses are constitutional, whether voting must be secret, and whether qualifications for voting are consistent with the First Amendment, will be now subject to First Amendment scrutiny.

The *Doe* decision also has implications for the constitutionality of disclosure requirements and the First Amendment right to anonymity in one's political speech. It will be impossible for the *Citizens United* prodisclosure language to be reconciled with the *Doe* and *McIntyre* anonymity holdings; one or the other will have to give way at the behest of the Supreme Court. Is it appropriate for the Supreme Court to effectively control this aspect of political reform efforts too?

The other case that raises difficulties in the consequences area is *Boy Scouts v. Dale*. There the consequences concern the quite radical transformation of the free-speech paradigm for cognitive (political, for example) speech, eliminating the need for a speaker who intends a specific message to be communicated. The problem with the *Dale* speech holding is that the Court seems not to have seen or anticipated the change being effected—indeed, one might wonder whether the Court intended it at all were it not for Justice Stevens's dissent on the very point. The *Dale* decision is just a single opinion, and it may be one of those that the Court simply ignores in the future. One can hope, anyway.

■ ■ ■

We can answer the "too much free speech" question in constitutional terms. Free speech is largely the creation of the Supreme Court. The Supreme Court is created by the Constitution and *its* power is limited *by* the Constitution. For our purposes, those limits are twofold. First, the Court can exercise only judicial power, which means that the Court may only decide specific cases whose resolution can be achieved through the neutral exercise of *judicial* power. Second, in exercising that power in a judicial manner the Court must follow methodologies of the judicial process, including public judgment, arrived at through reasoned and generalizable principles, based on the Constitution and enforceable by a judgment binding on the parties to the case.

I leave the reader, armed with these criteria and a deep familiarity with each case, to render final judgment. I don't believe that my views are a mystery to those who have read this book. For me there is in these cases (not all of them, of course) too much haste to decide, too little open, honest and revealing reasoning, too little humility, too much enthusiasm for the law-creating process, and too little sober reflection about the limits of judicial power. Consequences—even foreseen ones—have been ignored, including the failure to appreciate the proper roles of the other, elected branches upon which the Court relies for its building, its budget, and enforcement of its decisions.

The Supreme Court must continually earn its reputation and support. Right now, with free speech, it's not doing a very good job of it.

Too Much Free Speech?

The "too much free speech" question can be addressed also in a larger frame.

Justice Scalia claims that "there is no such thing as too much speech." Do we believe it? Does he believe it? What does he mean?

If he means nothing other than that speech that is *already* constitutionally protected should not be restricted, the statement is vacuous and tautological and contributes nothing new at all. It is also, technically, wrong, because the sheer quantity of speech can be limited in order to prevent other speech from being drowned out and thus not heard. But even this limited meaning of his statement is clearly not what he seemed intent on expressing, and it has nothing to do with our question about too much free speech.

If, instead, Justice Scalia means to say that speech should not be limited, definitionally or otherwise—more speech always being the better alternative to less—then he is saying something that even he doesn't agree with. There are many ways in which "free speech" is limited and restricted—speech that is acknowledged to be an act of individual liberty under the First Amendment. Incitement to violence or intimidation can be prohibited. So also false speech that produces harm. Speech can be prohibited or limited in many places—free speech in a theater during a performance; free speech in my classroom, or in airport gate areas, or in the streets during most times of the day, or in government property devoted to government speech or to government monuments, to name just a few examples. Conduct that is illegal can be prohibited no matter how expressive it is intended to be. Speech communicated while trespassing on others' (or government's) property can be prohibited. Justice Scalia has been an approving party to many of these relatively commonplace limitations on free speech.

The cases we have looked at are of a different ilk, however. They involve definitional expansions of the meaning of speech—to include corporations as individual speakers, voting as speech, government speech, and expression "out of thin air" that is counted as speech despite the absence of an author with a message understood by an audience. Justice Scalia's statement of course applies to these kinds of protections for speech too. Indeed, his statement applies particularly to these kinds of definitional expansions, for it was made in his opinion in the *McConnell* campaign reform act case and was quoted and used forcefully in the opinion he joined in *Citizens United.*

Should we agree with him that the expansion of speech, too, is subject to the principle that there is no such thing as too much free speech? Certainly not, at least not for this reason alone. So we should examine why and how the expansions took place. Here we can say a lot of things.

First, the expansions were not clear or obvious. They were not, in other words, simply instances of conventional speech that the Supreme Court had inadvertently or mistakenly failed to recognize earlier.

Second, the expansions were not the product of conventional First Amendment interpretation of the meaning of "speech" in the First Amendment.

Third, in the *Citizens United* case, there was little need to reach out to decide the corporation-speech question. There were ample narrower grounds on which the same result could have been reached. More basically, however, there was no dearth of corporate speech and involvement in the political process. Corporations could and did speak regularly and effectively. They need no constitutional right to individual free speech to do so. As important and powerful actors in the national political and economic order, they could, they did, and they still can protect themselves and their power to speak.

The law at issue was narrow and limited. It was designed to give voters a brief respite from the constant drone of independent political ads, and to give the candidates a time to speak for themselves. The law wasn't the most well-crafted way to do that, and maybe it should have been declared unconstitutional because of its sloppiness—overbreadth and underinclusiveness, as lawyers put it. But in no other way did it impede corporations from speaking and lobbying and involvement in politics. Why not leave it there? Why reach out to transform and greatly expand the foundational meaning of speech?

Fourth, and finally, the analytical means used by the Court are often peculiar and disturbing. The expansions were rationalized as mere applications of the Court's established precedent developed in *other* speech settings. For instance, the rule against discrimination based on speaker identity (itself never absolute) had been developed in the setting of individual speech at a time when the question of corporations qualifying as individual speakers wasn't even on anyone's agenda. And the principle that action which is expressive in character should qualify as First Amendment speech had likewise been forged in the individual speech liberty setting, not in the constitutionally distinct and quite different setting of voting. Government speech, it might be said, came out of nowhere. And speech "out of thin air" might be said to have come from a conviction that artistic speech should be protected, not from any thought about its application to cognitive and political speech.

The benign explanations for the cases, and especially *Citizens United*, would be that the Court just got swept up in the hydraulic force of ideas it has applied in other speech settings. The result was that the "speech" interpretation became a product of the Court's doctrine, not of the First Amendment. But even this generous explanation does not forgive the Court for its serious error. To say that because a regulation discriminates on the basis of speaker identity, so therefore business corporation speech is fully protected by the First Amendment, is a non sequitur of the worst sort.

The question of whether speech by nonindividual legal business entities should be fully protected by the First Amendment is radically different than the question of whether limiting corporation speech and not similar individual speech is a restriction based on speaker identity. The Court only answered the latter question—and didn't even answer that one too well. It never answered the first except to say, without any real reasoning, that the First Amendment protects "speech," not speaking, based again on claimed support in prior noncorporate speech cases.

Whether the outcome of the cases was right or wrong is frankly beside the point. The decisions and opinions in the cases were analytically and methodologically flawed and, therefore, simply wrong. There will be a great deal of analytical resuscitation to do when the Court begins to consider the implications of its decisions in future cases.

▪ ▪ ▪

Freedom of Speech is, for all practical purposes, the exclusive domain of the Supreme Court. The Court applies and enforces speech freedom. More basically, it creates it.

All of us have our own personal views about free-speech decisions or doctrines or definitions. But if that's all we do, we must understand that we are making a political argument that belongs in the realms of debates, political theory, and ultimately legislative or executive action. In these areas the Supreme Court holds all of the trump cards and our opinions may amount to just that and no more.

But the Supreme Court has duties and responsibilities, too. Humility, open and full reasoning, principled judgment, and judicial power and authority are basic ones. In meeting those duties and expectations, the Supreme Court has failed us. In the process it has given us "too much free speech."

Notes

Introduction

1. McConnell v. Federal Election Commission, 540 U.S. 93, 259 (2003) (Scalia, J., dissenting).

Chapter One. Corporations as Speakers

1. Available at www.whitehouse.gov/photos-and-video/video/2010-state-union-address (accessed January 24, 2012).
2. First National Bank of Boston v. Bellotti, 435 U.S. 765 (1978), upheld a Boston bank's First Amendment right to make a political contribution in connection with a voter referendum.
3. For example, Pacific Gas & Elec. Co. v. Public Utilities Commission of California, 475 U.S. 1, 33–35 (1986) (Rehnquist, dissenting).
4. The Snow-Jeffords Amendment was approved by Congress as an alternative to the categorical ban on corporate and union electioneering, should the categorical ban be struck down. The amendment permitted electioneering by ideological organizations in corporate form—the NRA, for example. The Court's categorical opinion in *Citizens United* made the amendment irrelevant and thus played no part in the Court's decision; it would have functioned much like the *Austin* case, which the Court overruled.
5. For example, White v. Regester, 412 U.S. 755 (1973).
6. McIntyre v. Ohio Elections Commission, 514 U.S. 334 (1995), involved Margaret McIntyre's claim that she had a right to distribute an inadvertently anonymous leaflet opposing a school bond issue at a public meeting on the bonding proposal. Her failure to identify herself on the leaflet was a criminal act under Ohio law. The Supreme Court held that the law violated the First Amendment.

7. A CENTURY OF LAWMAKING FOR A NEW NATION: U.S. CONGRESSIONAL DOCUMENTS AND DEBATES, 1774–1875, *Annals of Congress*, House of Representatives, 1st Congress, 1st Session, OF DEBATES IN CONGRESS, AMENDMENTS TO THE CONSTITUTION, June 8, 1783, 451.

8. Poe v. Ullman. 367 U.S. 497, 542 (1961) (Harlan, J., dissenting).

Chapter Two. Government and Its Speech Forum

1. Available at http://www.summum.us/philosophy/principles.shtml (accessed January 24, 2012).

2. ALEXANDER MEIKLEJOHN, FREE SPEECH AND ITS RELATION TO SELF-GOVERNMENT 26–27 (1948).

Chapter Three. Expressive Conduct Unleashed

1. The following discussion of Hurley is drawn in part from R. Bezanson and M. Choe, *Speaking out of Thin Air: A Comment on Hurley v. Irish-American Gay, Lesbian and Bisexual Group of Boston*, 25 COMM/ENT (2003), and is an adaptation of a chapter in the author's previous book, ART AND FREEDOM OF SPEECH (University of Illinois Press, 2009).

2. Charles Simic, *Making It New*, THE NEW YORK REVIEW OF BOOKS, at 10, August 10, 2006; citing HUGO BALL, FLIGHT OUT OF TOWN 64 (1996).

3. The council itself applies for and receives a permit from the city every year to organize and conduct the parade. Through 1992, however, the city allowed the council to use the city's official seal and directly funded the parade. *Id.* Ball at 560–61.

4. Kevin Dwyer, "Do Your Job": A Talk with Wacko Hurley, South Boston Online, http://www.southbostononline.com [archives] (accessed July 29, 2006).

5. *Id.* at 561.

6. At the time of the *Hurley* case, the Supreme Court was still following its long-standing custom of not identifying the Justice who is asking the question. That practice has since changed.

7. J. L. AUSTIN, HOW TO DO THINGS WITH WORDS 6 (J. O. Urmson and Marina Sbisà, eds) (1975, 2d ed.).

8. Austin refers to verifiable statements of fact–statements that *do* nothing in themselves, or that have no necessary force–as "constative" statements. *Id.* at 1–3.

9. Some background discussion of Austin's speech-act theory is in order here. When Austin began the Harvard lecture series documented in the book, *How To Do Things With Words*, he crafted a dichotomy between a performative and constative statement, suggesting that no overlap existed between the two senses of speech. See *id.*, at 1–11. By the end of the lecture series, Austin rejects this dichotomy in favor of a more generalized speech-act theory that tracks the various degrees of illocutionary force effected by various statements:

> We said long ago that we needed a list of "explicit performative verbs"; but in the light of the more general theory we now see that what we need is a list of *illocutionary forces* of an utterance. The old distinction, however, between *primary* and *explicit* will survive the sea change from the performative/constative distinction to the theory of speech-acts quite successfully. For we have since seen reason to suppose that . . . [we can sort] out those verbs which make explicit . . . the illocutionary force of an utterance . . . What will *not* survive the transition . . . is the notion of the purity of performatives: this was essentially based upon a belief in the dichotomy of performatives and constatives, which we see has to be abandoned in favour of more general *families* of related and overlapping speech acts . . . (*Id.* at 149–50).

For additional discussion of Austin's speech act theory and a critique of the constative/performative dichotomy, see generally STANLEY FISH, DOING WHAT COMES NATURALLY: CHANGE, RHETORIC, AND THE PRACTICE OF THEORY IN LITERARY AND LEGAL STUDIES 37–67 (1989).

10. *Id.* at 568 (emphasis added).

11. *Id.* (emphasis added).

12. ERIC DONALD HIRSCH, JR., VALIDITY IN INTERPRETATION 5–6 (1967).

13. 515 U.S. at 570–71.

14. 515 U.S. at 575 (emphasis added).

15. 515 U.S. at 574.

16. JOHN DURHAM PETERS, SPEAKING INTO THE AIR: A HISTORY OF THE IDEA OF COMMUNICATION 61 (1999) (noting that "[t]he Christian doctrine of communication is a doctrine of broadcasting, of single turns, expended without the expectation that one good turn deserves another").

17. JAMES W. CAREY, COMMUNICATION AS CULTURE 15 (1988).

18. *Id.* at 9.

19. *Id.* at 23.

20. *Id.* at 25.

21. *Id.* at 34.

22. *Id.* Carey explains:

> [A] ritual view conceives communication as a process through which a shared culture is created, modified, and transformed. The archetypal case of communication is ritual and mythology . . . art and literature. . . . A ritual view of communication is directed not toward the extension of messages in space but the maintenance of society in time . . .; not the act of imparting information or influence but the creation, representation, and celebration of shared even if illusory beliefs.

23. *Id.* at 28.

24. *Id.* at 33.

25. *Id.* at 44. LEE BOLLINGER, THE TOLERANT SOCIETY: FREEDOM OF SPEECH AND EXTREMIST SPEECH IN AMERICA 67–71(1986). The Supreme Court understands the premise that communicative practices are central to the existence of a democratic polity, in part because linguistic connectivity is a basic element of the tissue of civility and a precursor to democratic enfranchisement. Precisely because of this realization, the Court in *NAACP v. Button*, 371 U.S. 415 (1963), held that membership in the NAACP (plus its affiliates and staff) constituted a "mode[] of expression and association" protected by the First Amendment. *Id.* at 428–429. Justice Harlan dissented, arguing that the activities of the NAACP are more akin to conduct than speech and should not be protected. *Id.* at 453–55. Participation in the organization articulated an effective political statement (especially given the historical context of 1963) and constituted a legitimate form of political expression.

Awareness of linkages between communicative practices and democratic culture may also lend credence to the notion of "low value" speech articulated most recently by Justice Stevens. *R.A.V. v. City of St. Paul*, 505 U.S. 377, 416 *et seq*. (1992) (Stevens, J., concurring in the judgment). In *Young v. American Mini Theatres*, 427 U.S. 50 (1976), and *Renton v. Playtime Theatres*, 475 U.S. 41 (1986), sexually explicit, nonobscene speech was thought to have less social value than political speech because sexually explicit nonobscene speech failed to occupy a "core" position in relationship to democracy. Cases from *Valentine v. Chrestensen*, 316 U.S. 52 (1942), to *Central Hudson Gas v. Public Service Commission*, 447 U.S. 557 (1980), also demonstrate a belief, at least by a majority of the Court, that commercial speech is less valuable to a democratic ideal than, for example, traditionally conceived political speech.

26. Carey, *supra* note 98, at 17.

27. *Id.* at 573.

Chapter Four. Speech out of Thin Air

This chapter is an adaptation of an earlier article and a chapter in the author's book *Art and Freedom of Speech* (University of Illinois Press 2009).

1. Benoit Lewis-Denizet, *The Model Boy Scout*, THE ADVOCATE, April 14, 1998.

2. *Id.*

3. *Id.*

4. *Id.*

5. The Supreme Court's answer in the license plate case, *Wooley v. Maynard*, 430 U.S. 705 (1977), was that the pacifist was protected against liability for covering the motto on his license plate.

6. The status or existence of the "message" itself is, in fact, an open question that should have been dealt with more thoroughly by the Court. *Dale* did not speak, nor did he intend to speak; the same goes for the Boy Scouts. The case seems to involve a totally fabricated message—indeed, the Court is really talking about stigma. And the problem with stigma is that it's the effect of broader social structures. Neither the

Boy Scouts nor Dale, as individuals can *will* it into existence as some finite message intended to be expressed.

7. ALEXANDER MEIKELJOHN, POLITICAL FREEDOM (1960); Owen Fiss, *Why The State?*, 100 HARV. L. REV. 781 (1987); CASS R. SUNSTEIN, DEMOCRACY AND THE PROBLEM OF FREE SPEECH (1993); Daniel A. Farber, *Free Speech Without Romance: Public Choice and the First Amendment*, 105 HARV. L. REV. 554 (1990); Red Lion Broadcasting Co. v. FCC, 395 U.S. 367 (1969); Virginia State Board of Pharmacy v. Virginia Citizens Consumer Council, 425 U.S. 748 (1976); Miller v. Calif., 413 U.S. 15 (1973).

8. C. EDWIN BAKER, HUMAN FREEDOM AND LIBERTY OF SPEECH (1989); Martin Redish, *The Value of Free Speech*, 130 U. Pa. L. Rev. 591 (1982); STEVEN H. SHIFFRIN, THE FIRST AMENDMENT, DEMOCRACY, AND ROMANCE (1990); Abrams v. United States, 250 U.S.616, (1919) (Holmes, J. dissenting).

9. Citizens United at 907.

10. The classic formulation of this approach is found in the definition of obscenity, which excludes from the constitutional definition of speech material that "lacks serious literary, artistic, political or scientific value." Miller v. California, 413 U.S. 15, 24 (1973). Commercial speech, in contrast, is given some constitutional stature under the First Amendment, but only because of its instrumental informational value, and thus not if it misleads or is false. Virginia State Board of Pharmacy v. Virginia Citizens Consumer Council, 425 U.S. 748 (1976).

11. Robert C. Post, *Meikeljohn's Mistake: Individual Autonomy and the Reform of Public Discourse*, 64 U. Colo. L. Rev. 1109 (1993); Robert C. Post, *Managing Deliberation: The Quandary of Democratic Dialogue*, 103 Ethics 654 (1993).

12. ANTONIO DAMASIO, DESCARTE'S ERROR: EMOTION, REASON AND THE HUMAN BRAIN (1995); ANTONIO DAMASIO, THE FEELING OF WHAT HAPPENS: BODY AND EMOTION IN THE MAKING OF CONSCIOUSNESS (1999).

Chapter Five. The Secret Ballot: Voting as Speech

1. Available at http://www.npr.org/templates/story/story.php?storyid=126290385 (accessed January 24, 2012).

2. *Id.*

3. This is a fairly technical legal point, but it is important to the case. Most free-speech cases are "as applied" challenges, which focus on the particular speaker's action only and relief is limited to the speaker. For instance, I might challenge a local noise ordinance on the ground that it was unconstitutionally applied to my speech, which I claim was inherently and valuably noisy. My relief, should I succeed, would be to allow me to give my speech or to award me damages for having been unconstitutionally restrained in making it.

Occasionally, though, I may be permitted to use my specific claim as a means of challenging the noise ordinance "on its face." In such a case I might challenge the noise ordinance itself, claiming that it was too broad or too vague and thus conferred too much discretion on the police to apply it differently in one situation than in another because the police like or dislike the ideas expressed in the particular speech. In a facial challenge, my relief would include striking down the entire ordinance in all its applications in order to prevent other speakers from being inhibited from speaking loudly in the future.

The *Doe* case involved both a facial challenge—public disclosure of petition signatures cannot be required in most instances—and an as-applied challenge—petition signatures cannot be disclosed for *this* referendum because there is a risk of intimidation or violence toward the signatories. The posture of the *Doe* case in the Supreme Court was only a facial challenge—in this case, as Bopp is arguing, a law like Washington's that makes no clear and practically available exception for risks of intimidation should be stricken in its entirety lest future referendum petitions, and future otherwise-willing petition signers, be inhibited in launching the campaign. Because only the facial challenge was tried in the courts below, the case must go back to the district court if the Supreme Court decides that the law is valid on its face. The issue then—it's called "on remand"—would be whether the otherwise valid Public Records Law requirement of public disclosure of names and addresses of signers was unconstitutionally applied in this case because an exception for likely intimidation was constitutionally required but not considered by the enforcement officials of the State of Washington.

V. Is There Such a Thing as Too Much Free Speech?

1. ALEXANDER BICKEL, THE LEAST DANGEROUS BRANCH 6–98, 2nd ed. (1986).

2. HERBERT WECHSLER, PRINCIPLES, POLITICS, AND FUNDAMENTAL LAW 21 (1961).

3. RANDALL BEZANSON, ART AND FREEDOM OF SPEECH (2009).

4. See Tushnet, Review of ART AND FREEDOM OF SPEECH, Jotwell blog, 2010, http://conlaw.jotwell.com/why-exactly-are-jackson-pollocks-paintings-shielded-by-the-first-amendment (accessed January 24, 2012).

Index

Randall P. Bezanson is the David H. Vernon Professor of Law at the University of Iowa and the author of *Art and Freedom of Speech*, *How Free Can Religion Be?*, and *How Free Can the Press Be?*

The University of Illinois Press
is a founding member of the
Association of American University Presses.

Composed in 10.5/13 Minion Pro
with Helvetica Neue display
by Celia Shapland
at the University of Illinois Press
Manufactured by Sheridan Books, Inc.

University of Illinois Press
1325 South Oak Street
Champaign, IL 61820-6903
www.press.uillinois.edu